ISAIAH
PROPHECIES, PROMISES, WARNINGS

Isaiah

Prophecies·Promises·Warnings

by W. E. Vine

Lamplighter
Books Grand Rapids, Michigan
Zondervan Publishing House

Lamplighter Books are published by Zondervan Publishing House, 1415 Lake Drive, S.E., Grand Rapids, Michigan 49506

Zondervan paperback edition, 1971

Reprinted by special arrangement with Oliphants Ltd.

ISBN 0-310-33771-2

Printed in the United States of America

89 90 91 92 93 94 / CH / 28 27 26 25 24 23

CONTENTS

PART III (b)

PART III (c)

PREFACE

THIS work is the outcome of the preparation of notes written on behalf of many of the Lord's servants abroad during a course of several years. The many expressions of appreciation received have encouraged the writer to produce the volume.

The notes have a twofold aim: firstly, to seek to unfold the Scriptures, secondly, to bring to bear upon the lives of believers the practical effects of the warnings, promises and prophecies of the book of Isaiah, since "all Scripture is profitable for teaching, for reproof, for correction, for instruction which is in righteousness: that the man of God (a description of every faithful believer) may be complete, furnished completely unto every good work" (2 Tim. 3: 16, 17). Introductory chapters on the life and times of Isaiah have been purposely omitted.

The writer unhesitatingly maintains the view that there was only one human author, the prophet Isaiah, of the sixty-six chapters of the book. Evidences of this unity are noted from time to time in the course of the commentary, and in the appendix, which gives a number of instances in which the same characteristic phraseology is used in both parts of the book.

W.E.V.

Bath.

INTRODUCTION

THE name Isaiah signifies "Jehovah's salvation", and this subject forms a prominent feature throughout his prophecies. Among his key words are "save" and "salvation". His call came in 756 B.C. in Uzziah's reign. There were three periods of his ministry: (1) in the reigns of Uzziah and Jotham; (2) from the beginning of the reign of Ahaz to that of Hezekiah; (3) from Hezekiah to the fifteenth year of his reign. After this he lived till the beginning of the reign of Manasseh. Tradition says that he was then sawn asunder (cp. Heb. 11: 37).

As with Amos in Israel so with Isaiah in Judah, they were called to declare that the time of God's longsuffering was coming to an end. His prophecies consist of two parts, (I) Chapters 1-39, (II) Chapters 40-66; but these are closely connected with (I).

The book may also be divided into three parts, (I) *Prophetic*, of Israel and Gentile nations, especially Assyria (chapters 1-35); (II) *Historic*, relating to the reign of Hezekiah (chapters 36-39); (III) *Messianic*, especially regarding the deliverance of a remnant in Israel (chapters 40-66). Part I has four main sections: (a) prophecies concerning Judah and Israel (chapters 1-12), (b) prophecies against Gentile nations (chapters 13-23), (c) concerning Divine judgments and deliverances and concerning woes (chapters 24-33), (d) the future of Gentile nations and Israel (chapters 34, 35). Part II has two main sections: (a) concerning the Assyrian Invasion and Hezekiah's distress and deliverance (chapters 36, 37), (b) concerning the Chaldeans and Hezekiah's sickness and sin (chapters 38, 39). Part III has three main sections: (a) concerning Israel and the Gentiles and Divine deliverance (chapters 40-48), (b) concerning Jehovah's Servant, His sufferings and glory (chapters 49-57), (c) concerning the godly and ungodly in Israel and the contrasted issues of their ways and doings (chapters 58-66).

The book has been the subject of much expenditure of Higher Critical and Modernistic energy in recent times. One of the underlying principles in this kind of teaching is the denial of the predictive element in the book. The various suppositions of the exponents of these theories have tended only to confirm the faith of those who maintain the view of the unity of the whole book as being the work of the one human author writing what is given him by inspiration of God. Deny the predictive element and the only conclusion resulting is the disunity of the book and the composition of certain parts by different writers; a conclusion derogatory to the Person of the Holy Spirit as being the Divine Author through whom the book is 'God-breathed'.

PART I (a)

PROPHECIES CONCERNING JUDAH AND ISRAEL
(Chapters I–XII)

CHAPTER I

THE prophet begins with the mention of his subject and the time of his writing. The subject is Judah and Jerusalem and it is to be noticed that this twofold theme is prominent in chapters 40–66 as much as in 1–39, and that it involves a constant reference throughout the book to the whole nation of Israel.

He invokes the heavens and the earth to be witnesses to what the Lord has spoken, just as Moses did in Deut. 32: 1, and, as also did Moses, he proceeds to declare the grievous ways of God's people. God had acted towards Israel as a Father, nourishing (R.V. marg., "exalting", i.e., making them great, as in natural growth) and bringing them up, and they had fallen away from Him (verse 3). Israel was His wayward son, Exod. 4: 22, 23; cp. Deut. 14: 1; 32: 20.

What He had done for them as a nation He has done for us individually and spiritually. The record of their apostasy is written "for our admonition" (1 Cor. 10: 11). How we need therefore to take heed lest we grieve Him, as they did, and suffer eternal loss!

In verse 3 the Lord declares that the way His people have behaved is worse than that of the brutes. " **The ox knoweth his owner, and the ass his master's** (a plural in the original, not of number, but expressive of fullness of authority, as in Exod. 21: 29) **crib: but Israel doth not know, My people doth not consider**", i.e., that the Lord was their Owner and Master, that they belonged to Him and were dependent upon Him for all they required.

This twofold relationship with God is ours and needs to be kept in mind at all times, in all our ways and service.

In *verse 4* Isaiah speaks, breaking out into stern denunciation and lamenting over Israel as sinful, guilt-laden, a race of evildoers, a family corrupt in their ways. Their guilt was threefold. Each description is set in contrast to what God had designed them to be. They are (*a*) a " **sinful nation** " ; the Lord had said "ye shall be unto Me . . . a holy nation", Exod. 19: 6; (*b*) " **a people laden with iniquity** " ; God had chosen them to be "a peculiar people unto Himself" (a people for His own possession), Deut. 14: 2; (*c*) " **a seed of evil doers** " ; God had made them the "seed of Abraham", Isa. 41: 8, of Isaac, Gen. 21: 12, of Jacob, Isa. 45: 19; (*d*) " **children that deal corruptly** " ; the Lord had declared to them "ye are the children of the Lord, your God", Deut. 14: 1.

All this is again admonitory for us upon whom the very 'height of the ages' has come. The description given concerning us in 1 Pet. 2: 9 is similar to that given to Israel as God's people just mentioned: "Ye are an elect race, a royal priesthood (as in Exod. 19: 6), a holy nation, a people for God's own possession, that ye may shew forth the excellencies of Him who called you out of darkness into His marvellous light." We should therefore take heed lest we fall as they did, lest there be in any of us "an evil heart of unbelief in departing from the living God".

The fourfold description is followed by a threefold declaration of the way in which Israel had acted towards God; they had become evil in heart, in speech, in act: (*a*) they had " **forsaken the Lord** ", their *heart* had turned away from Him; (*b*) they had " **despised the Holy One of Israel** " (the word signifies to mock, to scorn), they had sinned in *speech*, and that against the Holy One of Israel (a title which is especially connected with Isaiah's prophecies, see also 5: 19, 24; 10: 20; 12: 6; 29: 19; 30: 11, 12, 15; 31: 1; 37: 23; 41: 14, 16, 20, etc., and, finally, 60: 9); as the Holy One He was Israel's Sanctifier, and they should have sanctified themselves in response; He had said "ye shall be holy : for I the Lord your God, am holy", Lev. 19: 2; (*c*) they were " **estranged** " and had " **gone backward** ", they were guilty in *act*; they chose their own way instead of His.

This is followed in *verse 5*, by the remonstrance: " **Why will ye be still stricken, that ye revolt more and more ?** " (or rather, 'revolting continually'). Why reap the consequences of persistent rebellion, adding iniquity unto iniquity? How fearfully the spirit of rebellion had permeated the nation is vividly portrayed in *vv. 5 and 6*: " **the whole** (or rather, 'every') **head is sick, and the whole heart faint.**" The head represents the outward controlling power, the heart the inward emotions. The whole condition was a Divine judgment. They were like a diseased body throughout. If the head and the heart are unsound the entire body is affected. From the sole of the foot to the head there was nothing sound, but " **wounds, bruises, and festering sores** ".

The wounds needed binding up; the bruises needed mollifying with oil; the sores required closing (or pressing) so as to cleanse them and quicken their healing. The remedies are mentioned in almost the opposite order to that of the evils (thus forming a sort of chiasm, or reverse order, for the purpose of vividness or emphasis).

At *verse 7* Isaiah passes from metaphors to direct language, which recalls, no doubt purposively, the punishments threatened in Lev. 26: 33; Deut. 28: 49–52; 29: 22, 23. These things had come upon them. The land had been unprecedentedly productive under Uzziah (2 Chron. 26: 10), but now wickedness was prevalent to such a degree that in 9: 18 it is described as burning like a fire.

In *verse 8* the phrase " **the daughter of Zion** " depicts Zion as a daughter, not a mother; it means "Zion the daughter" (see Zech. 2: 10 and cp. Jer. 46: 19; 48: 18). It is expressive of the tenderness with which the Lord had regarded the relation which He had established between Jerusalem (as representing His people) and Himself.

Her diminished population and desolate state were "**as a cottage** (a mere hut) **in a vineyard, as a lodge** (or rather, a booth or hammock for a garden-keeper to use to scare animals away, and so corresponding to a scarecrow) **in a garden of cucumbers, as a besieged city** ", a picture of isolation and difficulty.

Only a remnant was left. There always has been, and there will be in the coming time of Jacob's trouble, "a very small remnant". Were it not so, says the prophet, " **we should have been as Sodom, we should have been like unto Gomorrah** " (*verse 9*).

We should take heed lest what was literally true of Israel becomes spiritually true of us, lest we be diminished, not it may be in numbers but in spiritual power and fruitfulness. If we yield to sin in our own hearts and lives, we are bound to make way for the enemy against us collectively as the Lord's people.

In Rev. 11: 8 Jerusalem is described as Sodom. Isaiah now addresses the authorities and people as " **rulers of Sodom** " and " **people of Gomorrah** " (*verse 10*).

Ezek. 16: 49 shows that the sins of Sodom were pride, lust, luxury and cruelty, and now rulers and people under them in Jerusalem were guilty of the same sins. But there was something additional. Over all the abominations there was a garb of religion, a perfunctory discharge of certain details of the law. They presented their offerings to God, but of what value were they in His sight? They were simply trampling His courts (*verse 12*). Their observance of the appointed days and feasts was hateful: " **I cannot away with iniquity and the solemn meeting**," He says (*verse 13, R.V.*); in other words, 'I cannot bear ungodliness and gatherings at festivals'.

Mere external religion is ever a cloak to cover iniquity. The Lord exposed all that in His strong denunciations in Matt. 23. The guilty combination in Judaism has largely developed in Christendom. The conscience of a believer may become so seared that a person can practise religion while yet living in sin.

The Lord warns His people in *verse 15* that, if they stretch out their hands to Him, He has to hide His eyes from them. If they make ever so many prayers He does not hear, for their hands are full of blood. God listens to those who lift up holy hands (1 Tim. 2: 8 and see Ps. 24: 4, 5). The word "blood" is plural, which points, not merely to murder, but to acts of violence akin to murder, and to bribes which purchased the ruin of widows and orphans (cp. Micah 3: 9–11). They are therefore called upon to wash and cleanse themselves, and put away the evil of their doings in His sight, to " **cease to do evil and learn to do well, and seek judgment, relieve the oppressed, judge the fatherless, plead for the widow** " (*vv. 16, 17*). Let them learn the first principles of well-doing. God has a special care for widows and orphans, Exod. 22: 22–24; Deut. 10: 18; Ps. 68: 5; Jas. 1: 27.

If they would do this and turn from their evil ways, there was mercy for them, both in the removal of their sins and in the prospect of eating the good of the land. The message of *verse 18* invites them to realize both the graciousness of His appeal and the justice of His demands: " **Come now** (or Come, I pray you), **and let us reason together** (as if challenging them to a trial), **saith the Lord: though your sins be as scarlet, they shall be as white as snow; though they be red like crimson, they shall be as wool.**" The scarlet may suggest the deep-dyed character of sin. There would seem to be a reference to Num. 19: 2, 6, 9, where scarlet was burnt in the sacrifice, and thus there is an intimation as to the atoning efficacy of the blood of Christ. The glaring character of sin is certainly in view, and for the whiteness of snow see Ps. 51: 7. Some regard the scarlet and white as emblematic of the relation of fire to light, i.e., of the wrath of God against sin to His pardoning grace.

" **If ye be willing and obedient, ye shall eat the good of the land** " (*verse 19*).

The offer of justifying grace is designed to lead to repentance not to be repented of. True repentance leads to willingness and obedience, to listen to the voice of God and do His will. This leads to spiritual blessing. What was the good of the land for Israel is to us the provision made for us in Christ as the nourishing and sustaining power of our life by the Holy Spirit. Refusal must bring judgment (*verse 20*).

The lamentation which follows bewails the apostate state of the nation. The once faithful wife (pictured as a strong citadel) had become a harlot. Judgment had given place to violence and murder. The pure silver of righteousness had become dross, an amalgam of formal religion and vileness. The wine of Divinely imparted wisdom (Prov. 9: 5) was diluted with the water of mere tradition. The princes, forsaking righteous judgment and the cause of the widow, had become lawless (*vv.* 21–23).

There was One who acted as the righteous judge, " **the Lord, Jehovah of hosts, the mighty One of Israel** ". This last title is used here only. He was mighty to deal with these adversaries and to restore the nation (*verse 24*). Promises are therefore given to Zion: " I will turn My hand upon thee "; His strong hand would be outstretched to redeem from iniquity, to smelt out the dross and take away the tin (or lead), *verse 25*.

Righteous judges and counsellors would be installed as in the earliest days, e.g., of the reigns of David and Solomon. The day is approaching when Zion shall be called " **The city of righteousness, the faithful city** " (or 'citadel'), a different word from that rendered "city" in the preceding clause. Cp. 60: 14. The names express the nature. These glorious characteristics will result from the great basic acts of God in redeeming Zion with judgment and her converts (those who have looked on Him Whom they pierced and turned to Him in repentance) with righteousness (*vv. 26, 27*).

It will be all God's doing. God's justifying grace in Christ leads to righteousness and steadfastness in the lives of the justified. These are the evidences of genuine conversion.

In contrast to these converts who will enjoy the Millennial Kingdom, those who have followed the Antichrist will be destroyed together and consumed (*verse 28*).

In *verse 29* the "oaks" which they have desired represent the the mighty ones of earth, the Man of Sin and the leaders under him. The "gardens" which they have chosen symbolize the pleasures and glories of the world (*verse 29*). They themselves will be as a fading oak and a waterless garden (*verse 30*). They forsake "the Fountain of living waters" (Jer. 2: 13). To choose anything but the will and way of God results only in loss and shame.

The close of this first chapter (*verse 31*) points on to the close of the whole book and speaks of the time of the end. The strong man is a phrase suggestive of the two great "beasts" of Rev. 13, the final Gentile world ruler and his colleague (perhaps a Jew). He shall be " **as tow, and his work** (R.V.) **as a spark** "; his sin will kindle the fire of the punishment that will fall upon him; " **they shall both burn together, none shall quench them** " (see Rev. 19: 20).

CHAPTER II

THE opening word of this chapter resumes what Isaiah stated at the beginning of his prophecies (*1: 1*), but now introduces the subject of chapters 2 to 5. In 1: 1 he spoke of seeing a vision, now he speaks of seeing a word. This marks the communication as supernatural. When men speak to one another they hear; God's word was seen. This suggests two things: firstly, the word of God is "living", its energizing effect is to impart a revelation impossible to the merely natural mind; therefore, secondly, it involves a mind prepared and qualified to behold intelligently what God has to reveal.

The seeing of the word will lead to a vision of the Lord's glory in chapter 6. In chapter 1 Divine justice deals with rejected mercy; in 2: 5 Divine mercy restores holiness. Accordingly the prophecy opens, not with denunciation of sin (that is to be renewed at verse 6), but with the promise of blessing " **in the last days** ".

" **It shall come to pass** " does not begin a quotation from Micah 4: 1–3; it is a direct revelation to Isaiah. What is now in view is the glory of the Millennial Kingdom. " **The mountain of the Lord's House shall be established in the top of the mountains, and shall be exalted above the hills** " (*verse 2*). The Temple will apparently have a loftier site than formerly. There may be also an indication of the domination exercised therefrom over all other earthly powers (cp. Ps. 76: 4, 5). " **All nations shall flow unto it,** " a metaphor from the peaceful flowing of a river, in contrast to the tossings of the sea of national strife and upheaval. The builders of Babel who sought to establish a world centre found their scheme brought to confusion under Divine judgment, and were scattered abroad. Mount Zion and the Lord's House will become a gathering centre for the nations in their recognition of His power and His claims.

There will be a mutual agreement and decision among many (not all, it would seem) of the nations to go up to Mount Zion, " **to the House of the God of Jacob** ", with a genuine desire to be taught His ways and to walk in His paths: " **for out of Zion shall go forth the law, and the word of the Lord from Jerusalem** " *(verse 3)*. Gen. 22: 14 will be fulfilled. See also chapter 51: 4; Mic. 4: 2; Zech. 8: 3.

" **He shall judge among** (i.e., between) **the nations** " *(verse 4)*. He will administer justice regarding international questions and difficulties, which now so often give rise to war. He will " **rebuke** (or reprove) **many peoples** ", rectifying their mistaken and selfish ideas, with the result that, after the tremendous clash of arms at Armageddon (Har-magedon) at the close of the great tribulation (the time of Jacob's trouble), the manufacture of weapons of war will cease and agriculture shall flourish. No longer will they learn war.

In *verse 5* the glorious future prospect assured to Israel stirs up Isaiah to plead with his people to return to God immediately, and to walk " **in the light of the Lord** ". Hence the renewal of the lamentation for their deplorable apostasy. *Verse 6* should begin with "For" (not "Therefore"): " **For Thou hast forsaken Thy people, the house of Jacob** " (not here the noble title of "Israel"). They were filled with customs and ways from the east (cp. Num. 23: 7) and had adopted from the Philistines the arts of divination, and had joined hands with the sons of strangers (that is the meaning of " **please themselves** ").

That gold and silver and horses and chariots *(verse 7)* filled the land was a complete ignoring of the command given in Deut. 17: 16, 17. Solomon had erred in this respect, and from the throne downwards the nation thereby became permeated with idolatry under the influence of pagan peoples; high and low engaged in it; the mean man bowed down to what his hands had made, and the great man degraded himself *(vv. 8, 9)*. Hence the intercessor was now compelled to plead against his people that they might not be forgiven (cp. Hos. 1: 6).

The answer is given. Judgment is impending. They had forsaken the Rock (Deut. 32: 4; Isa. 17: 10; 26: 4; 30: 29); they must therefore flee to the natural rock and hide in the dust of the earth, from before the terror of the Lord and " **the glory of His majesty** " *(verse 10)*. Pride must be humbled. They had bowed down to idols; now their haughtiness must be bowed down, that the Lord alone might be exalted *(verse 11)*.

Where God is not given His rightful place everything falls into ruin.

The passage from here to the end of the chapter passes from immediate circumstances to the end of Gentile dominion and to the judgments which must fall upon the nations at the time of the Second Advent, preliminarily to the setting up of the Millennial Kingdom.

The period is described as " **the day of the Lord** ". The word "day", when used in this way, in the O.T. and the N.T., has the twofold significance of time and judgment. The natural day brings into light that which has been in darkness. The present period is called "man's day" (1 Cor. 4: 3, A.V. and R.V. margins, for the text "man's judgment"), for now man passes his benighted and often perverted judgment upon things. There have been days of the Lord in His judicial dealings with Israel in the past, especially by victory over the foes, Jer. 46: 10; Ezek. 13: 5; 30: 3.

Here, however, as in Joel 2: 31 and Mal. 4: 5, the period indicated is yet future. It will see the complete overthrow of Gentile power (Isa. 13: 9–11; 34; Dan. 2: 34, 44; Obad. 15) and the deliverance of the Jews.

In *verse 13* the cedars of Lebanon and the oaks of Bashan, illustrative of natural glory and power, are symbolic of military leaders of the nations gathered finally against the Jews.

In *verse 14* the mountains and hills, likewise emblematic of natural power, symbolize the mighty kingdoms of the nations. All that they have accomplished, in their pride and independence of God, both by way of strongholds on land (*verse 15*) and in traffic and commerce by sea (*verse 16*), is to be brought to nought. The self-exaltation of man must yield place to the exaltation of God alone (*verse 17*).

Idolatry will be stopped (*verse 18*), and men who gloried in their prowess and strength will flee to underground shelters, to " **the holes of the rocks, and into the caves of the earth, for fear of the Lord, and for the glory of His majesty, when He ariseth to shake terribly the earth** " (*vv. 19, 20*). See 13: 9–13; Joel 2: 30, 31; 3: 16; Hag. 2: 6, 7; Matt. 24: 29, 30; Rev. 6: 12–17; 16: 18–20.

Pagans, convinced of the futility and delusions of their idols, will hide them in the haunts of moles and bats, as if disgusted with them under their revulsion of feeling, and under the terror of Divine judgments. They themselves will flee to the cavities and crevices (the real meaning of the word rendered "tops") of the rocks—not that these will afford protection from the wrath of God.

Verse 22 exposes the impotency of the Antichrist, the Man of Sin, the leader of the great confederacy of the nations, the would-be conqueror of the world, the determined destroyer of the Jewish people, the man upon whom the nations had set their hopes of world-organization and prosperity, the man who 'set himself forth as God' (2 Thess. 2: 3, 4). His " **breath is in his nostrils : for wherein is he to be accounted of ?** "—an exposure of his human frailty in face of the almighty power of the true God. For his doom see Deut. 32: 42, R.V.; 2 Thess. 2: 8; Rev. 19: 19.

CHAPTER III

JUDGMENT must begin at the House of God. Israel would suffer almost 'immediately at the hand of the Chaldeans, and the chapter gives warning of this. The people had provoked the Lord. Cruelty and oppression were practised by their rulers (*vv. 14, 15*) and godless gaiety and luxury characterized the ways of the " **daughters of Zion** " (*vv. 16–23*). In the future the nations cannot be blessed till Divine Judgment has been wrought upon God's earthly people in "the time of Jacob's trouble" and upon their Gentile aggressors.

The opening verses give a testimony to the effects of national sins. The Divine titles " **the Lord, Jehovah of hosts** " combine the supreme and absolute authority and power of God as Ruler and Judge. "Stay" and "staff" are different forms of the same Hebrew word, and denote every sort of support. The removal must produce famine conditions, natural and spiritual, and not only so, it would mean the removal of every kind of national leader and official, every counsellor and guide, as well as every skilled labourer (*vv. 2, 3*). The nation would be stripped of all organization and power. Inexperienced youths and babes (lit., childish things, or puerilities) would govern (*verse 4*).

Utter confusion must result. Men would ask for help from one another, but all would be helpless, unable to provide remedies or sustenance, or to rule (*vv. 6, 7*). A few faithful men would remain, and acknowledge that the whole situation was the result of iniquity and the provocation of the Lord (*verse 8*). In *verse 9* " **the shew of their countenance** " means their glaring effrontery (cp. Hos. 5: 5; 7: 10). They openly avow their sin, as the people of Sodom did. But like them they must bring retribution upon themselves (cp. Amos 5: 10–20).

Amidst it all there is a word for the godly by way of a contrasting parallel: " **Say ye to the righteous, that it shall be well with him** (lit., 'it is good', the same phrase as in Gen. 1: 4, 10, 18, etc.); **for they shall eat the fruit of their doings.**" "Whatsoever a man soweth, that shall he also reap." What seems so terrible for the godly will be found to be for their eternal good. The apparent prosperity of the wicked will eventuate in his own destruction: " **the reward of his hands shall be given him** " (*vv. 10, 11*).

Verses 12 to 16 describe further the degraded condition of the people. Mere youths, with all their inexperience, governed them with oppression, and women ruled over them, as had Maachah (1 Kings 15: 13) and Athaliah (2 Kings 11: 1, 13). These leaders did nothing but mislead; they destroyed (lit., 'swallow up', cp. Job 39: 24) the paths appointed for Israel, obliterating and hiding them. Therefore Jehovah would interpose to judge the peoples (the word is plural in *verse 13*), the nations in general and especially the rulers of His own nation, dealing with them for crushing His people and 'grinding the face' of the suffering, a vivid metaphor, not found elsewhere, taken from the action of the millstone and describing unmerciful severity.

The general worldliness found its great expression in the ways and doings of the females, in their luxurious style of dress, and adornment, adopted partly by imitating the priestly vestments and partly from idolatry. Dire retribution must ensue. The "scab" (*verse 17*) is a word connected with leprosy. The word rendered "discover" is used in Ps. 137: 7 of razing a city. The men (civilians) would fall by the sword and the mighty men (lit., 'might', i.e., the entire military body) would perish in war. The gates, places where worshippers thronged and ceremonies were held, would become scenes of mourning, and the city being "desolate" or purged (the word is rendered "be free" in Num. 5: 19, 28, in connection with the water of jealousy), would sit upon the ground, a phrase expressive of utter humiliation, used in 47: 1 and Job 2: 13.

When worldliness comes into a church, the Lord has to administer rebuke and chastening and takes an outside place

(Rev. 3: 19, 20). Let the individual backslider repent with earnest zeal, and the Lord's desire to re-enter will be fulfilled.

CHAPTER IV

THE first verse of this chapter probably belongs to the end of the preceding chapter, and continues the effects of the Divine judgments upon the proud, godless daughters of Zion. The prevailing conditions would be reversed. Whereas the young women had each gloried in being an attraction to suitors, the time of humbling was coming when seven women would make suit to the same man, whoever he might be, saying " **We will eat our own bread, and wear our own clothes** (renouncing the claim established by the law for provision of food and clothing by the husband, Exod. 21: 10); **only let us be called by thy name ; to take away our reproach,**" i.e., the reproach of being single. The number seven is here suggestive of the fullness of Divine judgments.

But mercy rejoices against judgment, and the second verse introduces a passage dealing with eventual restoration. "In that day" marks the yet future part of the long period of God's dealings with His earthly people. When the sinners in Zion have been removed, a remnant will be brought forth in the glory of their fidelity. "The escaped of Israel" will constitute the reigning earthly power under the King of Kings.

It is He Who is called in *verse 2* " **the Branch of Jehovah** ", and " **the fruit of the earth** ". This twofold description combines His Deity and His humanity. He will be revealed as " **beautiful and glorious** ", lit. 'for beauty (ornament) and glory', the same two words as describe the priestly robes in Exod. 28: 2, 40. He will be a Melchizedek Priest. With the phrase "the fruit of the earth" cp. the statement "our Lord sprang out of Judah" (Heb. 7: 14). He will be " **excellent and comely** ", or "majesty and splendour" (cp. 28: 5). "Except a grain of wheat," He said, "fall into the earth and die, it abideth by itself alone; but if it die, it beareth much fruit" (John 12: 24, R.V.). Accordingly here it says that He will, in all this glory, be " **for them that are escaped of Israel** ".

Just as Christ, when He comes to receive the dead saints and change the living, will be "our Deliverer from the coming wrath" (as the rendering should be in 1 Thess. 1: 10), i.e., the wrath of God upon the world at the end of this age, so when He comes in glory with the angels and the Church He will be "the Deliverer" of the godly remnant in Israel (the same phrase and title in Rom. 11: 26), not from wrath but from their foes.

Then those who are " **left in Zion** ", those who are " **written among the living in Jerusalem** " (cp. Luke 10: 20; Phil. 4: 3; Heb. 12: 23; Rev. 17: 8), will be called "holy" (*verse 3*), Israel's primary and real vocation (Exod. 19: 6).

This is our vocation too; it involves a life of complete separation to God, an identification with His character (1 Pet. 1: 16). Let us therefore who are written among the living "cleanse ourselves from all defilement of the flesh and spirit, perfecting holiness in the fear of the Lord".

The people failed to obey the command " **Wash you, make you clean** " (1: 16). In the coming day the Lord will Himself " **wash away the filth of the daughters of Zion** " and purge " **the blood of Jerusalem** ", and that " **by the spirit** (or blast) **of judgment, and by the spirit of burning** " (*verse 4*). This will be the baptism of fire, foretold by John the Baptist (Matt. 3: 11).

In the wilderness the Lord provided for the journeying of the people a pillar of cloud and fire. In the coming Millennium there will be, not a pillar, but a " **canopy** " of cloud by day and fire by night " **over the whole habitation** " and upon the festal assemblies of the people. The figure is that of a wedding canopy carried above the bridegroom. " **Upon all the glory shall be a covering** (not "a defence"), *verse 5*. The term gives an intimation of the Lord's joy over His redeemed people, as the rejoicing of a bridegroom over his bride. There is likewise a suggestion of the close association of the Church in its Heavenly position with the restored earthly nation.

" **And there shall be a tabernacle** (or rather, a pavilion) **for a place of refuge, and for a covert from storm and from rain** " (*verse 6*). Nature will continue its activities during the Millennial age. The most glorious feature of the whole scene will be the conjoint existence of the restored and glorious Jerusalem on earth, "the city of the Great King", and the Heavenly Jerusalem, consisting of all the glorified saints, and described figuratively in Rev. 21: 10 to 22: 5, the great City-Bride, the wife of the Lamb, the "Light-Giver" of which is Christ Himself.

CHAPTER V

ISAIAH is now led to adopt a new mode of appeal to Israel. He is in the closest fellowship with Jehovah, Who gives him a song to record concerning His vineyard. It is " a song of My Beloved " (not addressed to Him). The vineyard belongs to Jehovah, and there is an intimation that His Well-Beloved is Christ.

The vineyard is " the house of Israel ", and the vine is " the men of Judah, His pleasant plant (lit. the plant of His pleasures)." God had done everything for His people that they might be blessed in glorifying His Name and fulfilling His will. He had fenced His vineyard (*verse 2*). He had given Israel His Law, separating them from all other nations. He had gathered out the stones, dealing with the Canaanites, who rendered the land barren. He had planted " the choicest vine " (the word is found elsewhere only in Gen. 49: 11 and Jer. 2: 21, rendered "noble"). He had built a tower, the central city of Jerusalem, where He would place His Name (cp. Prov. 18: 10), a tower from which His appointed priests and prophets could watch against spiritual foes. He had hewed out a wine-vat to receive the juice of the grapes, symbolic of the Temple, where the offerings, worship and praise would be rendered to Him by the operation of His Holy Spirit.

For all this fruit the Lord "looked", waiting patiently for the prosperous outcome of His dealings. There appeared instead the small bitter berries of the wild vine (*verse 2*).

Let the inhabitants of Jerusalem and the men of Judah judge the matter, taking the circumstances into careful consideration. Let them have regard to what Jehovah had wrought for them, and what they had done in their rebellion against Him and the dishonour done to His Name (*vv. 3, 4*). Divine retribution was impending and inevitable. The hedge must be removed and eaten up (devoted to grazing). The fence must be broken down and be trodden upon by the G ntiles (*verse 5*).

The whole must be laid waste. Pruning and hoeing would be futile. Rainless clouds would produce barrenness. What might have been so fruitful must yield briers and thorns, the very emblems of stunted growth.

The Lord's doctrine "drops as the rain" and His speech "distils as the dew"; but where there is no heart to receive it, how can there be anything but unproductiveness and blights? (*verse 6*).

Verse 7 also interprets the metaphor of the wild grapes. God **" looked for judgment, but behold oppression ; for righteousness, but behold a cry."** It has been pointed out that the fact that the Hebrew pair of contrasting words have a certain similarity of sound, gives an intimation that as the wild grapes have a certain resemblance to the good, so in mere outward appearance the evildoers seemed religious, while actually they were full of iniquity. Cp. Matt. 23: 28.

The lesson from this passage is clear. It is possible to become so familiar with the routine of religious exercises that, while outwardly conformed to what has been learnt from Scripture, real heart devotion to Christ Himself has waned; the first love has been lost, and with it true spiritual power. The declension may open the way for grosser forms of evil, and the Lord has to stand at the door and knock, waiting for a response from any who really desire to enjoy communion with Him, and real conformity to His will and way.

This parable of the vineyard is followed by six denunciatory woes. In much the same way the Lord in dealing with the leaders of the people followed His parable of the vineyard, in Matt. 21: 33 to 41, by a sevenfold series of "woes" in 23: 13 to 36.
The first "woe" uttered by Isaiah, is against covetousness and greed (*verse 8*). There were those who added house to house and field to field, aiming at monopolies, and violating the law of property laid down in Num. 36: 7. Desolation and scarcity must follow (*vv. 9, 10*). The land was the Lord's, not theirs.

Failure to realize that all that we are and have belong to Christ leads to such misuse of what has been entrusted to us, that we seek to serve our own ends thereby and bring the disaster upon ourselves of spiritual barrenness and want.

The second woe is against self-indulgence and pleasure seeking (*vv. 11, 12*; with *verse 12* cp. Amos 6: 4, 5). They heeded not the work of the Lord and were blind to the operation of His hands. Hence captivity without knowledge. The phrase rendered " **for lack of knowledge** " (*verse 13, R.V.*) may mean 'without knowing it', i.e., without discerning the reason for, and the meaning of, the Lord's dealings. As a result their glory (the high and mighty in the nation) would become 'men of starvation', and the multitude (the riotous mass of the people) would be men parched with thirst.

Self-indulgence dulls the spiritual sense by which we understand the ways of the Lord.

But a further consequence would ensue. Death follows famine. The foe would be cruel. Sheol (the under-world) would open wide its jaws, and the glory (the men of note) and their multitude (the people in general), with all the pomp and godless rejoicing, would descend into it. The mean man would be brought down and the mighty humbled (the order is chiasmic, or inverse, in contrast to that in *verse 14*). The eyes of the lofty, open to anything but the Lord, would be humbled (*verse 15*). Cp. 2: 9, 11, 17.

When men are persistently blind to God's dealings in grace and longsuffering, He manifests Himself in righteous retributive judgment. So it was with Israel and its captivity. So it will be with the world at the end of this age. Jehovah of Hosts will be (lit., will show Himself) " **exalted in judgment** ", and God the Holy One will be " **sanctified** (lit., will sanctify Himself) **in righteousness** " (*verse 16*). He will compel recognition of His attributes and claims. Jew and Gentile alike will be made to give Him the glory which is His alone. Cp. Phil. 2: 9–11.

And as to the land that remained after the nation had gone into captivity, it would be occupied by foreign nomad shepherds; lambs would feed " **as in their pasture** " (*verse 17, R.V.*) and the places left waste by the removal of the nation, would be eaten by strangers. For centuries Arabs have literally fulfilled this, and Jerusalem has been given up to Islam.

The third woe (*vv. 18, 19*) is against daring presumption and defiance against God. They " **draw iniquity with cords of vanity** (not pride, but lying and seductive teaching), **and sin as it were with a cart rope** ". The figure is that of beasts of burden roped to a wagon. Iniquity was the burden they dragged by their vain delusions, and sin the wagon to which they were roped. However presumptuously they might glory in their ungodliness, it would bring the inevitable punishment. The description is sarcastic. Vaunting themselves in their evil in word and deed they failed all the time to apprehend the retribution it was bringing upon them.

They scoffed at God's Word and derided His Name. " **They say, Let Him make speed, and hasten His work, that we may see it** (i.e., let Him fulfil what He has foretold, let us see whether He can actually carry it out); **and let the counsel of the Holy One of Israel draw nigh and come, that we may know it** (i.e., experience its fulfilment)!" This way of taking God's Name in vain was a gibe at Isaiah's use of it (1: 4; 5: 24; 30: 10, 11). Such taunts were the very height of defiance. They would be repeated at the Cross, and will be repeated by the Antichrist. See also 2 Pet. 3: 3, 4.

The fourth woe (*verse 20*) denounces those who subvert moral principles. They " **call evil good, and good evil.**" They put " **darkness for light, and light for darkness** "; " **bitter for sweet, and sweet for bitter.**" Evil loves darkness and delights in sin, the bitter thing. To forsake the Lord is evil (Jer. 2: 19); they pronounce it good. It is good to draw nigh to God (Ps. 73: 28); they declare it to be evil. Thus they flagrantly contradicted the very precepts and revealed will of the Lord.

The fifth woe (*verse 21*) denounces the pride and self-complacency of those who are " **wise in their own eyes, and prudent in their own sight** " (in contradiction to Prov. 3: 7). This condition is closely connected with those mentioned under the two preceding woes. It is the natural concomitant of the rejection of God's Word and the subversion of morals.

The sixth woe (*vv. 22, 23*) denounces those who pervert justice and use their administrative powers to enrich themselves by bribes and to indulge in drunken debauchery. The prophet is again sarcastic. They are "mighty", i.e., men of renown, in their twofold criminality.

The Divine judgment upon all this is likened to a fire (lit., a

tongue of fire, a phrase here only in the O.T.) devouring stubble,
a flame consuming chaff (or rather, dry grass sinking down in
flame). All that they gloried in would be as mouldy rottenness
and vanishing dust (*verse 24*). They despised Jehovah's law and
scornfully rejected " **the word** (the speech, as in Deut. 32: 2)
of the Holy One of Israel ". Hence the righteous and irrevocable
anger of the Lord and the stretching forth of His hand in wrath.
The hills would tremble by the marching of hostile armies, and
the carcases of the people would be like street sweepings (*verse 25*).

What is foretold in *vv. 26–30* came to pass in the invasions of
Nebuchadnezzar, the first of which took place in 589 B.C. God
is described as lifting up " **an ensign to the nations from far** ",
i.e., planting a banner to summon them to Jerusalem as His
military *rendezvous*, to fight His battles against His apostate
people. How great the change from the time when He Himself
was their banner (Jehovah-nissi) against their first foe after the
overthrow of Pharaoh and his hosts (Exod. 17: 15)! Secondly,
that He would " **hiss unto them** (the Chaldeans) **from the end
of the earth** " presents the figure of a bee-keeper enticing the
bees, by hissing, to leave their hives and settle on the ground.

The foe would roar over it (*verse 30*), i.e., over Judah and
Jerusalem, and God's nation would look to the earth and see
only darkness and tribulation, and in the heavens the darkness
of night instead of light.

The general description given in these verses points not only
to the Chaldean invasions but to those by subsequent powers,
reaching a climax in the Roman conquest and eventual destruction of the city and the scattering of the people.

This 5th chapter thus has three parts; (1) Jehovah's planting
and care of His vineyard, and His disappointment in its failure,
vv. 1–7, (2) the actual transgressions of both rulers and people,
denounced under the six woes, *vv. 8–23*, (3) the judgments
which would fall upon them, *vv. 26–30*.

All has its warnings against departure from the Word of God,
and against the adoption of evil practices, the inevitable result
of such departure. So it has been in the history of Christendom.
All must meet with Divine retribution at the hands of the
nations. For this see Rev. 17: 16–18.

God in His grace has left nothing undone to enable us to
be fruitful for His glory, by His Spirit and His Word. Once

we turn from this we not only become unfruitful but open our hearts to many forms of evil, and "judgment must begin at the House of God".

CHAPTER VI

THIS chapter is closely connected with chapter 5. The sad condition of things described in that chapter existed in Uzziah's reign, and now in the year of his death (a jubilee year, which began on the evening of the Day of Atonement—that was the fourteenth jubilee since Israel occupied Canaan) Isaiah is given a vision of the Lord's glory, in contrast to the nation's shame. The glory was about to depart from the earthly Temple. It has never returned nationally since. In this connection it is significant that shortly after Uzziah's death Rome was founded, the power that was destined to consummate the devastation of Jerusalem and the scattering of the Jews.

The vision was of " **the Lord** (Adonai, sovereign or absolute Lord) **sitting upon a throne, high and lifted up** " (*verse 1*). The Apostle John makes it known that the glory seen by the prophet was that of Christ Himself (John 12: 41). "High and lifted up" almost certainly refers to the Throne. Some would regard it as descriptive of the Lord. The word rendered "train" means the hem or fringe of His robe, as in Exod. 28: 33, 34. His garment consists of light (Ps. 104) and fills the Heavenly Temple, just as the cloud filled the Tabernacle (Exod. 40: 35).

That the seraphim stood "above" (*verse 2*) signifies that they were in attendance (not in a superior position). They differ from the cherubim. They are the fiery guardians of the holiness of the Lord, and are possessed of certain human features. With two wings they covered their faces, in awe that dared not gaze at the glory. With two they covered their feet, in acknowledgment of the lowliness of their glorious service. With twain they were flying, or hovering. The verbs are in the imperfect tense, describing what they were doing continually.

" **One cried unto another** " (*verse 3*). This suggests that their utterances were antiphonal, though not in song. There is no record in Scripture of angels singing. The worship offered is thus expressed: " **Holy, holy, holy, is Jehovah of hosts : the whole**

earth is full of His glory (or rather, His glory is the fullness of
the whole earth)." Possibly the first part was said by the seraphim on one side, the second part by those on the other.

As to the threefold utterance of the word "holy", three is the
number of unity expanded or developed. There is more than
mere emphasis here. What is suggested is probably the realization of the character of the Tri-unity, the Three in the one
Godhead, their attribute in its purity and perfection, rather than
three different modes of Their dealings.

The determinate counsel of God is not only that the earth
"shall be filled with His glory" (Num. 14: 21) but that "the
earth shall be filled with the knowledge of the glory of the Lord"
(Isa. 11: 9 and Hab. 2: 14). His glory stands for His character
and actings, and all this is to be manifested and is to receive
world-wide recognition and acknowledgment (Jer. 31: 34; cp.
Phil. 2: 11).

" **And the foundations of the thresholds** (R.V.) **were moved at
the voice of him** (a collective pronoun, signifying 'them', the
company of the seraphim) **that cried, and the house was filled
with smoke** " (*verse 4*). The smoke, the outcome of the worship
of the seraphim, arose from the altar of incense. It was therefore connected with the fire on the altar (*verse 6*) and was
indicative of the acceptance of Isaiah himself (*verse 7*) and the
preparation for his testimony (*verse 8*). This completes the vision
of the glory of the Lord as set in contrast to the dishonour done
to Him by the ways and doings of His people.

The effect upon Isaiah was to bring him down before the Lord
in the realization of his own natural state and in acknowledgment
of his identification with his nation in their evil condition (*verse 5*).

So should it ever be with us. The more we apprehend the
facts and character of the atoning sacrifice of Christ and the
glories of His Person the more deeply we realize our own sinfulness. The nearer we are to the Lord the greater the sense of
our utter unworthiness. Further, in this our own rightful
attitude before Him we learn to identify ourselves with the
condition of those fellow-members of the Body of Christ who
have proved unfaithful and have lapsed into evil ways, and to
confess their sins, as ours. Only so can we really be prepared
to give an effectual testimony. It is one thing to condemn the
saints, it is quite another to take upon ourselves the confession

of their sins as ours. It is that which causes the Holy Spirit to use us for real blessing amidst them.

The fire on the altar of incense did for Isaiah all that was necessary. The vision of the glory caused him to exclaim, " **Woe is me! for I am undone** (or, cut off), **because I am a man of unclean lips, and I dwell in the midst of a people of unclean lips : for mine eyes have seen the King, Jehovah of hosts** " (*verse 5*). Uzziah had been cut off, and had to cover his lip and cry "Unclean, unclean" (Lev. 13: 45). Now Isaiah feels himself in the like condition spiritually. No man could see God without suffering death (Exod. 33: 20). His vision of the glory had reduced him, in his own estimate, to the level of his guilty and defiled nation.

For such a contrite heart there was immediate mercy (see 57: 15). A seraph became a ministering spirit, in the vision. He brought in his hand a burning coal taken from the incense altar by the tongs of the sanctuary (*verse 6*). A seraph could not touch the sacrifice or that which arose from it, he brought the effects of it. With the coals he touched the prophet's mouth, that member the uncleanness of which he had deplored (cp. Jer. 1: 9). His iniquity was removed, and his sin expiated (*verse 7*).

The whole vision and the Divine dealings were the appointed preparation for the solemn testimony he was to deliver. This was not the beginning of his witness, the occasion was a special one. If we are to engage in any particular service for the Lord, we can render it effectively only as we freshly appropriate to ourselves the efficacy of the atoning sacrifice of Christ for the cleansing of our hearts from sin. For each occasion we must come to the Throne by way of the Cross. We must come to the Mercy-Seat (Christ Himself) "that we may obtain mercy".

All was now clear for the prophet to deliver his solemn message. He hears the voice of the Lord (*Adonai*, as twice elsewhere in this chapter, *vv. 1 and 11*, the supreme Ruler and Judge), saying " **Whom shall I send, and who will go for us ?** " (*verse 8*). The plural is suggestive of the Tri-unity of Persons in the Godhead. This was not a question of mere deliberation, it was directed to the heart of Isaiah himself, whom the Lord had already prepared

for the purpose. The response was immediate. Isaiah was standing in unhindered communion with his Master. " Here am I ;
send me," he says. There was no questioning or reasoning. No
burden would be too cumbersome, if the Lord committed it to him.

> There is no task laid upon us by the Lord which we shall
> not have power from Him to fulfil, when everything that would
> hinder our communion with Him has been removed.

Nothing could be more solemn than the message he was
commissioned to give: " Go, and tell this people, Hear ye indeed
(or hear ye still), but understand not; and see ye indeed, but
perceive not " (verse 9). They were "this people", not "My
people" (cp., e.g., Exod. 32: 9, 21, 31; Num. 11: 11–14), and
thus frequently in subsequent chapters of Isaiah. They were
"a people of unclean lips".

The message was not only for immediate purposes, it pointed
on to the time when Christ Himself, in the days of His flesh,
pronounced this very doom upon the apostate nation (Matt. 13:
14, 15).

The commands in verse 10, to make the heart of the people
fat, to make their ears heavy, and to shut their eyes, involved
the punitive measures which God Himself would carry out.
Isaiah's message would be God's own instrument in doing it.
Prophets were often said to do themselves by their messages
what God actually did through them. See, e.g., Jer. 1: 10;
31: 28; Ezek. 43: 3; Hos. 6: 5.

What follows is in the inverse order of what has just preceded:
" lest they see with their eyes, and hear with their ears, and
understand with their heart." This inverted parallelism is called
Chiasm, from the shape of the Greek letter Chi (X). It lends
vigour and emphasis in the handling of a subject. For a simple
example see Matt. 12: 22.

> The people had so persistently perverted their ways that
> they had gone beyond the possibility of conversion and healing.
> A man may so harden himself in evil as to render his condition
> irremediable, and this by God's retributive judgment upon him.

> The prophet, while willing and obedient, was so weighed down
> by the nature of his message, that he cried, " Lord, how long ? "

For Isaiah knew that He would not cast off His people for ever (cp. Exod. 32: 9–14). The Lord responds by foretelling the wasted, depopulated condition of the cities, the uninhabited state of the houses, the utter desolation of the land, the removal of the people far away, and a multitude of forsaken places in the very heart of the country (vv. 11, 12).

There is always a "remnant" of faithful ones in the nation and God shows His mercy to it in and through such. Accordingly He now says, " **But in it shall be a tenth, and it shall again be eaten up.** " Even so this remnant will come through a time of trouble. It will be "eaten" (or "burnt"), i.e., by a purifying fire (see Mal. 3: 3). This was the case with those who returned from captivity by the decree of Cyrus, as recorded in the books of Ezra and Nehemiah. So in the coming day, in "the time of Jacob's trouble" under the Antichrist (Jer. 30: 7).

It will be " **as a terebinth and as an oak, whose stock remaineth, when they are felled** (or when the branches are cut off and only a stump remains); **so the holy seed is the stock thereof** " (verse 13). The stump has life in it after the cutting off of the branches; it can shoot out into verdure again. All this describes, in a twofold application, the circumstances of the remnant both after the return from captivity and hereafter in the great tribulation. The nation, consisting of the remnant, will, under the hand of their Messiah—Deliverer, revive and be glorified (see 11: 1).

CHAPTER VII

AFTER the death of Uzziah (6: 1) and during the reign of Jotham, Isaiah was given no written prophecy to record. Jotham, probably exercised by his father's death, sought to be conformed to God's Law. Evil went on in the nation (2 Chron. 27: 2), and Ahaz broke out into open defiance of God. And now a new series of prophecies is committed to His messenger.

The kings of Syria and Israel combined to invade Judah and attack Jerusalem, but were frustrated. The northern tribes were at least as guilty as Judah. In verse 2 Ephraim stands for Israel (as distinct from Judah), for Ephraim was the paramount tribe of Israel and was a rival to Judah. A second expedition was planned by the allies, and the house of David was moved, that is to say, trembled with fear, " **as trees are moved with the wind.**"

Isaiah was therefore commanded to take his son Shear-jashub and to go to meet Ahaz at the end of the aqueduct of the upper pool, at the road of the fuller's field (*verse 3*). This would be on the west of Jerusalem, and the king was probably carrying out operations to prevent the foe from a water supply, while yet retaining its use for the city.

Shear-jashub means "the remnant shall return (or turn)." This forms a continuation of the message given in 6: 13, marking the unity of the distinct prophecies. The name was designed to be to Ahaz both an inducement to him to turn to God himself, and a warning that, if he refused to do so, he would have no part in the restoration of that part of the nation described as the remnant.

God in His longsuffering was showing Ahaz mercy in spite of his iniquity. He promises him that the northern confederacy will be overthrown, and Ephraim would be broken in pieces (*vv. 4–9*). Yet let him beware lest, persisting in his unbelief, he would be excluded from the promised blessing: " **If ye will not believe, surely ye shall not be established,**" or, to bring out the similarity of the expressions in the two clauses, 'If ye are not firm in faith, ye shall not be made firm in fact.'

This warning serves to remind us, positively, of the power of faith. Faith is encouraged and strengthened by difficulties. Faith faces what to the natural mind are impossibilities, and, resting on the promises of God, relies upon Him to fulfil His counsel concerning them and to turn the obstacles to account for His glory.

Ahaz did the opposite. He was no true child of Abraham. When the Lord invited him to ask a sign from Him, as a pledge of the fulfilment of His word, seeking it whether from below " **the depth** ", an allusive remonstrance against his resort to necromancy), or from heaven (" **the height above** "), he replied, " **I will not ask, neither will I tempt the Lord** " (*vv. 11, 12*).

This was selfwill under the guise of piety, and received the Lord's rebuke through Isaiah, " **And he said** (addressing Ahaz),

Hear ye now, O house of David (the royal line of privilege and honour, now represented by this degenerate king); **is it a small thing for you to weary men** (i.e., Isaiah, himself and others with him, who mourned over the rebellious attitude of the king), **but will ye weary my God also?** " (*verse 13*). Would he make it impossible for God to grant the mercy of repentance and restoration?

As Ahaz refused to ask for a sign, the Lord would give one of His own choosing, and a sign the range of which would extend to circumstances far beyond those of the time of Ahaz, and would bring to a culmination the prophecies and promises relating to "the house of David". Ahaz and men of that sort would have no share in the blessings and glories of the fulfilment of the sign: " **behold, a** (Heb., the) **virgin shall conceive, and bear a son** (the present tenses in the Hebrew vividly convey the future event in its certainty, as if it were already accomplished), **and shall call His Name Immanuel** " (*verse 14*).

"Behold", in Isaiah, always introduces something relating to future circumstances. The choice of the word *almah* is significant, as distinct from *bethulah* (a maiden living with her parents and whose marriage was not impending); it denotes one who is mature and ready for marriage. The various conditions relating to the prophecy are such that the only possible fulfilment is that recorded in Matt. 1: 22, 23 and Luke 1: 31-35. An outstanding feature of O.T. prophecies is that they connect events chronologically separated. Conditions more immediately relating to Assyria were developed under subsequent powers successively, culminating in the Roman, under which Immanuel was born. The circumstances depicted by Isaiah as prevailing in the land continued up to and in Immanuel's day.

This sign would be " **in the depth** ", for Immanuel (God with us, or, as in the order in the original, with us is God) would be one condescending to become man, and to go down into the depths of vicarious judgment and death. It would be also " **in the height** ", for Immanuel would be "very God". See verse 11 and 8:10.

" **Butter and honey shall He eat when He knoweth to refuse the evil, and choose the good** " (*verse 15, R.V.*). This is indicative of impoverishment. Thickened milk and honey were the food of desert wanderers. They were, of course, not the only articles of food; but instead of abundance of provisions there would be comparative scarcity. Such was the condition at the birth and in the childhood of Christ. There was no luxury in the home in Nazareth. "He became poor." The R.V. correctly gives the time indication, that, namely, of the days of his childhood.

This rendering is confirmed by the context in *verse 16*. Before the period of the early lifetime of Immanuel, He the only One who alone perfectly knew to refuse evil and choose good, the land, instead of being full of olive-yards, cornfields and vineyards, would be reduced to comparative poverty.

The desolation began in the time of Ahaz. The two kings of Syria and Israel, of whom Ahaz was afraid, were overpowered by the Assyrians. Their attack upon Judah followed (*verse 17*), and though recovery was granted in Hezekiah's reign, it was only temporary. The Egyptians (" **the fly** ") and the Assyrians (" **the bee** ") jointly devastated the land, fulfilling *vv. 18 and 19*. The King of Assyria is spoken of as a hired razor (*verse 20*). Ahaz had determined to hire him for help. God would hire him (the sarcasm is noteworthy) for destruction. Judah would be shaved in a manner bringing the utmost shame. The head, the hair of the feet, the beard would be shorn, indicating respectively the removal of kingly authority, national independence and the priesthood.

Again the Nazirite had to shave his head, were he defiled (Num. 6: 9). Israel as a Nazirite nation, set apart to God, had become defiled. The leper had to shave all his hair (Lev. 14: 9). Israel had become leprous. The Levite, after contact with the dead, had to be completely shaved (Num. 8: 7). Levitical service must be made to cease. But not for ever. "God did not cast off (i.e., irremediably) His people whom He foreknew."

Yet as a result of the destruction wrought by national foes, there would be poverty; instead of a well-stocked farm, " **a young cow and two sheep** " ; instead of abundance of milk, just the thickened milk, or curd, and wild honey; instead of a flourishing vineyard, " **briers and thorns** ". As for the hills formerly digged with the mattock (the verb in the first clause of verse 25 should be rendered in the past tense), men would go there apprehensive of briers and thorns, not for agricultural purposes, but with arrows and bows. Oxen would roam about wherever they could, and lesser cattle would tread down any growth (*vv. 21–25*).

Where a company of God's people departs from the right ways of the Lord, fruitless and noxious products are sure to develop, and there will be spiritual barrenness instead of the fertility that glorifies God. Bows and arrows suggest strife, instead of "the whole armour of God" that wards off and defeats the spiritual foe.

CHAPTER VIII

WARNINGS concerning Assyria are now given by means of a significant undertaking enjoined upon Isaiah. He was commanded to take a great tablet, or slab (not a parchment roll), and write on it " with a man's pen " (i.e., in common or popular characters, for all to read without difficulty) " for in Maher-shalal-hash-baz ", i.e., plunder speedeth, booty hasteth (*verse 1*). This was confirmed by the granting of a second son to the prophet (for the eldest see 7: 3) to whom he was bidden to give the same name as on the tablet.

Moreover, since the fulfilment of the prophecy would arouse the people to the fact that God had spoken through him by the mysterious name, the Lord himself says " I will take (as the R.V. rightly renders it) unto Me faithful witnesses to record, Uriah the priest, and Zechariah the son of Jeberechiah " (see 2 Kings 16: 10 and 2 Chron. 29: 1 and 13). These would tell the people how Isaiah had long before foretold, by his inscription and by the name of his son, what had now come to pass (*vv. 2, 3*).

Before the child, i.e., Isaiah's, not Immanuel, had learned to say in baby language " my father, my mother ", the king of Assyria, Tiglath-Pileser, would have despoiled the capitals of Syria and the northern Israelitic ally (*verse 4*). His prophecy was not designed to be, nor was it actually, a comfort to Ahaz, for the success of the Assyrian King would be only the stepping-stone to his attack upon Judah, and that is confirmed in verses 5 to 8. The nation, both Israel and Judah ("this people"), refused the softly-flowing waters of Shiloah ('that which is sent'), Divinely provided at Zion and Moriah and symbolic of God's promises concerning the throne and lineage of David, and rejoiced in setting their hopes upon earthly powers, Israel and its

ruler Remaliah's son, of Samaria, rejoicing in its alliance with
Rezin, King of Syria, and Judah relying upon Assyria (*verse 6*).

Both Israel and Judah, and Syria with them would therefore
suffer at the hands of the King of Assyria, symbolically depicted
as the rushing overflowing waters of the eastern river, in contrast
to the waters of Shiloah (*verse 7*). But Judah in a different way
and to a less extent than Israel. For the Assyrian power, instead
of completely overflowing Judah, would reach only to the neck
—a dangerous height, but kept under Divine restraint, inasmuch
as Immanuel would eventually come to Judah, and the land is
His possession. Hence the sudden address to him, " **Thy land,
O Immanuel** " (*verse 8*).

God did through Isaiah what He has' done ever since, and
will do, through His completed Word, confirming the truth of
its prophecies by their fulfilment in the course of human events.
We may not read Scripture in the light of events, but we can
see, as Judah did in Isaiah's day, the veracity and power of
the Divine revelations in their fulfilment.

In *verse 9*, in view of the glory of Immanuel, the prophecy
points on to the final gathering of the nations under the Antichrist
against the Jews in "the war of Har-mageddon" and the utter
overthrow of their confederate effort to annihilate them:
"**Associate yourselves, O ye peoples** " (plural R.V.). Another
version gives the meaning "Disquiet yourselves", i.e., "raise
the war cry". Let them gird themselves for the attempt. Three
times their doom is pronounced, " **Ye shall be broken in pieces** ".

Their counsel will be brought to naught. Their propaganda
will fail of realization. The scene and the circumstances are the
same as those in Ps. 2: 1–5; Joel 3: 2; Zech. 14: 1–3; Rev. 19:
15–21.

In this *10th verse* of Isaiah 8 the nations are bidden to speak
the word, i.e., "utter your sentence". It will not stand. The
secret of the overflow lies in the great Name Immanuel.

Verses 11 and 12 continue the remonstrance against the reliance
upon Assyria instead of upon God. Isaiah declares that Jehovah
had spoken to him, overpowering him with His hand (see margin),
instructing him not to walk in the way of his people. The command in verse 12 is addressed to Isaiah and the few with him
who feared God and dissociated themselves from the apostasy

of the time. The true meaning of the verse is unfolded if the accurate rendering "A conspiracy" is substituted for "A confederacy". The reference here is not to the alliance between Pekah and Rezin. Isaiah and his associates were being accused of a conspiracy against Ahaz and Judah under him, because of the prophet's denunciation of the alliance with Assyria. This kind of calumny was what prophets had to endure whenever they opposed an appeal by God's people for the help of Gentile aid (Amos 7: 10).

While, then, Isaiah was comforting the faithful with the promises concerning Immanuel, he was to warn them against the popular idea, and against sharing in fears of the people. 'Call ye not conspiracy all that this people calls conspiracy. What they fear, fear ye not, nor regard it as dreadful': this seems the true rendering of the verse. *Verse 13* sets a positive command in direct contrast: " **Sanctify Jehovah of hosts Himself, and let Him be your fear, and let Him be your dread.**"

To sanctify the Lord is so to live that He has absolute authority and control over the heart and will, over every activity of the life, to walk in His fear, dreading to displease Him. This is the due response to His redeeming grace and love in Christ. "Sanctify in your hearts Christ as Lord," 1 Pet. 3: 15, R.V. See Isa. 29: 23 and contrast Num. 20: 12.

The effect of the fulfilment of this is that the Lord becomes "a sanctuary" to us (*verse 14*). Just as the Temple was designed to be to Israel the centre of their spiritual life, their joy in worship and praise, a place of holiness and peace as well as a defence, so Christ Himself is to the believer. "We live in Him." Our life is "hid with Christ in God".

To unbelieving Israel He has become " **a stone of stumbling ... a rock of offence ... for a gin and for a snare** ". They have been "broken" on the stone and "taken" in the snare (*verse 15*). That was the case with Judah and Israel in Isaiah's day in their attitude towards Jehovah. So Christ became to them and still is (Rom. 9: 33; 1 Pet. 2: 8), till the veil is removed from their heart.

In *verse 16* the testimony refers to what has preceded, concerning both Immanuel and the future condition of Israel. It was to be secured and kept for the godly remnant then and in

the coming generation. The law, which the people had cast away
(5: 24), was similarly to be sealed among the faithful disciples,
those who humbly sought to know and follow it (possibly this
verse is Isaiah's prayer instead of the continuation of God's word
to him, and in that case his disciples are "the children" given
him by the Lord, *verse 18*). Amidst the darkness of the people
from whom God hid his face, Isaiah determines the more steadfastly to wait upon (or for) God and look for Him.

There is a helpful lesson for us in this. Conditions of declension from God and refusal to listen to His Word will be the
means, if we abide faithful and stand in His counsels, of
directing our hearts the more steadfastly to wait upon Him,
that our expectation may be from Him. The backsliding state
of some who once gave hopes of being blessed and made fruitful through our ministry, tends to depress the spirit. In these
circumstances, and amidst difficulties of whatever nature, the
Spirit of God would draw us nearer to Him, that we may ever
find our resources in His power still to glorify His Name
through us.

The prophet finds comfort and assurance in the children the
Lord had given Him (*verse 18*), Shear-jashub and Maher-shalal-
hash-baz were "**for signs and wonders in Israel from Jehovah
of hosts, which dwelleth in Mount Zion**". The one was a sign
that 'a remnant would return', the other that 'plunder would
speed and booty would haste'. The *sign* was a token or pledge
by word and deed portending the fulfilment of an event; the
wonder was an indication of the Divinely supernatural source
and cause of it. Thus the two children were tokens of redemption
for Israel through judgment.

The first part of this verse is quoted in Heb. 2: 13, where the
Spirit of God (who is a law to Himself in the matter of quotations
from the O.T.) applies it to the spiritual children of God in
relationship to Christ. Isaiah's natural children were symbolically representative of believers, who likewise are to be a testimony
in the world.

Instead of accepting the signs and messages given by God, the
people made application to those who had "familiar spirits",
i.e., to spiritist mediums, as Saul did at Endor, and indulged
in the arts of necromancy and wizardry (*verse 19*). The Lord's

remonstrance is twofold; " should not a people seek unto their God ? On behalf of the living should they seek unto the dead ? " This is the folly of Spiritism. The disastrous character of it is that its dupes, both the mediums and the applicants, put themselves into the delusive and destructive power of evil spirits.

Before every great crisis in human affairs there has been an outburst of spiritism. So it was in Judah and Israel just before the captivity. So it was at the time of Christ's Incarnation and atoning Death. So it is to-day. God has provided all that is requisite for our guidance and spiritual needs in the Scriptures of truth (2 Tim. 3: 16, 17).

So it was in the nation of Israel, ere even the Old Testament was completed: " **To the law** (i.e., the teaching, *thorah*) **and to the testimony! if they speak not according to this word, surely there is no morning for them** " (*verse 20*) or 'they are a people for whom no morning dawns'; they abide in perpetual darkness. "**And they shall pass through it** (or rather, 'they, the rebellious nation, shall go about therein', i.e., in the darkness), **hardly bestead** (i.e., hard pressed or hardened) **and hungry.**" Then, instead of repenting, they would fret themselves, curse the king and curse God (or rather curse by the king and by God), and would "look upward", turning their face in despair towards heaven, to see if light would come from thence, and look downward to the earth, to find relief therefrom: and behold, distress and darkness, the gloom of anguish, and into thick darkness they shall be driven away, i.e., cast out of Immanuel's land.

CHAPTER IX

THE "Nevertheless" marks an immediate connection with the close of chapter 8, and a contrast to the judicial darkness there foretold. God had provided (and would provide) a light if the rebellious nation would receive it. Here again the prophecy passes from the immediately subsequent calamities of invasion to the shining light of the Incarnate Christ amidst the people, and especially in Galilee.

That district, the region of Zebulon and Naphtali, was to
suffer from the invasions of the Syrians and then the Assyrians.
Yet in contrast to that "**former time**" of contempt, "**in the
latter time**" God would 'make it (the region) glorious' (see the
R.V.). "**The people that walk** (the tense is prophetic present)
**in darkness see a great light : they that dwell in the land of the
shadow of death, upon them a light shines**" (*verse 2*). The
fulfilment of this is described in Matt. 4: 12 to 25, where the
Evangelist writer quotes this passage. How the Light shone in
Cana of Galilee is recorded in John 2: 1–11.

From this point to the end of *verse 7* the prophecy stretches
across another interval and passes to the overthrow of the
Antichrist, the oppressor, and the establishment of the Messiah's
Kingdom of peace and righteousness.

Verse 3 is correctly rendered in the R.V. There is no word
"not" (see the A.V. margin). "**Thou hast multiplied the nation,
Thou hast increased their joy : they joy before Thee according
to the joy in harvest, as men rejoice when they divide the spoil.**"
This has never been fulfilled in the nation yet. Only a remnant
returned from the captivity. The very opposite of these conditions has prevailed under successive Gentile domination. At
the close of the coming great tribulation, when the Lord comes
in Person to deliver His earthly people, they will joy over blessings granted and destruction averted. The Millennium will see
a vast increase in the nation's population.

They will joy before the Lord. That ever should be the
character of our joy—not mere exuberance of natural feeling,
not merely joy in mercy and prosperity, in deliverance and
supply, but joy before the Lord, a joy that exults in Him,
His power and presence.

In *verse 4* the past tense looks upon the future event as an
assured accomplishment. The pronoun "his", thrice in the verse,
refers to Israel. The Lord will break "**the yoke of his burden**",
i.e., the burden inflicted upon it by the oppressor; "**the staff
of his shoulder**", i.e., the stout stick of the yoke burdening and
chafing the shoulder; and "**the rod of his oppressor**", the
sceptre of the imperial tyrant, the emblem of tyranny. The
"**day of Midian**" was the time of Gideon's victory (Judges 6
and 7). God saved the nation, not by its military power or

prowess, but by His own choice of a small company and by means far otherwise than that of human might, so that they could not boast in their own strength (Judges 7: 2). So in the coming day, it will be all the Lord's personal act, for the nation will be in its extremity of weakness.

The lesson for us is clear. What we seek to accomplish by our own devices and in our own strength, only plays into the hands of our spiritual foe. It is when we are weak that we are strong (2 Cor. 12: 10). Cp. what is recorded of Ahaz himself in 2 Chron. 28: 21. His self-efforts "helped him not".

Verse 5 points directly to the war of Har-magedon (Rev. 16: 14, R.V.). That climax will see " **all the armour of the armed man in the tumult** " (Joel 3: 9-14; Zech. 14: 13), " **the garments rolled in blood** " (Isa. 63: 3; Rev. 14: 20), " **burning** ", and " **fuel of fire** " (Isa. 66: 15, 16; Joel 2: 30).

But all this victory, deliverance and joy is based upon the Birth of Christ. *Verse 6* is an expansion of the meaning of "Immanuel" in 7: 14. There He was spoken of as a sign, here He is a gift: " **For unto us a child is born** "; He is partaker with " **the children** " of flesh and blood (Heb. 2: 14); " **unto us a son is given** ", One who grows up into Manhood, qualified to exercise the power and reveal His nature and character now to be mentioned: " **and the government shall be upon His shoulder : and His Name shall be called** (cp. 7: 14) **Wonderful, Counsellor, The mighty God, The everlasting Father, The Prince of Peace.** "

For the first of these titles cp. Judges 13: 18 (R.V. and A.V. margin); for the second, see Isa. 11: 2; and for the two together, 25: 1. These two are not to be combined into one phrase as if the first was an adjective describing the Counsellor as wonderful: each is a noun. Contrast 28: 29, where the phrase is different.

In the next title, "The mighty God," "God" is *El*, the last syllable of Immanuel, and again the Deity of Christ is declared. El is contrasted with man in 31: 3 and Hos. 11: 9. "Mighty" is used of God in Deut. 10: 17 and elsewhere. "The everlasting Father" is, lit., 'The Father of eternity.' There is a twofold revelation in this: (1) He inhabits and possesses eternity (57: 15); (2) He is loving, tender, compassionate, an all wise Instructor, Trainer and Provider.

The title "The Prince of Peace" comprehends His actings in respect of each of the four preceding titles. His eternity and His provision of peace are combined in 57: 15–19. He is a Prince who will in Person completely subdue every opposing foe, banish every disturbing element and thus bring peace to His people and to the nations. This the angels heralded at His Birth (Luke 2: 14).

To the extension of His government and to peace there will be no limit (*verse 7*). He will Himself establish " **the throne of David** ", in fulfilment of 2 Sam. 7: 16, ordering and establishing it with judgment and righteousness unending. " **The zeal** (or rather, the jealousy) **of Jehovah of hosts shall perform this.**" His jealousy has two objects. It is a fire of indignation against all who maltreat His chosen earthly people, and a fire that burns with such a love for them and zeal for their welfare that it must consume all unfaithfulness in their midst. Cp. Song of Sol. 8: 6, 7, and see Deut. 4: 24; 5: 9; 6: 15.

The jealousy of the apostle Paul concerning the church at Corinth was but the expression of the Lord's own jealousy on their behalf. "I am jealous," he says, "over you with a jealousy of God: for I espoused you to one Husband, that I might present you as a pure virgin to Christ" (2 Cor. 11: 2). The cup of jealousy had been put into the hand of that church in the first Epistle. She had drunk it and had cleared herself (2 Cor. 7: 11). See Num. 5: 11–21. What the Lord does with a local church He does with the individual members of the church, and in the coming day He will similarly deal with Israel.

The promises of *vv. 6, 7* are now followed in *vv. 8 to 10: 4* by further denunciations of evil and warnings of impending judgments (just as the promise in 7: 14 had been followed). The nation had to be reminded again and again that such was its condition that evil and consequent trouble and darkness would reach a climax before the promised blessing and light could be given. Though Ephraim is especially mentioned the passage deals with the whole nation, as is clear from *verse 9*. Ephraim was guilty of persistent hardness of heart. In spite of the utter failure of their alliance with Syria, which broke down under the attacks of the Assyrian, Tiglath-Pileser, there was no repentance.

In their pride and stout-heartedness they said, " **The bricks are fallen down, but we will build with hewn stones : the sycomores are cut down, but we will replace them with cedars** " (*verse 10*).

For this cause fresh adversaries were raised up (Philistines against Judah and Syrians against the other tribes); the Lord's indignation was continued, and His hand was still stretched out in judgment (not in pleading with them, as some would interpret it), *vv. 11, 12*.

In *vv. 13–16* the prophet gives a second exposure of the causes of, and necessity for, the Divine judgments. In spite of these they refused to turn and seek the Lord. Those who were chiefly responsible were the elders and men of prominent position ("the ancient and honourable"); they are described as the "head". Then there were the false prophets, teaching lies. These were the "tail" (i.e., the wagging tail of a dog), delighting in their guileful flatteries. The former were the palm-branch, waving aloft; the latter were the "rush", down in the marshy ground. Each must be " **cut off . . . in one day** ". In *verse 16* they are directly called "the leaders", and the people that follow them are destroyed (lit., 'swallowed up').

Such was the evil that the Lord could have no joy in their young men (those who should have become powerful to maintain the spiritual vitality of the nation), and the fatherless and the widows (ordinarily the special objects of Divine compassion, Deut. 10: 18) would obtain no mercy. All were profligate, evildoers and blasphemers. Hence a second time Isaiah has to say that the Lord's anger was not turned away, but His hand is still stretched out in judgment (*verse 17*).

And now a third time warnings of Divine vengeance are given. Wickedness, whether in an individual or a nation, brings its own retribution. It becomes a burning fire consuming the evil-doers themselves. As thorns and thickets are ready for the burning, so hardened sinners are ripe for judgment (*verse 18*).

The land would be "darkness" (the word here means turned like coal into fuel for the fire). With the civil war (see *verse 21*) there would be cruelty, famine, and self-destruction (*verse 20*). And a third time the solemn declaration is uttered that the Lord's anger continues and His hand is still stretched out in judgment. The whole circumstances, and all that led up to these calamities, are described in Nehemiah, chapter 9.

We need to beware of despising our higher privileges, of turning away from the right ways of the Lord, and, in a spirit of self-satisfaction, of rejecting God's commandments, "which if a man do, he shall live in them" (Neh. 9: 29).

CHAPTER X

THE first four verses of this chapter are a continuation of chapter 9. Evil is again denounced, fresh sins are exposed, and warning of impending judgment is given. Injustice, robbery of the poor, the fatherless, the widows, will bring the day of visitation and desolation. There will be no one to whom to flee for help. His presence in their midst had been their "glory" (*verse 3*). Now it would "fly away as a bird" (Hos. 9: 11). They would suffer desolation, shame and captivity (*verse 3*).

The presence of the Lord in the midst of His people is their highest glory, their greatest privilege. It is the secret of blessing, of power in testimony, of strength against the spiritual foe. At the same time His presence is intensely solemn. It is designed to enable us to live in His fear, not the fear that shrinks from Him, but the fear that shrinks from grieving the Holy Spirit. Failure to apprehend this leads to spiritual declension, resulting either in a mere form of godliness without the power, or in manifest ungodliness. So it was in Israel.

Verses 5 to 19 give a striking example of how God has used Gentile nations to chastise His earthly people, permitting these nations to attain to a high degree of domination. They on their part have prided themselves on what they consider to be their own attainments, and on this account have brought upon themselves the retributive judgments of the Lord.

That was the case with Assyria, "**the rod of His anger**", against His "**hypocritical nation**", "**the people of His wrath**". *Verses 7 to 11 and 13 and 14* recount his self-glorying and pride, his determination to found a universal empire. So it has been with recent tyrants and their schemes. So it will be with the **Man of Sin, who will achieve a greater measure of success than** all his predecessors. What an axe or rod is in relation to him who handles it, so is a mere man to Almighty God Who uses him. A stick unused is virtually " **not wood** " (*verse 15*).

When therefore the Lord had accomplished " **His whole work upon mount Zion and on Jerusalem,**" purging out its abominations, He punished " **the stout heart of the king of Assyria, and the glory of his high looks** ". Cp. Hab. 1: 11. This likewise applies to the final events of the present age.

The Divine titles in *verse 16* are significant. "The Lord" (*Ha-Adon*) is used by Isaiah always in connection with the power exerted judicially and penally. *Adonai Sabaoth*, "the Lord of hosts", is used here only, and indicates His absolute Sovereignty.

The fat men of Assyria would be made lean. Under its boasted glory God, as " **the light of Israel** " (*verse 17*), and " **His Holy One** " would be a consuming fire, making a bonfire of the mighty ones as of briers and thorns (just as with Israel, 9: 18). The armed forces, " **the glory of his forest and of his fruitful field** ", would be consumed " **from the soul even to the flesh** ", i.e., internally, externally, and therefore "utterly", the whole army being demolished. In *verse 19* the fewness of " **his forest** " depicts the scattered remnants of the army that march against Jerusalem, so few that a boy could easily count them.

On the other hand, the remnant of Israel (Shear-jashub, 7: 3) would no more rely upon the Gentile power, the Assyrian, that smote them, but upon God (*vv. 20, 21*); see 2 Chron. 30: 6.

Verse 22 makes clear that here again (as often in O.T. prophecy) the passage points not merely to the immediate fulfilment, as in the case of the Assyrian invasion, but looks on to later circumstances. For the Apostle Paul in Rom. 9: 27 applies vv. 22, 23 to the yet future time, when Israel, passing through the great tribulation, will be reduced in number to a mere remnant, the nucleus of the redeemed nation at the inception of the Millennium. This will be the issue of " **the consumption decreed** ", i.e., the judgments of "the time of Jacob's trouble", executed " **with righteousness** " in the midst of all the land. Accordingly the prophecy relates to the future time of "the Day of the Lord".

The remainder of the chapter is occupied with a prediction of the actual details of the Assyrian invasion and the overthrow of the invader. On which account God's people were not to be afraid of him. The rod must be used, but the smiter must himself be smitten. So it was with Egypt (*vv. 24, 26*). Assyria and Egypt are coupled again in 52: 4.

In *verse 27* the statement " **the yoke shall be destroyed because of the anointing** " is understood in two ways. The English Version points to the anointing of the kings and priests in Jerusalem as those who were consecrated to God, on account of which God would destroy the foe. The mention of the yoke and the neck, however (metaphors from the wooden yoke on the ox), suggests that the neck of the bullock is so fat that the yoke will not go round it. So Israel would grow strong and assert its freedom. Accordingly the rendering will be, "the yoke shall be destroyed by reason of the fat" (cp. Deut. 32: 15). The whole scene foreshadows the doom of the Antichrist.

CHAPTER XI

THIS chapter introduces a striking contrast to the close of chapter 10, a contrast between a proud cedar of Lebanon and a twig out of a hewn-down stock, a shoot from its roots. The former was symbolic both of the Assyrian and his final antitype the Antichrist, the latter is descriptive of the Christ, His lowly birth, His growth under the delighted eyes of Jehovah, and eventually of His mighty power to overthrow the very Antichrist and rule in righteousness and peace.

"**And there shall come forth a shoot** (or, a twig) **out of the stem** (the stock or stump) **of Jesse, and a Branch** (a shoot) **out of his roots shall bear fruit** " (*verse 1*, *R.V.*). The house of David had become so degenerate that it resembled the stump of a tree that had been felled. There would, however, grow out of it a twig which would take the place of the whole trunk. To confirm this promise another figure is used. Springing up from the earth-covered roots there would arise a green shoot (*netzer*, from *natzer*, to shine or blossom, and hence the word "Nazarene", Matt. 2: 23) which would develop and bear fruit (cp. Phil. 2: 7–9).

Verse 2 gives a glorious description of Christ's perfect character and virtues. " **The Spirit of Jehovah shall rest upon Him**", expressive of the complete and complacent delight of the **Father** in Him, and of the abiding nature of His virtues; cp. John 1: 32, 33. The statement contains a mention of the Three Persons of the Trinity. The Spirit of Jehovah is the Holy Spirit, operating in the fullness of the Divine powers (cp. Col. 2: 9).

Following this are six spirits in three pairs. The first, " **the spirit of wisdom and understanding**", relates to powers of mind: wisdom discerns the nature of things, understanding discerns their differences. The second, " **the spirit of counsel and might**", relates to practical activity: counsel is the ability to adopt right conclusions, might is the power exercised in carrying them out. The third pair, " **the spirit of knowledge and of the fear of the Lord**", relates to fellowship with Jehovah; knowledge is here a knowledge of Jehovah (both details of this pair go with "of Jehovah"); Christ Himself said "ye have not known Him (*ginōskō*, i.e., ye have not begun to know Him), but I know Him (*oida*, i.e., I know Him intuitively and fully)", John 8: 5; the fear is that which, enjoying the presence of the Lord, refrains, therefore, from displeasing Him. Christ said "I do always the things that are pleasing to Him", John 8: 29.

These seven correspond to the seven-lighted lampstand, with its main shaft and the three pairs of branches from its sides (Exod. 25: 31, 32). See also Rev. 1: 4; 4: 5; 5: 6.

These powers and virtues would " **make Him of quick understanding** (*rewach*, scent) **in the fear of the Lord** " (*verse 3*), i.e., quick to appreciate as fragrance " **all that is of the fear of the Lord** ", or, as it is otherwise rendered, "the fear of the Lord shall be fragrance to Him". Accordingly He will not judge by mere appearance, nor will He pass sentence on mere hearsay, but by reason of His possession of the Spirit of Jehovah He will judge the poor with righteousness, and pass sentence equitably on behalf of the meek, the humble, those who cannot undertake their own cause.

Before peace is established, He will " **smite the earth with the rod of His mouth, and with the breath of His lips shall He slay the wicked** " (*verse 4*), i.e., the Antichrist. This prophecy is expanded in 34: 1-10 and 63: 1-6 (where see notes), a testimony to the unity of the book of Isaiah. The rod of the Lord's mouth and the breath of His lips are elsewhere described as "the voice of the Lord" (cp. 2 Thess. 2: 8).

The rest of this chapter depicts Millennial conditions. The new era which Christ will introduce will see the exercise of

" righteousness as the girdle of His loins, and faithfulness as
the girdle of His reins " (the same word as that rendered "loins"
in 5: 27, and denoting the hips), emblematic of the energetic
activity of His powers and attributes in fulfilling the Divine will.

Verses 6 to 9 are not to be regarded as symbolic. The actual
fulfilment of the conditions in the animal world will be the
natural outcome of the presence and authority of Christ. In
verse 8 the cockatrice is probably the adder (see Jer. 8: 17, R.V.
marg.). In *verse 9* the " holy mountain " stands for the land,
with Zion as its governmental centre. The phrase " as the
waters cover the sea " signifies the covering of the bed of the
ocean by its waters, a symbol of the depth and fullness of the
experimental knowledge of Jehovah.

Verse 10 describes again the lowliness and exaltation of Christ.
He Who had been in obscurity as the sprout from the root of
Jesse, figurative of His lowly birth, will " stand for an ensign
of the peoples " (plural), a banner, summoning them, not to war,
but to Himself as the benign Ruler, exercising His authority in
righteousness and peace. To Him the nations will seek, and
His resting-place, the seat of His authority, " shall be glorious ",
lit., 'shall be glory'. So it was with the Shekinah glory in the
Tabernacle, Num. 10: 33; cp. 2 Chron. 6: 41 and Ps. 132: 8, 14.

Then will the Lord gather "a second time" the scattered
remnant of Israel (*vv. 11, 12*). There was a gathering of His
people at the return from captivity in the time of Ezra. True,
the Lord delivered Israel from Egypt under Moses, but that was
not the gathering of a remnant. There will be peace and unity
in the nation (*verse 13*) and they will subdue surrounding foes
(*vv. 14, 15*).

There will be geographical changes, making for the welfare of
Israel. The sea between Egypt and Arabia will be destroyed
(lit., 'be under a ban'), and the river Euphrates will be smitten
into seven shallow brooks. From Egypt to Assyria there will be
a highway for traffic (*verse 16*). Cp. Zech. 10: 11.

CHAPTER XII

THIS foretells the redeemed nation's song of praise at the inception of the Millennial reign of their Messiah-Deliverer, after His overthrow of their Antichristian foes. The song will be the earthly counterpart of the Heavenly doxology sung as preliminary to the judgments preceding and issuing in the overthrow (Rev. 5: 9, 10, 12, 13; 15: 3, 4), and as an immediate counterpart to the doxology in Rev. 19: 6, 7.

The Lord's righteous anger in His retributive dealings with His people, culminating in their great tribulation, will be followed by the mercy by which He becomes their strength, their song and their salvation (*verse 2*). Cp. Exod. 15: 2. The double title " **Jah Jehovah** " is found only here and in 26: 4.

The promise follows that with joy (rapturous joy) they shall " **draw water out of the wells of salvation** " (*verse 3*), all found in Him Whom they once rejected, ''the waters of Shiloah'' (8: 6), and Who invites the thirsty to come to Him and drink (John 7: 37).

They will call upon themselves to declare His doings among the peoples (the Gentiles), glorifying Him in the proclamation to them that " **His Name is exalted** " (*verse 4*). All the earth must know of His " **excellent things** ", His "manifested Majesty". For God has determined that the salvation of Israel shall mean the bringing of salvation to the Gentiles, and this by reason of the fact yet to be fulfilled, " **great is the Holy One of Israel in the midst of thee** " (*verse 6*).

It is the presence of the Lord in the midst that here and now satisfies the desires of His people, produces their worship, provides the power of their testimony. His realized presence is the gladsome dominating factor in their assembling. Where this is lost sight of all is mere routine, though there may be enthusiasm for a cause, and resounding jubilation.

PART I (b)

PROPHECIES AGAINST GENTILE NATIONS
(Chapters XIII–XXIII)

CHAPTER XIII

CHAPTERS 13 to 23 consist of oracles concerning surrounding Gentile nations. These come appropriately after the great subject of Messianic prophecies in chapters 7 to 12. It had been foretold therein that the authority of the Messiah will be exercised over all the kingdoms of the world, and consolatory messages had been given concerning the ultimate blessing and glory of Israel. Accordingly the doom of these Gentile powers one after another is predicted.

First comes Babylon. For the Chaldean rule would succeed the already doomed Assyrian. It must, however, be borne in mind that many of the utterances go beyond the more immediate judgment upon that power.

Verses 2 to 5 are descriptive of the Medes, who are mentioned in verse 17, and of the Persians; *verse 4* speaks of kingdoms (plural). These combined powers are called " **My consecrated ones** ", .i.e., those chosen by God for the fulfilment of His counsels against Babylon (*verse 3*). That they 'rejoice in His highness', or excellency, does not necessarily imply a consciousness on their part that they are acting for God's glory. Yet the Persians regarded the destruction of idols as part of their vocation, and Cyrus the Persian did rejoice in the recognition of God and the fulfilment of His mind. Cp. 44: 28; 45: 1, and see Ezra 1: 1–4. The Medo-Persian powers were to be " **the weapons of His indignation, to destroy the whole land** " (i.e., Chaldea).

From *verse 6 to verse 13* the prophecy passes from the doom of Babylon to the future judgments of God upon the whole world at the end of this age, in the time of the coming "Day of the Lord ". This is indicated by the mention of "the world" (*tebel*, not *eretz*, land) in *verse 11*. In *verse 9* "the land" should be "the earth". With this passage the following should be compared: 34: 1–8; Joel 2: 31; 3: 15; Matt. 24: 29; Mark 13: 24; Luke 21: 35.

Verse 12 foretells the reduction of the world's population at the time of the end, as the Lord Himself has foretold in Matt. 24: 22.

Verse 14, if rightly translated, returns to the destruction of Babylon, as the rest of the chapter makes clear: **"And it shall come to pass** (the "it" is not a pronoun, referring to the earth), **as with a gazelle which is scared, and as a flock without gatherers, they shall turn every one to his own people, and flee every one to his own land."** That is to say, all foreigners would escape from the city, which attracted them as being the market of the world. The Medes, under Darius, began a work of destruction. Alexander the Great purposed rebuilding it, but his early death prevented it. In 20 B.C., Strabo described the site as "a vast desolation".

And yet *vv. 19 to 22* have never had a complete fulfilment. Its destruction has never been like that of Sodom and Gomorrah. Here again the principle of expanded prophecy in a twofold fulfilment is exemplified. The key to the question as to whether Babylon is yet to be a fresh centre and to receive its complete destruction, is provided at the beginning of chapter 14, which begins with the word "For", i.e., as an explanation of what has preceded. Chapter 14 introduces the day of Israel's deliverance and Millennial blessing, and it is in the day that the Lord gives them rest from sorrow and fear and bondage, that they will rejoice in the destruction of Babylon and utter their taunt against the city's oppressor.

There would be little or no point in Israel's glorious note of triumph over the destruction that took place over two thousand years ago. See, too, the prophecy of Zech. 5: 11. It is not at all unlikely that part of the coming Antichristian policy of defiance of God, will be the resuscitation of the great city, and that the prophecy of this passage in Isaiah will then have its complete fulfilment. See also Rev. chap. 18.

CHAPTER XIV

As we have pointed out, the explanatory word "For", which continues the subject of the preceding chapter, introduces a reason for the overthrow of the Gentile oppressor. This illustrates the following principles of the Divine dealings with God's chosen people Israel: (a) the self-will and rebellion of His people causes Him to use Gentile powers to chastise them: (b) the arrogance and outrageous cruelty of these Gentile nations in the permitted exercise of their power, brings His judgments upon them, when the chastisement of Israel has accomplished its purpose: (c) His covenant mercy in the fulfilment of His promises to the "fathers" means the eventual restoration of Israel: (d) this in turn makes them instrumental in blessing to Gentile nations.

Verse 1 tells of Jehovah's purposes for Israel in a fourfold way: mercy, choice, establishment, influence. *Verse 2* shows that those who remain of their former oppressors, after the Divine judgment upon them, will become servants and handmaids to Israel.

At the same time the nation, in its rest from sorrow, bondage and affliction, will rejoice over the destruction of Babylon and its king, with a note of taunting triumph (for the fact of this immediately preceding overthrow of the revived city, see notes at the end of chapter 13), *vv. 3–6.*

In *verse 8* the statement as to the fir (or rather, the cypress) trees and the cedars, is to be taken literally. The Chaldeans had cut down large parts of the forests to make use of the timber for a great variety of purposes.

Another circumstance is now predicted concerning the final overthrow of Babylon. The spirits of the slain potentates and people of the city are seen entering Sheol, the region of departed spirits, here the lost. Those who are there already address them at their arrival. Sheol is the Hebrew word in *verse 9* (wrongly translated "Hell" and "the grave"); it is not Gehenna, but what the corresponding Greek word in the N.T. calls Hades. " **Sheol from beneath is moved** (or violently disquieted) **for** (i.e., on account of) **thee : it stirreth up the dead** (the rephaim, the spirits of those who had been mighty among men, the giants) **for thee, even all the chief ones** (the leaders, lit., he-goats, i.e., leading goats among herds) **of the earth; it hath raised up** (raiseth up) **from their thrones** (a word which retrospectively contemplates their position when on earth) **all the kings of the nations."**

This passage demonstrates the fact of the conscious state of the souls of the dead in Hades, their power to exchange thoughts, and their vivid recollection of their past circumstances on earth. There is no Scripture to support the supposition of the unconsciousness of the soul.

"All they shall speak and say unto thee, Art thou also become weak as we? art thou become like unto us?" This is all the spirits in Sheol have to say to the newcomers. *Verse 11* resumes the triumphant taunt of redeemed Israel as from *verse 4*. Babylon's pomp is cast down to the grave (not Sheol here). The "viols" refer to the instruments of music, as in Dan. 3: 5. The statements **"the worm is spread under thee, and the worms cover thee,"** are sarcastically figurative allusions to the luxurious cushions and pillows on which the inhabitants of Babylon lay and to the gorgeous rugs and coverlets under which they rested. All were now maggot-eaten.

In *verse 12* Lucifer, lit., "light-bringer", is primarily symbolic of the fallen monarch of Babylon. The language which describes him is used of Satan (Luke 10: 18; Rev. 12: 8, 9), who spiritually energized the founder of Babylon, Satan's great seat, from which the world has been corrupted. Pride was Satan's sin and caused his downfall; so with Babylon (*verse 13*), the boasting purpose of the king who was to defy God in heaven and rule over the utmost limits of the earth ("the north"), and to rival His power (*verse 14*). Yet Babylon's doom is Sheol, and the sides (or corner) of the pit (in contrast to the sides of the north), *verse 15*.

In *verse 16* **"they that see thee"** are not the spirits in Sheol, but people on earth, astonished at the downfall of the tyrant. *Verse 18* is the prediction of Isaiah, introducing the retribution foretold by Jehovah Himself (*vv. 22–25*). First there is a contrast. Other kings **"lie in glory"**, i.e., have an honourable burial. But Babylon's monarch, Belshazzar, lies cast away from (not "out of") his prepared sepulchre. Other corpses of those slain in the battle, their blood-stained raiment gathered in heaps, are thrown into holes filled up with stones and earth. But his carcase lies unburied, trodden under foot, for he had destroyed his land, and slain his people. His dynasty would perish, without renown, an example of the doom of all evil-doers (*vv. 20–22*).

Afterwards, the bittern (or the hedgehog) in place of inhabitants, and marshland in place of palaces! And the city swept away with the besom of destruction!

In *verse 24* the scene passes back to the doom of Assyria (presenting a contrast to that of Babylon), to be followed by that of other foes of Israel (for the order see Jer. 1: 18, 19). All this is introduced by a general declaration of the unthwartable purpose of Jehovah of hosts. "Man proposes, but God disposes." See 46: 10; Ps. 33: 11; Prov. 21: 30; Acts 2: 23; 4: 28; Eph. 1: 11; Heb. 6: 17.

The breaking of the yoke of Assyria is mentioned as a sample of the similar purposes of God concerning all the nations of the earth (*vv. 26, 27*). Not an event can take place out of the line of God's predetermined counsels.

Verse 28, recording the death of Ahaz, is to be taken with what follows, not with what has preceded. This burden (or oracle) refers to the doom of Philistia (R.V., for A.V., Palestina). Upon the death of Ahaz, Hezekiah ascended the throne. He it was who utterly defeated the Philistines (2 Kings 18: 8).

In *verse 29* the rod is the sceptre of David. That had been broken by all that had taken place in and against Judah, and over this the Philistines gloated. The cockatrice (or basilisk) is Hezekiah. The closing phrase is, lit., 'a fiery flying one.' This points on to the benign government of the Messiah, when the poor and the needy will be satisfied (*verse 30*). *Verse 31* likewise points to the time of the end (see Dan. 11: 40–2).

In *verse 32* the word rendered "nation" is plural, and the question is, "What answer do the messengers of the nations, bring?" Are not these Jews, who will declare the mighty acts of Jehovah? The answer is that " **The LORD hath founded Zion.**" All the foes in the long history of their efforts to destroy it will have been foiled in their attempts, and Zion will be the peaceful refuge of His people.

CHAPTERS XV, XVI

THESE chapters contain the Divine oracle concerning Moab. Isaiah mourns over its doom. For fuller details of this see Jer. 48, which ends with a promise of eventual restoration in the Millennial day. Accordingly the prophet's heart is roused to pity, unlike his pronouncements concerning Assyria and Babylon. Moab's pride procured its punishment (15: 6).

In 15: 5 Zoar, a fortress in the south, is described as " an heifer (or ox) of three years old ", i.e., an ox in the fulness of its powers (cp. Jer. 46: 20; 50: 11). To this unconquered stronghold Moab's fugitives would flee from the northern foe.

In 16: 1 " the ruler of the land " is the occupant of the throne of David, to whom the tribute of lambs is to be paid by Moab, here represented by Selah (or Petra). This tribute had been sent to Samaria (2 Kings 3: 4); now the lambs must be sent to Jerusalem and this will be the case, by way of Gentile tribute, when Christ comes to deliver Israel (see verse 5).

The exhortation to Moab to be a refuge for the outcasts of Israel, that is to say, the godly remnant, is deeply significant prophetically. The time indicated is that of the future great tribulation, "the time of Jacob's trouble". At the end of the warfare of Har-Magedon, the King of the North will pass through Palestine, "the glorious land", on his way to conquer Egypt, but Edom, Moab and Ammon will "be delivered" (Dan. 11: 41, R.V.). Satan will have instigated the Antichrist to lead the armies of the Roman power to endeavour to exterminate the Jewish people, and particularly the godly remnant. These will have fled to the mountains of Moab from Jerusalem, fulfilling the Lord's word in Matt. 24: 16 to flee from Jerusalem to the mountains. They are to be guarded and nourished there for three and a half years (Rev. 12: 14, with verse 6). The serpent will cause a flood, perhaps symbolic of a military expedition, to rush forth, with the endeavour to destroy them (verse 15), but the earth (probably the desert region between Palestine and the mountains) will swallow up the army. The sandy nature of the district could easily be made to accomplish this.

The very nature of the deep rocky gorges in that region of

the mountains, enormous depths where Kings of ancient times
have had their palaces, as, e.g., at Petra, will afford a complete
refuge to the thousands of this remnant of Jews, appointed to
form the very nucleus of the race when Christ comes in glory
at His Second Advent, to set up His Kingdom on earth. Cp.
Jer. 48: 47. This explains the decree, "Let Mine outcasts dwell
with thee, Moab; be thou a covert to them from the face of the
spoiler," the Antichrist, Isa. 16: 4. The fact that David put his
father and mother in Moab to safeguard them from Saul, was
a typical foreshadowing of this (1 Sam. 22: 3). The Antichrist
oppressors will be consumed. The throne will be established in
mercy, and One will sit thereon, "**judging, and seeking judgment** (or rather, zealous for right) **and hasting** (or practising)
righteousness" (*verse 5*).

Thus, as so constantly, the prophecy looks on from the near
fulfilment to the final accomplishment at the end of this age
and the establishment of Messiah's Kingdom.

Verses 6 to 14 revert to the impending doom of Moab, as a
result of his pride, wrath and lying. "Pride goeth before destruction, and an haughty spirit before a fall" (Prov. 16: 18). At
the end of *verse 10* God speaks in fellowship with Isaiah, who
thereupon resumes his lamentations.

Moab's prayers to his idols would be unavailing. Judgment
would come in three years, "**as the years of a hireling**", i.e.,
exactly at the time predicted; for a hireling does not exceed
his period of labour, and his employer will not allow him to
leave earlier.

CHAPTER XVII

THIS chapter gives a brief oracle concerning Damascus, and
proceeds with judgment upon Israel, and especially Ephraim,
because it had allied itself with Damascus against Judah. Only
a remnant would be left (*vv. 4–6*); this would turn steadfastly
to God (*verse 7*), and abandon idolatry (*verse 8*).

Forgetfulness of God brings barrenness; there may be much
labour and activity in the spirit of self-reliance, but it produces
no real fruit (*vv. 9–11*). Let us never be unmindful of the

true Source of our strength, " **the Rock** ", Christ Jesus, lest we bring upon ourselves " **grief** " and " **desperate sorrow** " (*verse 11*), the sorrow not of contrition but of remorse.

Again, consistently with the prophetic principle the oracle points, in *vv. 12–14*, to the time yet future, when the nations, rushing like mighty waters, gather together "against the Lord and against His Anointed" (Ps. 2: 2), only to be driven like chaff, and "like the whirling dust before the storm" (*verse 13, R.V.*). Cp. Joel 3: 11, 12; Zech. 9: 14; 14: 2, 3; Ps. 46: 2.

CHAPTER XVIII

THE beginning of this chapter seems best understood with reference to the fact that Assyria was threatening the nations. The word rendered "Woe" is the same word as that rendered "Ho" in 55: 1, and is expressive of a summons to hear the word of God. Many interpretations have been suggested of the phrase "**shadowing with wings**". The most probable seems to be that indicating protection. The land is mentioned as beyond or outside the rivers of Ethiopia, and therefore may be regarded as a region outside the activities of the lands overrun by the powers that had attacked or would attack Israel and the surrounding nations.

The idea of protecting care is confirmed by the command to the outside nation to go as swift messengers to Israel. Israel is " **scattered and peeled** " (other suggested renderings do not appeal as suitable). Israel was terrible from its beginning, terrible to the Egyptians, terrible to the Canaanites. Israel is " **meted out** " by God's decrees and dealings of righteousness, and " **trodden down** " under Divine judgments. Israel's land was destined to be temporarily spoiled (or divided) by nations famed for their rivers, e.g., the Nile, the Euphrates, and even the Tiber, the "rivers" standing for the oppressing Gentile powers.

The outside nations were to go with messages to Israel. They will take part in gathering the scattered outcasts of God's people, as Isaiah's prophecies declare, e.g., 11: 12, which speaks of the same ensign as here in *verse 3*.

Verse 4 intimates that for the time being He will wait while, under His control, circumstances are developing until the actual time of His intervention, the time figuratively described as "harvest", before which the bud appears and the sour or unripe grape. In due course the Lord would do His pruning upon the foes of Israel and cut down their branches, for fowls and beasts to dwell among them. So it happened in the case of Sennacherib.

So it has been, and will be, in every crisis of the strife of nations, and especially when efforts have been put forth to crush God's chosen people. The passage gives us lessons of confident patience to await God's time of direct interposition for deliverance, assured that in all our experiences everything is under His absolute control. "The bud may have a bitter taste, But sweet will be the flower." Trials and difficulties are sent to cast us upon God in simple and unwavering dependence upon Him.

The nations outside Ethiopia (a comprehensive term) were to wait till God acts and will present Israel itself as an offering to Jehovah of hosts, a beautiful description of the combined act of Gentile nations in helping to assemble the people of Israel at the beginning of the Millennial period. This is confirmed by the closing sentence of the chapter, and the tremendous significance of the event is indicated by the repetition in *verse 7* of the facts concerning Israel.

CHAPTERS XIX, XX

THESE give the oracle concerning Egypt. Jehovah " **rideth upon a swift** (or light) **cloud** ", that is to say, He is about to display His judicial dealings. Civil war would ruin the nation (*verse 2*). Idolatry and spiritism were rampant among the Egyptians, but the futility of all this would become evident. The cruel lord, the fierce king (*verse 4*) was probably not a foreign invader, such as Sargon or Nebuchadnezzar, but an Egyptian monarch himself, as, e.g., Pharaoh Necho.

There were to be further calamities, in connection with the sea and the Nile, i.e., the commerce carried on in regard to them. The various characteristic occupations would come to grief (*vv. 5–10*). The princes of Zoan (an ancient capital of Egypt), advisers and wise men would all be of no avail. So with Noph, or Memphis, a renowned city near Cairo. God can judicially impart a perverse spirit of self-will to rulers, to their own doom (*verse 14*). Hardness of heart would give place to timidity and fear (*verse 16*).

The rest of the 19th chapter points, as in other prophecies, first to a more immediate fulfilment and then to the yet future time of the Millennial Kingdom. There are five paragraphs each beginning with " **In that day** ". The day consists of a period extending from the impending judgments upon Egypt to the end of the present age and the Second Advent of Christ.

Firstly, Judah was about to be the Divine instrument of judgment (*vv. 16, 17*). Secondly, the attitude of Egypt towards Israel would be changed. There would come a time when the language spoken in Canaan would be the language spoken in Egypt, to a limited extent ("five cities"). This was fulfilled when in the empire founded by Alexander the Great the Hellenistic Greek language became the common tongue in Canaan and elsewhere and was adopted in Egypt (where the Septuagint Version was produced). " **The city of destruction** " (lit., the city Ir-ha-heres) probably indicates the destruction of idolatry (*verse 18*). That took place, after the successive invasions of the Assyrians, Chaldeans, Persians and Greeks.

Thirdly, there would come a time when an altar would be erected to the Lord in the midst of the land, and " **a pillar** " at the border. The Jewish religion actually spread in Egypt (*verse 21*). Synagogues were built, and one especially at Heliopolis, and later on a church was erected at Alexandria. Subsequently Egypt was smitten (*verse 22*) by the power of Islam. Islam will not prevail permanently. There will be healing.

Fourthly, we are directed to the change to take place at the beginning of the Millennial reign of Christ. A road will run from Egypt to Assyria. Both nations, whose separate aim had been the conquest of the world, will unite to serve the Lord.

Fifthly, Israel will be the intermediary in the Assyrian-Egyptian combine. Instead of being subdued by each, as formerly, God's people will reach their destined height of power and glory;

they will be " a blessing in the midst of the earth ", and will be God's own inheritance. Cp. Acts 2: 39 and 3: 25, 26.

In chapter 20 we are taken back to the conquest of Egypt by Assyria. As Philistia was allied with Egypt, Tartan, Sennacherib's chief of command, subdued that country (represented by Ashdod) on the way (*verse 1*). Isaiah himself was appointed as a sign of the impending overthrow of Egypt and Ethiopia. The coastland ("isle") in *verse 6* stands for all Palestine.

CHAPTER XXI

THREE oracles are pronounced in this chapter, concerning Babylon, Edom and Arabia. " The desert of the sea " (*verse 1*) is Babylon (cp. Jer. 50: 38; 51: 13, 36, 55). It was soon to be conquered by the Medes (Elam, *verse 2*, is Media), who would come upon it with violence and rapidity, like the storms which in Chaldea spring up from the south. Isaiah was overcome with emotion at the prospect (*vv. 3, 4*). He was deprived of the pleasure of rest at night in realizing the horror of the destruction.

The Babylonians would be indulging in luxury and debauchery when the calamity fell upon them (*verse 5*). So it came to pass, as described in Dan. 5. The prophet was to employ a watchman, (in *verse 11* he is himself the watchman; cp. Hab. 2: 1, 2).

The watchman is one who stands in God's counsels, knows what is coming and looks out for the event. So now, he who learns from the completed Scriptures what God has foretold, discerning His purposes, not by speculative interpretation, but by comparing Scripture with Scripture, and accepting what is therein made plain, is able to warn and exhort others. He stands upon the watch-tower (*verse 7*) in fellowship with God.

What the watchman saw was a procession of chariots, driving in pairs (R.V.). Contemplating the vision carefully, he discerned the impending calamity, and cried " as a lion " (R.V.). He beheld "a troop (or cavalcade) of men, horsemen in pairs" (*verse 9*).

In *verse 10* the " threshing, and child of my threshing-floor " is figurative of crushing oppression (41: 15; Mic. 4: 12, 13), and of Divine judgment (Jer. 51: 33), and this reference is to God's use of Babylon as an instrument of chastisement upon His people Israel.

In *verse 11* Dumah is Edom. Dumah means "silence" (i.e., of death). Isaiah, the watchman, receives an enquiry, earnest in its repetition, " **How far on is it in the night ?** " The reply is to the effect that while the morning is coming, night will yet envelop it. If they wish to enquire, let them do so, but the one thing necessary is that they should turn to God in repentance.

For Israel and the world the morning is coming, the dawn of the Millennial day; but there must come the Day of the Lord in judgment, and Israel must pass through the night of the great tribulation.

As to Arabia (*vv. 13–17*), the caravans of the Dedanites must pass the night in the forest (or wilderness). The inhabitants of Arabian Tema must bring (margin) them water and bread. In *verse 16* Kedar stands for the Arabian tribes. First the Assyrians and then the Chaldeans would subdue Arabia (see Jer. 49: 28–33). The time was predicted precisely: for the phrase " **according to the years of an hireling** ", see on 16: 14.

CHAPTER XXII

THE valley of vision, concerning which this oracle is uttered, is not Samaria (as suggested by some) but Jerusalem. Though not exactly situated in a valley, yet there are mountains round about it (Ps. 125: 2), and God had chosen it as a place shut in, so to speak, from the world, a place where He would give, through his prophets, visions of His will and purposes. Man's cities are spiritually and morally deserts.

Judgments were about to fall on Jerusalem, through Gentile powers, but the chapter is not confined to events of the then near future. Much of the opening verses will be fulfilled when the nations are gathered together against the city at the end of this age. There will be " **a day of trouble, and of treading down, and of perplexity** " (*verse 5*) such as Jerusalem has never experienced.

Elam and Kir (*verse 6*) were strategic places in Assyria, and the passage primarily refers to the Assyrian invasion. *Verses 8*

to 11 describe what was done in Hezekiah's time (2 Kings 20:
12–21; 2 Chron. 32: 2–7, 30). While God blessed Hezekiah's
efforts, he did some scheming; but the people were in such a
state of apostasy from God that He could not purge their iniquity
(verse 14). They had no idea of looking to their Maker (verse 11),
and when He called for mourning and repentance, they indulged
in feasting and entire carelessness as to the judgments impending,
even though they were aware of their doom (vv. 12, 13).

The lesson of the passage, vv. 8 to 11, is of the utmost
importance. Whatever we attempt by our own efforts is futile
and disastrous unless directed by God and wrought by His
power. Evil can never be averted by means adopted by our
natural wisdom. Forgetfulness of God leads to reliance upon
human resources and means, and ends in disappointment and
misery.

In vv. 15 to 19 we learn facts about Shebna additional to
those in chapters 36 and 37 and 2 Kings 19. He was a sort of
vizier, or chamberlain, over the king's household, with charge
of his treasury. The word "this" (verse 15) expresses Divine
contempt. His arrogance led him to hew out a sepulchre for
himself, hollowed out in the rocks of the city, copying the high
and mighty of earth. His doom of captivity would prevent him
from lying there. Jehovah would turn (lit., coil) him violently,
and toss him like a ball into a land far and wide. The state-
carriages which he had provided for himself would go too, and
become the shame of Hezekiah's house. In captivity he would
meet his death. So is he who "layeth up treasure for himself
and is not rich toward God" (Luke 12: 21).

His place would be filled by Eliakim, who would have a still
more honourable and extensive position. What is said of him
in vv. 22 to 24 marks him as a type of Christ, of whom what is
mentioned in verse 22 is spoken by Christ Himself in Rev. 3: 7,
while Shebna, whose doom is repeated in verse 25, foreshadows
the Antichrist. As Eliakim replaced Shebna, so will Christ
replace the Man of Sin.

Eliakim's family would be benefited by his position, as metaphorically described in vv. 23, 24, a foreshadowing of the effect
of Christ's coming glory upon those who, spiritually, being born
of God, are related to Christ.

CHAPTER XXIII

THE oracle concerning Tyre is the last of the series concerning the nations. Babylon represented imperial power. Tyre stood for commercial power. Its influence, with that of the older city Zidon, here spoken of as a mother in relation to Tyre, (*vv. 4 and 12*) exercised a more potent effect in this respect than any other nation. Tarshish was in the west of the Mediterranean, and perhaps stood here for the whole of that sea.

In *verse 3* Sihor is the Hebrew name for Siris, the upper Nile (here called "the river"), the region of which was a grain mart for the nations. Egypt and Tyre are associated in *verse 5*. In *verse 9* Tyre is made an example of a Divine purpose concerning all potentates who glory in their prowess and their attainments of power and domination. Jehovah of hosts will "**stain the pride of all glory, and bring into contempt all the honourable (the chief men) of the earth.**"

In *verse 10* Tarshish is set free. Just as the Nile overflows its banks, so the people can now enjoy liberty and be independent of the mother city. It can exercise no more restraining girdle (see margin) of authority. Let the Zidonians escape to Cyprus (Chittim); they will have no rest there (*verse 12*). The Chaldeans, who succeeded the Assyrians (*verse 13*), would desolate Tyre and bring it to ruin (Ezek. 29: 17, 18). During the seventy years of Chaldean supremacy (Jer. 25: 9, 11; 29: 10) it would be forgotten. "**The days of one king**" marks a fixed period. After this the Lord would permit the restoration. Not that Tyre would turn to God. She could renew her melodies and, like a harlot, attract nations again to herself by her traffic and enterprise (*verse 17*).

Verse 18 received a fulfilment in that Tyre and Sidon assisted in the building of the Temple after the captivity (Ezra 3: 7).

PART I (c)

DIVINE JUDGMENTS AND DELIVERANCES
(Chapters XXIV–XXXIII)

CHAPTER XXIV

THIS chapter, following the account of the dealings of God with the individual nations one after another, takes into view the whole scene, all the nations, including Israel, as destined to come under the judgments of the Lord at the end of this age.

The separate nations, reviewed in chapters 13 to 23, display differing conditions of the world's alienation from God, influenced and directed by the hosts of spiritual wickedness in the heavenlies. All must meet the Divine retribution in the coming Day of the Lord. Babylon represents systematized corruption and oppression in all the earth; Assyria, antagonism against God's people; Philistia, constant and closer hostility; Moab, human pride; Damascus, the ally of apostasy; Dumah, self-reliance; Jerusalem, mere profession; Tyre, worldly glory.

All that is represented in the world by these characteristics must hereafter experience the judgments foretold in the opening verses. Everything is to be overturned (*verse 1*). In *verse 4* the earth and the world are broadly synonymous; speaking generally the distinction may lie in this, that *the earth* is that especially in which God's governmental dealings have been manifested, *the world* is the same scene presenting man's condition in its alienation from God. The rendering "earth" sometimes should be "land", with reference to the land of Israel. This is apparently the case in *verse 5*. The inhabitants of the world have not broken the covenant of Genesis 9: 16. That covenant was virtually a Divine promise, God alone undertaking the fulfilment. Israel it was who broke the Covenant of God's Law (see Deut. 31: 16–20; Jer. 11: 10). And as to the future, the agreement which the apostate nation (the godly remnant excluded) will make with the Man of Sin, will absolutely fulfil all that is stated in verse 5. The judgments which follow will depopulate the earth, so that 'few men will be left' (*verse 6*) fulfilling the Lord's word that "except the Lord shortened the days no flesh would be saved." For the elect's sake He will do so. This depopulation is figuratively described in *verse 13*.

Verses 14, 15 and the first part of *16* describe the exultation and praise after the judgments upon the Antichrist and his worshippers have been executed, Israel is delivered and peace brought to the diminished nations. The words for "sing" and "cry aloud" in *verse 14* are the same as those used of Zion in 12: 6.

In the latter part of *verse 16* Isaiah mourns over all that is to happen to his people, especially in "the great tribulation", resulting from two cases of treachery, first the treachery of Israel in turning from God to make a covenant with the Antichrist, and secondly the treachery of the Antichrist in breaking that covenant and endeavouring to exterminate the Jews.

The final judgments upon the nations under the Satanic rule of the Beast and the False Prophet (Rev. 13) are foretold in the rest of the chapter, the consummation being the Personal intervention of Christ at the Second Advent (*verse 23*).

CHAPTER XXV

THIS and most of chapter 26 consist of the song of praise which will arise from the godly remnant after "the great tribulation", the nucleus of redeemed Israel. There is first a praiseful recognition of God's faithfulness in view of His relation to His earthly people (*verse 1*), and of His overthrow of the hostile city of the nations, a reference probably to Rome (*verse 3*), while *verse 2* points to Babylon. All the proud organizations of man are doomed. God will be a stronghold to the poor and needy in the perils and distress of the times of the Antichrist (*verse 4*). The Gentile peoples which remain will come to mount Zion to share the festal provision Jehovah will make for Israel (*verse 6*). The veil that has blinded the nations under Satanic delusions, will there be cast away (*verse 7*). Death will be 'swallowed up in victory'; the quotation of this in 1 Cor. 15: 54 shows that resurrection is in view. These who have been slaughtered by the Antichrist and his agents during the great tribulation will

be raised to share the reign of Christ. Tears will be wiped away,
and the "rebuke" (i.e., the shame) of Israel will be removed
(*verse 8*). The godly remnant will celebrate their deliverance
(*verse 9*). Moab with its pride and plunder will be utterly humbled
(*vv. 10–12*).

CHAPTER XXVI

THE first eighteen verses of this chapter consist of the song of
the delivered remnant in Israel as they enter upon Millennial
peace and blessedness. The whole land is called the land of
Judah, in view of the concentration of power and domination in
Jerusalem. The strong city is set in contrast to "the city of
the nations" (25: 3). Israel, redeemed and converted to their
Messiah, is " **the righteous nation** " (*vv. 1, 2*).

Verse 3 primarily applies to the members of the redeemed
nation. They in their great deliverance will realize the assurance,
" **Thou will keep him in perfect peace** (lit., peace, peace), **whose
mind is stayed on Thee** (or firmly established in Thee): **because
he trusteth in Thee.**"

This is to be enjoyed at all times by those who, instead of
being overcome by difficulties or by yielding to the pressure
of spiritual foes and human antagonism, put their trust in the
Lord, staying their mind upon Him. The peace possessed is
not the outcome of mere self-determination, it is ministered
by the keeping power of the Lord Himself. It is that peace
which essentially characterized Christ, and of which He said
"Peace I leave with you, My peace (lit., the peace which is
Mine) I give unto you."

The experience of this leads the possessor to utter the
exhortation, " **Trust ye in the Lord for ever: for in the Lord
JEHOVAH is the rock of ages** " (*verse 4*). Cp. 17: 10; 30: 29,
marg.; Deut. 32: 4, 15.

Verse 5 provides a reason for trusting Him and a proof of
His strength, and *verse 6* tells how He will impart it to His
people. *Verse 7* is a further comment on verse 4.

God makes smooth the path of His people. Not only so, He imparts His character to them. He is upright; so are they. This is not mere moral rectitude, it is fellowship with Him.

This is confirmed in *verse 8*. Israel will have learned to wait for God in the way of His judgments. God rewards the patience of those who, discerning His counsels and purposes, await His time. Their desire is not simply for deliverance, but for the honour of His Name, that is to say, His character, and towards the remembrance of what He has done in the past.

Verse 9 continues the song of the redeemed remnant. In the night of their tribulation they had desired Him. They had learned to seek Him early, that is, earnestly. This is ever the response of the trusting soul in times of affliction.

In the coming judgments of the Day of the Lord the nations that are left will learn righteousness. Yet there will be many who refuse to do so (*verse 10*), and will retain their animosity against the Jews (*verse 11*). The Lord will deal with them in Person, and fire will devour the adversaries. The bestowment of peace upon His people will be the consummation of His mercies in accomplishing all their works for them (the same word "for" as in the preceding clause), *verse 12*.

In *verse 13* they review the various tyrants who have oppressed them throughout "the times of the Gentiles", but the intervention of Christ on their behalf will call forth their praise in ascribing the glory to His Name. While the enemies are overthrown God's people will be increased. The R.V. gives the correct rendering of the end of *verse 15*: " **Thou hast enlarged all the borders of the land** "; cp. 54: 2, 3. The land allotted to Israel in the Millennium will be extended.

Verses 16 to 18 depict the agonies and supplications of the godly in Israel during their time of trouble under the Antichrist, in the realization and acknowledgment of their utter helplessness to deliver themselves or others. *Verse 19* gives the Divine promise of the revival of the nation. The word rendered " **My dead body** " is used in a collective sense (some would therefore render it "my dead bodies"). Israel will, so to speak, be brought to life, as from the dead.

At the close of the pouring out of the wrath of God upon the nations under the Antichrist (Rev. 6 to 16) during the great

tribulation, the Lord is coming forth in Person to visit the
iniquity of the inhabitants of the earth upon them (*verse 21*) for
the fulfilment of which see especially Rev. 19: 11–21. A place
of refuge will be provided for the godly remnant, who will form
the nucleus of the redeemed nation (*verse 20*).

———————

CHAPTER XXVII

In *verse 1* the leviathans (there are two, R.V.), the swift serpent
and the crooked, or winding, serpent, and the dragon are doubtless symbolic both of the great world powers at the end of this
age and of the evil one who will instigate them; he is spoken of
both as the serpent and the dragon, Gen. 3: 1; Rev. 20: 2, 10,
the latter of which foretells his punishment. The passages in
Isaiah and Revelation are parallel as to the course of events:
Rev. 19 corresponds to Isaiah 26 to 21, and Rev. 20 to Isa. 27: 1.

For the third time a prophetic song hymns the happiness of
redeemed Israel (*vv. 2–5*). There are four, but the first (ch. 5)
was of a different character. Here Jehovah rejoices over His
people. They are a vineyard of red (or fiery) vine (some manuscripts have "pleasant". Cp. Amos 5: 11), constantly kept and
watered by Him. 'Wrath have I none,' He says. That will be
a thing of the past for them. If enemies rise up against them
again, they will be but thorns and thistles for the burning. Nay,
let the would-be foe take the wise alternative, and take hold of
His strength for protection, and make peace with Him.

On the contrary, Israel is to take root, blossom, bud, and
" fill the face of the world with fruit," thus becoming "the
riches of the Gentiles" (Rom. 11: 12), *verse 6*.

This, spiritually, is the Lord's purpose and desire for believers
during the present period till the Church is complete (John 15:
1–16). Filling the earth with fruit is suggestive of the effects
of missionary service in all nations.

The Lord had to smite His people, but not as He smote their
foes (*verse 7*). How He smote Israel is now described (*vv. 8–11*)
and all with a view to their restoration. His covenant promises

remain unalterable. How God has, and will have, chastised His people is described in *verse 8, R.V.*: "**In measure** (i.e., not in fullness of wrath, but by indignation tempered by forbearance) **when Thou sendest her away, Thou dost contend with her: He hath removed her with His rough blast in the day of the east wind.**" He sifted His chosen people among the nations. He blew violently upon them, sifting them but not destroying them; and all this with a view to purging their iniquity (*verse 9*). The fruit of God's dealings is that the stones of idol altars are made like chalk stones broken in pieces. The images of Astarte and the sun images will never be set up again. These are suggestive of everything substituted for God.

As it is the punishment which causes the sin of Israel to cease, the prophet now gives, as a warning, details of the nature of the punishment (*vv. 10, 11*). Jerusalem, once so populous, would be left like a wilderness; animals would browse off the bits of foliage growing among the ruins, and their women would gather sticks for their fires, since the hostile armies, having accomplished their aim, would have left.

Yet mercy will rejoice against judgment, and Israel, repentant, shall be gathered. Just as in the year of jubilee, the trumpet sounded on the evening of the Day of Atonement, and every man returned to his own possession (Lev. 25), so will scattered Israel return to worship at Jerusalem when the Lord gives His signal among the nations (*verse 13*; cp. 11: 12).

CHAPTER XXVIII

THIS chapter introduces a fresh series of "Woes". There were six in chapter 5. There are six now from this chapter to chapter 33. The first five are pronounced against Israel and especially Judah and Jerusalem. The sixth is against Assyria.

The chapter may be divided into three parts, (1) vv. 1–13; (2) vv. 14–22; (3) vv. 23–29.

In the first section there is a record of the grievous condition of the leading men in Israel at that time.

In the first verses of the chapter Samaria is denounced. It is called (1) "**the crown of pride**", in which the intoxicated

Ephraim has gloried, (2) "a fading flower" (cp. 1: 30; 40: 7, 8).
The "fat valley" (R.V.) refers to the situation of the town.
The people were given to luxury and self-indulgence. All must
meet the judgments of the Lord (vv. 2–4), the Assyrian, "the
mighty and strong one", being the instrument. Samaria would
be to him "as a firstripe fig" (R.V.), ripe in June instead of
August, easily plucked and immediately swallowed.

This throws light upon the incident of the fig-tree recorded in
Matt. 21 and Mark 11. After the figs are gathered and stored
away in August or September, there is still sap in the tree, which
puts forth a second crop of figs through the winter. This begins
to ripen in the spring, but does not come to anything. You can
eat the figs, but they are not worth storing.

Now Palestine lay between Assyria and Egypt, and armies
passing from either side must traverse it, hence the reference to
the overflowing scourge. God's people were tempted to go to one
or the other for help, but the Lord constantly warned them
against this, and to trust in Him. That is the great teaching of
the first thirteen verses of this chapter.

It has its lessons for us. The Lord teaches us to avoid seeking help from man and to trust in Him alone. On the other
hand we are to guard against the spirit of selfish ease and luxury
which characterized Israel of old.

In verse 5 the residue of His people are the faithful in Judah,
and to them Jehovah would be "a crown of glory" (in contrast
to the crown of pride of Samaria), a spirit of judgment to those
who acted justly in their seat of judgment, and a strength against
the foe (verse 6).

This holds good for those who walk in the fear of the Lord,
in a day of widespread declension, as at the present time.
Righteousness and strength are their portion from the Lord.
We need to see to it that we deal righteously with our fellows,
and are overcomers by the power of the Holy Spirit.

Judah as a whole had gone astray (vv. 7, 8) and must receive
retribution, and this is confirmed in vv. 9–15. The questions
asked in verse 9 are a remonstrance against the self-satisfied,
self-righteous, ungodly people of Judah, and especially their

priests and prophets (they were like the scribes and Pharisees of a later date). Instead of being so superior in knowledge and attainment, as they imagined they were, in reality they were like tiny children, who must be taught the very elements of knowledge. Just as with children, precept must be upon precept, line upon line, here a little and there a little. The retributive side comes out in *verse 11*, in the incomprehensible way God would speak to them. Their sneers at His prophet made it impossible for them to receive the truth He would speak to them by the Assyrians, people of "another tongue". Cp. 29: 9–12 and see Jer. 6: 10. The Lord had offered them rest and refreshing, and the means of giving rest to the weary, but they would not hear. Therefore they must suffer the retribution appointed (*verse 13*).

The second section (*vv. 14–22*) gives the foreign policy of the leaders of the people. They thought that their predecessors did not know how to deal with Egypt and Assyria. They themselves had done better than that, and made treaties with both, and boasted that they had hoodwinked them. Their name for Egypt was Death and for Assyria, Hell. God again gives them warning, offering them wise counsel, but showing them to what their ways will lead. The third section (*vv. 23–29*) deals with the faithful in the nation. They would be strongly criticized for lack of patriotism, then when instead of peace foreign troops are in the country accompanying famine, the faithful will not have a better time.

Whatever the circumstances are, those who fear God and trust in Him will never have an easy time of it, but there is an end to the trial and God never goes beyond what is necessary, and so He promises instruction and guidance if we will be faithful to Him and rely upon Him whatever may happen.

But the rulers of Jerusalem had gone further in their defiance of God. They scornfully imagined that they need have no fear of death and Hades. As for the Assyrians they proposed a secret alliance with Egypt, boasting in their false attitude towards God and His messengers (*vv. 14, 15*).

In contrast to this the Lord again points to the future deliverance to be wrought by Christ, and to the glories of His Person and work (*verse 16*). He is to be in Zion a foundation stone, tried (lit., a stone of proof), not only proved Himself but able

to bear up and sustain those who trust in Him, a corner stone
of the building. The last statement has also been rendered
"shall hasten it to," or, again, "will not have to move." However it might be translated it presents Christ as the sure confidence
of the believer. Judgment and righteousness will be the plumb-
line to test everything, instead of injustice and iniquity. The lies
and the hiding place referred to in verse 15 will be swept away
(*verse 17*).

In *verse 18* the covenant with death and agreement with Hades,
while referring to the immediate circumstances, also point to the
future agreement of the nation as a whole with the Antichrist.
The ungodly in Israel who have entered into this covenant will
meet their merited doom. The infliction of the scourge will be
constant, and, whereas the rulers and people refused to listen to
Isaiah's message, in the coming time the nation will understand
the truth only to their own vexation (*verse 19*).

They thought that in getting help from Egypt they would
prepare a comfortable bed and a nice coverlet for their rest from
danger. But they would find to their dismay that their prepara-
tions would be futile, the bed too short, the coverlet too narrow
(*v. 20*).

So is it ever with any of God's people. Reliance upon the
world will only beget shame, misery and disaster. It is faith
that triumphs. Christ is a "sure foundation" for us upon
which to build our hope. "Blessed are all they that wait for
Him." "He that believeth shall not make haste."

The Lord would have to act against His people as He had
acted in past days against their foes at Perazim and Gibeon
(*verse 21*). Let them turn from their mockery lest their fetters
be strengthened. The time would come, and yet will, when a
"consumption", a destructive judgment, would fall upon the
whole earth (*verse 22*; cp. 26: 21).

The third section (*vv. 23–29*) contains God's appeal to the
faithful ones suffering for their loyalty to Him. It conveys His
promise and His covenant. He uses the illustration of the
husbandman, somewhat as the Apostle Paul does in 1 Cor. 3: 9.
God does not go on ploughing indefinitely, nor does He indefinitely
exercise discipline. He has gracious purposes for all, and there
is an end to the time of trial.

In the figurative questions and statements in *vv. 24 to 28* Israel is the Lord's farm land and threshing floor. His chastisements and punishments are the harrow and ploughshare. But He does not continue the use of these indefinitely, any more than the farmer continues ploughing. There is the resultant sowing and reaping. Again, Israel is His threshing, the corn of His floor (see 21: 10).

The husks of iniquity must be separated from the wheat of the persons dealt with. This is not a never ending process either in God's dealings or in the farmer's occupation. The Lord of hosts, who as Creator provides the farmer with the instinct and discretion necessary for his work, knows how to act in His perfect wisdom in dealing with His people. He will not destroy them. They remain His own possession. He chastens us "for our profit, that we may be partakers of His holiness," and His chastening yields "peaceable fruit unto them that have been exercised thereby, even the fruit of righteousness" (Heb. 12: 10, 11).

CHAPTER XXIX

AT the beginning of the last chapter Samaria was symbolized as a fading crown of flowers. Now the woe-judgment is pronounced against Jerusalem, symbolized as the hearth (i.e., altar) of God. Ariel may have its other meaning of "lion of God", but in 31: 9 the Lord is stated to have His fire and furnace (or hearth) there. Moreover in Ezek. 43: 15, 16, Ariel is the altarhearth of God (R.V. marg.).

Let them continue their formal religion, their round of feasts and sacrifices (*verse 1*). Judgment must come, and Ariel would become a veritable altar-hearth of slaughter and fiery indignation (*verse 2*). National foes would reduce them to utter weakness (*vv. 3, 4*). Yet deliverance is assured. All nations that rise against Zion must be brought to nought under the mighty hand of God (*vv. 5-8*).

Verses 9 to 16 contain a remonstrance against the condition of God's people, and a description of the inevitable and terrible judgments to be inflicted upon them because of their apostasy, luxury and hardness of heart. In *verse 9* the prophet judicially bids them carry on in their perverseness: " **Tarry ye** (i.e., do as Lot did when he lingered in the doomed city) **and wonder, take your pleasure** (or, as in the margin, blind yourselves) **and be blind.**" That is, 'go on in your heedless ways.'

The waywardness of the rulers, seers and people had brought upon them spiritual slumber and blindness. The revealed will of God had become like a sealed book or letter, so that even one who could understand writing could not open it, and when it was unsealed and handed to an illiterate man to read he had to refuse owing to his inability to make out the words (*vv. 10–12*).

Mere lip worship and external conformity while the heart was alienated, and all this the effects of "the precept of men", must result in the loss of the wisdom of the wise and the hiding of the understanding of the intelligent (*vv. 13, 14*). The same state of things prevailed when Christ was on earth (Matt. 15: 3; Mark 7: 6).

How far into the dark the backslider can go is revealed in *verse 15*. *Verse 16* really begins with an exclamation of sorrow: "**Alas for your perversity** "! They had in their ideas turned upside down the relation between the creature and the Creator: " **Shall the potter be counted as clay, that the thing made should say of him that made it, He made me not, or the thing framed say of Him that framed it, He hath no understanding ?** (R.V.)." They thought they had no need of Jehovah, they could manage for themselves, as if a pot should inform its maker and owner that it could itself do all that was required of it. Such is the preposterous attitude of all who seek to act independently of God.

But God would expose their folly. He Himself would turn things upside down (the paragraph begins at *verse 17*, not 18; 18 explains 17). The Lebanon forest would be changed into a fruitful field, and the fruitful field would be regarded as a forest. The deaf would hear the words of the book, in contrast to the sinners mentioned in *vv. 11, 12*, and the blind would see out of obscurity and darkness.

This and what follows bear reference to the coming Millennial reign of Christ. The meek will joy in Jehovah, the poor will rejoice in Christ, "the Holy One of Israel".

So it is now. It is the meek and the poor, those among believers who are conscious of spiritual need, who have the greatest joy in the Lord. For the Holy Spirit ministers the fulness of Christ especially to such. See Isaiah 61: 1; Zeph. 3: 12; Matt. 5: 3-5.

In the day to come " **the terrible one** ", the Man of Sin, will have been brought to nought, the scoffer destroyed, plotters of evil cut off, those who act unrighteously and pervert justice (*vv. 19-21*).

Jehovah's covenant relationship with Abraham as his Redeemer is made the basis of the blessings promised to the seed of Jacob (*verse 22*). His house, freed from shame and terror, will rejoice in being surrounded by their redeemed children, and "sanctify" (i.e., pay due and reverent regard to) the Name of Jehovah and Christ as " **the Holy One of Jacob** " and, unlike the rebels against whom Isaiah was protesting, will " **fear the God of Israel.**" Instead of erring in spirit they will come to understanding and instead of murmuring they will rejoice in receiving instruction.

CHAPTER XXX

Woe is now pronounced against Judah for seeking help from Egypt against Assyria. This the northern kingdom of Israel had done with disastrous results. In *verse 1* the phrase rendered " **that cover with a covering** " may also be translated "that weave an alliance" (some would render it "that form a molten image"; this seems less suitable). The counsel was contrary to that of the Spirit of God. It was adding sin to the sin of their hardness of heart, their self-will and apostasy from God. The effect would be shame and reproach (*verse 5*).

In *verse 6* Isaiah utters an oracle (R.V. marg.) concerning " **the beasts of the south** " not the beasts that are going southward, as in the end of the verse, but the beasts that are native to Egypt, such as the hippopotamus; there too are the lioness and lion, the viper and the flying serpent. Just as all these are dangerous and troublesome, so would the rulers of Egypt prove to be. To bring treasures on camels and asses so as to

secure the help of the country from which God had long before
delivered His people, would procure no help at all. " **For Egypt
helpeth in vain, and to no purpose : therefore have I called her
Rahab that sitteth still** " (verse 7, R.V.). Rahab signifies
"arrogance". Proud aloofness prevented help from that quarter.

The next verse shows that this warning against going to
Egypt for help was intended not merely for God's people in
Isaiah's day, but for all in every period. It was to be written on
a tablet and inscribed in a book " **that it may be for the time
to come, for ever and ever.**" To seek help and counsel from the
Egypt world instead of from God can result only in disaster.

Verses 9 to 11 reveal the utter perverseness of the nation in
their rejection of the testimony of the prophets of God and their
determination to do without the Lord Himself. They preferred
oppression (or fraud) and iniquity, the effect of which would be
like that of a falling breach in a towering wall (*verse 13*). They
would be broken in pieces like a potter's vessel (the destruction
which Gentiles will yet experience, Ps. 2).

Mercy was offered to those who would return to the Lord and
find rest. But they refused and would flee to Egypt on swift
steeds (*verse 16*). For this they would flee from their enemies,
one of whom would chase a thousand, and five chasing them all,
till they became like a single pine on a mountain top and a
single banner on a hill (*verse 17*).

In *verse 18* the "therefore" gives the key to the true meaning.
The Lord has been foretelling the judgments that must come
upon these guilty people. For this reason the eventual blessing
of the nation is delayed. He will " **wait** " (i.e., will delay) until
the right time comes for Him to be gracious, in the exercise of
His restoring mercy; He will " **be exalted** " (i.e., will withdraw
Himself on high), in His dealings in judgment, so that, when
this has fulfilled its purpose, and not till then, He may show
His mercy. The time has not come even yet. Israel has hindered
its own deliverance and salvation.

" **For Jehovah is a God of judgment.**" This forms a connecting
link between what has just been set forth as to His necessary
chastisements upon the backsliding, and what is now to be said
as to the assured mercy for those who, walking in fellowship
with Him, abide His time. In both cases He is righteous, both

in chastising and in showing mercy. He always has, and will have, until the day of deliverance, a remnant of godly ones. "Blessed are all they that wait for Him."

The people will dwell safely, will weep no more, and will receive the answer to their supplication. During the preceding time of adversity they will be supplied with bread, and with water in their affliction (*verse 20*). This is the true meaning of the first part of this verse. It continues the promises of mercy. The bread and water are not symbolic of adversity, they represent the promised supplies of need during the affliction. Moreover guidance and instruction will be imparted by God-sent teachers (*vv. 20, 21*). For the people will, in the spirit of repentance, purge themselves from their iniquities (*verse 22*).

All this is in harmony with other Scriptures which speak of the circumstances of the great tribulation and those who turn to Him therein and wait for the promised Deliverer. When He comes, *verses 23 to 26*, with their description of Millennial fruitfulness and glory, will be fulfilled.

Verses 27 to 32 foretell the outpouring of the wrath of God upon the gathered enemies. And, as in so many other passages, while the immediate foe was the Assyrian, the prophecy points on to the coming power of his antitype, the Antichrist. The very fact of the assurances of Millennial glory, which will follow, is sufficient to confirm this. The word rendered "people" in *verse 28*, A.V., is plural, and is the same as that rendered "nations" just before. God will put a bridle in their jaws, causing them to err under the deceptive Satanic power of the Man of Sin.

The godly in Israel will have a song in that night of tribulation, rejoicing in the prospect of the coming day. It will be an earnest of the "Songs of Ascents" when they come to Jerusalem, to the mountain of Jehovah, " **to the mighty One** (the Rock) **of Israel** " (*verse 29*).

Verses 30 to 32 depict the scene of the warfare of Armageddon. Tophet (*verse 33*) denotes, not the burning, but the abhorred. It is the place in the valley of Hinnom, where cruel and abominable sacrifices were offered to Moloch. There at the centre of the battle line of 200 miles (1,600 furlongs, Rev. 14: 20) of the gathered armies of the Antichrist, the breath of Jehovah will kindle the fire of His wrath, and Israel will be delivered. See 63: 1–6; Ps. 2: 1–6; Joel 2: 11; 3: 9–16; 2 Thess. 2: 8; Rev. 19: 11–21; Deut. 32: 42, R.V.

CHAPTER XXXI

AGAIN Isaiah denounces the evil of seeking help from Egypt instead of seeking the Lord. The scheme is wise in the eyes of apostate Israel; yet Jehovah is wise (*verse 2*), and will vindicate His wisdom in His judgment both upon the Egyptians and upon those who have sought their assistance (*verse 3*). " **He will arise against the house of the evil-doers and against the help of them that work iniquity** " (that is, the help afforded by the Egyptians to the evil-doers of Israel).

In *verse 3* the prophet speaks of the Egyptians as creatures of dust, in contrast to God, and their horses as mere flesh in contrast to spiritual power.

A message of the assurance of deliverance is given in *vv. 4–9*. The comparison of his interposition is that of lions roaring on their prey, a comparison of attack. In *verse 5* it is that of hovering or fluttering birds', a comparison of protection and deliverance. Hence there is a call in *verse 6* to turn in repentance to God, for the day is coming when never again will Israel be guilty of idolatry. Let the repentant therefore anticipate this. The Assyrian is to be utterly defeated (*verse 8*), for God's fire is in Zion and His furnace in Jerusalem, again an anticipation of the destruction of the Antichrist.

CHAPTER XXXII

THE first five verses of this chapter depict the issue of the deliverance, and foretell (1) the personal, Millennial reign of Christ, (2) the authority of those who rule under Him, (3) the protecting power of Christ as the One Who combines in Himself the prerogatives of Deity with the sympathy and compassion of humanity, (4) His protecting care, (5) His full supply of need, (6) His comfort for the weary, (7) the happy condition of the redeemed people with their clear vision, their attentive listening, their possession of knowledge and their ready testimony (vv. 1–4).

Until then there will be vile men practising deceit and cruelty. The word rendered "churl" signifies a crafty one.

Now follows a warning appeal, which is really a continuation of the fourth woe. It consists of a rousing remonstrance against the flippant self-security of the women in Jerusalem. Their carnal ease is doomed. Levity will give place to lamentation. Instead of luxurious dwellings, there will be weeds and briers, and instead of palaces desolation (vv. 9–14). So it was when king and people were carried away into captivity.

From this point Isaiah looks right on again to Millennial conditions, and identifies himself with his people in their redeemed state. The Holy Spirit will yet be poured upon the nation, and there will be abundance of righteousness, peace and fruitfulness. What was then valued as a fruit-garden will become more glorious. Even the uncultivated districts will be as full of verdure as a forest. Righteous judgment will be universal (verse 16). There will then be what the world has ever failed to establish, peace and safety (vv. 17, 18), but before this happy condition can obtain, there must be judgments upon the oppressor. The forest, in verse 19, represents the Antichristian foes, and the city their organized hostility.

While the closing verse gives a word of comfort to the godly in the nation who will live to see these times of blessedness, and will till the ground, free from all anxiety, it also gives a message of spiritual comfort to those who in the present time scatter the seeds of the Word of Life, and labour in doctrine.

CHAPTER XXXIII

In chapters 28 to 32 five woes were pronounced against Israel and Judah. The sixth woe is now uttered against Assyria, and again the prophecy looks on from Isaiah's own time to the yet future and final overthrow of the Antichristian powers and the day of Zion's deliverance (vv. 20–24), all being introductory to a fuller development of this twofold theme in chapter 34.

Primarily the time is that of the fourteenth year of Hezekiah.
The Assyrian has actually entered the land and God's judgments
are visiting " **the sinners in Zion** " (*verse 14*).

But the Assyrian must be brought low. There is to be retribution, point for point (*verse 1*), and Isaiah, after the denunciatory
woe, intercedes for his people in their time of trouble (*verse 2*).
The Divine response is sure, not only in Hezekiah's day, but at
the close of "man's day", the time of the great tribulation. The
gathered peoples (plural, *verse 3*) are to be scattered. Their
plunder will be seized and destroyed, as it were, before cater-
pillars and locusts.

Verses 5 and 6 form an interlude looking on to the establishment
of the Millennial Kingdom. No preceding period of deliverance
has filled this picture. The Lord will be exalted to His rightful
place amidst His people. Zion will be " **filled with judgment
and righteousness** ". He will Himself, as its " **wisdom and
knowledge** ", be the stability (i.e., security) of its times, its
strength (or wealth) of salvation (so the clauses are probably to
be rendered). Judah's treasure will be the fear of the Lord (a
striking contrast to Hezekiah's dealings as recorded in 2 Kings
18: 13–16).

The next verses describe Israel's pitiable state, not merely
under the Assyrian, but under the Antichrist. There is his
breaking of the covenant made with them (as in Daniel 9: 27),
the despair of the mighty ones among the Jews and their ambassadors, and the desolation of the land.

Yet the Lord will arise, the schemes of the enemy will be
rendered futile, and the Gentile nations ("peoples") will be
consumed (*vv. 10–12*).

The nations "far off", those not actually gathered at Armageddon, the Gentiles that remain after the worldwide judgments
of the day of God's wrath, are to hear what He has done, and
those that are near are to acknowledge His might (*verse 13*).

As for the Jews, there are "the sinners", "the hypocrites".
They will not escape the judgments. There is no partiality with
God (*verse 14*). There is the godly remnant; they shall dwell on
high, they shall be protected and nourished (*vv. 15, 16*). They
will see their King-Messiah " **in His beauty** " ; they will behold
" **the land of far distances** " (a greatly extended Israelitic
territory), *verse 17*. That is the reward of refusing to see evil
(*verse 15*).

They will muse on the terror they experienced during their great tribulation. The "scribe" (the political secretary) will be no more. The "receiver" (the Chancellor of the Exchequer) will be no more. "He that counted the towers" (the military commander) will be no more. The mighty foe with their foreign tongue will pass away (*vv. 18, 19*).

Zion will be seen in its glory, peaceful, permanent, prosperous, and all will centre in Him who is their Deliverer, the Bestower of peace and prosperity incalculable, the Judge, the Lawgiver, the King, the Saviour (*vv. 20–22*).

Verse 23 speaks of the weakness and inability of the people themselves, pictured whether as unable to guide the ship of state, or, what is more probable, arrange their tent as their dwelling place, with the necessary cord, tent pole and canvas. Yet it will be given them to divide the booty of the enemy, and the lame will take the prey (*verse 23*). Sickness, physical and spiritual, will be things of the past. The inhabitants 'shall have their sins forgiven' (*verse 24*).

God teaches us, as He will teach them, the impossibility of delivering ourselves by our own strength. He sends us weakness that out of weakness we may be made strong. Jacob had to learn this. Made physically lame, he proved more than ever the almighty power of the Lord. Paul learned to glory in his infirmities, that the power of Christ might rest upon him ('spread a tabernacle' over him), 2 Cor. 12: 9. In our trials and difficulties we are made to know the love of Christ in a way impossible without them. "In all these things we are more than conquerors through Him that loved us" (Rom. 8: 35–7).

PART I (d)

THE FUTURE OF GENTILE NATIONS AND ISRAEL
(Chapters XXXIV, XXXV)

CHAPTER XXXIV

THIS and the next chapter are an expansion of the two subjects of chapter 33, namely, the judgments of the Day of the Lord, and the subsequent Millennial blessedness of Israel and their land.

Under the Satanic power of the Beast and the False Prophet the armies of the nations will be gathered in one great effort to annihilate the Jews; see Rev. 19: 19–21, a passage which describes in detail what is here foretold in 34: 1–3. With *vv. 4–7* compare Rev. 6: 13, 14. In *verse 6* Idumea (i.e., Edom, always figurative of the natural state of man in his antagonism against God) is particularly mentioned as the great scene of the Divine intervention. Bozrah is a central stronghold of the country. It will be the culminating locality of the warfare of Armageddon (see 63: 1 and notes there). The judgments of this "day of the Lord's vengeance" will extend over 200 miles, the 1,600 furlongs of Rev. 14: 20, and the district of Bozrah will, it would seem, be the southernmost limit of the conflict. For there the King of the North, having gone to subdue Egypt, will be returning northward with a view to the destruction of Jerusalem and the Jews, because of tidings which will trouble him from the north. He will not reach Jerusalem, and that by reason of the Personal intervention of Christ (Dan. 11: 43, 44). He will pitch his military headquarters (not "palace", verse 45) in this Idumean region, and there will meet his doom at the Lord's hand, as will also the Antichrist further north of Jerusalem itself.

The figurative language of *vv. 6 and 7* describes the mighty leaders of these Gentile powers. "The times of the Gentiles" will have come to an end. " **It is the day of the Lord's vengeance, the year of recompence in the controversy of Zion** " (*verse 8*), i.e., to assert the rights of God's King. With *vv. 9, 10* cp. Rev. 18: 18 and 19: 3.

As for the land of Edom, it will be eternally barren, overgrown with nettles and thorns, and the habitation of wild beasts and birds of prey (*vv. 11–17*). The description is symbolic of the futility of the flesh and of all human schemes. Just as the creative power of the Lord assigns to animals their relation, condition and region ("no one of these shall fail, none shall want her mate"), so in the fulfilment of His prophetic word, each fulfilment will answer to the prophecy which has predicted it. His Spirit carries out the twofold design. He it is who governs the creatures and He it is who accomplishes the fiat of His unthwartable Word, detail for detail.

CHAPTER XXXV

THE Millennial conditions of peace and prosperity foretold in this chapter and the definite contrasts with what is predicted in chapter 34, make clear that the judgments of the wrath of God foretold in that chapter are those to be carried out at the close of the present age. The overthrow of the antichristian powers by the Second Advent of Christ will be followed by what is now set forth. In contrast to the barren condition of Edom, the land of Palestine will " **blossom as the rose** " (*verse 1*). " **The glory of the Lord, the excellency of our God** " will be manifested (cp. 40: 5). Weak hands are to be strong to work; tottering knees are to be confirmed. Fear will be banished. The vengeance of God upon the foe will be followed by permanent salvation. Blindness and deafness will be healed. The lame will leap, the dumb will sing (*vv. 3–5*). The woeful conditions of distress in the great tribulation will yield place to all that makes for the glory of God in the happiness of His redeemed.

The wilderness, the desert, the parched ground, the thirsty land, will all become fertile, for nature itself will reap the benefits of the removal of antagonistic powers, spiritual and human, and of the presence of the glory of the Lord and His people, earthly and heavenly (*verse 7*).

The very means of intercourse and communication will be consecrated to God. Both the highway and the ordinary road will be holy. The walk of life will be " **The way of holiness** ".

No unclean person will traverse it. It will be for those who have fellowship with God, those in whose heart are "the high ways to Zion" (Ps. 84: 5, R.V.). Even the simple folk will not go astray (*verse 8*).

The nature of the ravenous beasts will be changed. The lion will eat straw like the ox. There will be nothing to mar the peace of the redeemed (*verse 9*). The whole passage closes with a promise, which is repeated in 51: 11, the assurance marking both parts of the book with the same message of comfort: **"And the ransomed of the Lord shall return, and come to Zion with songs, and everlasting joy upon their heads ; they shall obtain joy and gladness, and sorrow and sighing shall flee away."**

PART II

THE ASSYRIANS, THE CHALDEANS, AND HEZEKIAH
(*Chapters XXXVI–XXXIX*)

CHAPTER XXXVI

A NEW section of the prophecies begins here. These and the two following chapters are suitably introduced in their historical setting. For the circumstances of Hezekiah's reign, mentioned in 2 Chron. 32: 32 as a part of the "vision" of Isaiah, are a fulfilment of what Isaiah had predicted nearly thirty years before (8: 5–10) and had alluded to subsequently (see 10: 12–19, 33, 34; 14: 24, 25; 30: 28–31; 31: 8).

The two chapters, dealing with the invasion and overthrow of the Assyrian, form, therefore, the historical consummation of chapters 7 to 35.

Chapters 38 and 39, on the other hand, with the account of Hezekiah's sickness, recovery and failure, form the historical basis of chapters 40 to 66. Chapters 36 and 37 are retrospective. Chapters 38 and 39 are prospective. The four are clearly in their Divinely appointed setting in the whole book. The fact that the whole passage is found in 2 Kings 18: 13 to 20: 19 provides no argument for the supposition that two or more authors compiled the book. The internal evidence is to the contrary. There are indications that these chapters form the original of the narrative in 2 Kings.

However that may be, the facts remain that chapters 36 and 37 record the judgments which began to descend upon the nation because of their persistent rejection of God's testimonies and their defiant rebellion against Him, judgments of which the prophet had warned them. On the other hand, while in Hezekiah's reign national corruption had been checked, and there was a measure of restoration, yet the very failure on the part of the king after the mercy of his recovery, provided evidence that Judah would have to be subjected to the disasters of the Captivity.

But, prospectively, all this only serves to call forth the assurance that God would not permanently cast away His people. Hence the opening of the latter part of the book, beginning with chapter 40, a great part of which is an extension of the promised blessings in chapter 35 and certain preceding passages. The whole book demonstrates God's pleasure in causing mercy to rejoice against judgment.

PART III

INTRODUCTORY NOTE ON CHAPTERS XL TO LXVI

THE latter half of Isaiah consists of three divisions, (a) chapters 40 to 48, (b) chapters 49 to 57, (c) chapters 58 to 66. The subject of the whole is twofold, the call to repentance and the promise of eventual deliverance. In connection with the former, each division closes with a solemn warning as to the state of the wicked: (a) **" There is no peace, saith the Lord, unto the wicked,"** 48: 22; (b) **" There is no peace, saith my God, to the wicked,"** 57: 21; (c) **" their worm shall not die, neither shall their fire be quenched ; and they shall be an abhorring to all flesh,"** 66: 24. In division (a) the contrast is between Jehovah and idols, and between Israel and the Gentiles, in (b) between the sufferings of the Servant of Jehovah and His future glory, in (c) between the hypocrites and the rebellious and the faithful and persecuted.

Other divisions have been suggested. The above seems the most likely. To all the themes in this latter portion of Isaiah the first thirty-nine chapters lead up.

PART III (a)

ISRAEL, THE GENTILES, AND DIVINE DELIVERANCE
(Chapters XL–XLVIII)

CHAPTER XL

IN chapter 40 the promise of deliverance opens with the consolatory message " **Comfort ye, comfort ye My people, saith your
God** ", and that and what follows to the end of *verse 11* form a
prologue to the rest of the book. The word rendered "comfort"
lit. means to cause to breathe again, and thus is expressive not
only of consolation but of enduring power, as a result of reviving
and relief. The repetition is indicative of urgency.

The phrase "saith your God" and other similar phrases are
found in both parts of the book (1: 11; 33: 10; 40: 1, 25; 41: 21;
66: 9). It here not only indicates the unthwartable decree of
God, but makes clear that the comfort to be bestowed is con-
ditioned by relationship to Him.

The command is repeated more emphatically: " **Speak ye
comfortably to** (Heb., 'Speak ye to the heart of') **Jerusalem.**"
The city stands for the people. The Lord desires not only to
minister comfort to us but to win our heart while doing so.

Three reasons for the comfort are given: (1) " **that her warfare is accomplished** "; the word primarily denotes military
service, then feudal service, and hence any wretched and miser-
able state (see Job 7: 1, R.V. and marg.); (2) " **that her iniquity
is pardoned** "; the verb signifies to receive satisfaction by the
payment of a debt; hence to pay off the debt of sin by enduring
punishment. This points to the sacrifice of Calvary; the justice
of God has been satisfied by atonement made; (3) " **that** (R.V.)
she hath received of the Lord's hand double for all her sins ";
this last states more fully the substance of the previous two.

Various ideas have been suggested as to the significance of
"double"; the meaning most in keeping with the context is
that punishment has been meted out in full measure (cp. Jer.
16: 18), not more nor less than had been deserved. The mercy

90

of God shines out in the words "for all"; nothing is left requiring punishment. God delights in the restoration of His people, on the ground that expiation has been accomplished. The meaning of liberation, by handing the counterpart or double of a bond, does not seem to be so appropriate to the scope of the passage.

Everything that hindered a right condition before God having been dealt with and removed, as in *verse 3*, the way is now opened for the blessing kept in store. A voice cries " **Prepare ye in the wilderness the way of the Lord, make straight in the desert a highway for our God**". It is like a king's courier appointed to see that his way is put in good condition. Of old God had led the way through "the wilderness from Egypt to Canaan. Now Israel has been in the wilderness of the peoples", the Gentile nations (Ezek. 20: 34, 35); there she will have passed through her great tribulation, and everything is prepared for Millennial deliverance, glory and blessing. Every valley is to be exalted (those who have been cast down and oppressed in the valley of humiliation are to be encouraged); every mountain and hill is to be made low (the self-righteous and presumptuous are to be humiliated); the crooked is to be made straight (double-mindedness is to give way to simplicity); the rough places are to be made plain (the ruggedness of pride is to be reduced to submission); the glory of the Lord is to be revealed, and all flesh shall see it together (*verse 5*). This is called in 2 Thess. 2: 8 "the manifestation of His Coming" (lit., the epiphany, or shining forth, of His Parousia). "Behold He cometh with the clouds; and every eye shall see Him, and they which pierced Him; and all the tribes of the earth shall mourn over Him" (Rev. 1: 7). Nothing can hinder it, " **for the mouth of the Lord hath spoken it** ".

How often, just when things seem to be at their darkest, and opposition and difficulty have risen to their highest height, this provides the occasion for the intervention of God! Faith has stood the test and receives its victorious reward.

Now another voice is heard, saying " **Cry** " ; and yet another: " **one said, What shall I cry ?** " The answering message declares the perishable nature of man and the imperishable nature of the Word of God. His word is one with Himself. What He says that He is. Hence, as He is everlasting, so His word shall stand for

ever (*verse 8*). Since Christ is the Word of God, this is all true
of Him, and is especially declared in His reply to the Jews in
John 8: 25, R.V., that He was what He had spoken to them
from the beginning (or completely, altogether). His teaching was
the expression of His nature and character.

So then the oppressors of Israel will fade and die as the grass,
under the retributive judgments of God.

What follows in *vv. 9 and 10* is really addressed to Zion and
Jerusalem, which again stand for the inhabitants thereof, and
the A.V. and R.V. margin are almost certainly right, " **O Zion
that tellest (bringest) good tidings . . . O Jerusalem, that . . .** "
(52: 7 and 62: 11 are in a different connection). The announce-
ment of the immediately impending Advent of the Messiah will
go forth from Zion; it will be known that such Scriptures as
Zech. 14: 3, 4 are about to be fulfilled. Hence a threefold
"Behold": first the proclamation " **Behold, your God** " (the
comma should be observed), and then the two assurances,
" **Behold, the Lord God will come as a mighty One, and His
arm shall rule for Him ; behold, His reward is with Him, and
His recompense before Him,** " the recompense being twofold in
character, both of retribution for the enemies of His people,
and for the compensation of the faithful.

All this is judicial; now follows that which is consolatory.
The figures of the Victor and the Judge are succeeded by that
of the Shepherd: " **He shall feed** (or rather, 'tend') **His flock
like a shepherd** " (John 10: 4–16), a sweet word of affectionate
consolation for those who have been scattered among the Gentiles
and have passed through fiery trial. " **He shall gather the lambs
in His arm, and carry them in His bosom** "; they could not
keep pace with the flock; " **and shall gently lead those that
give suck** "; for the mother sheep require special care (cp.
Gen. 33: 13). This is how the Lord will bring about the issues
from "the time of Jacob's trouble". Not a member of the godly
remnant in Israel, with their varied spiritual conditions, will go
unattended by their great Shepherd.

This verse provides lessons for those to whom, as under-
shepherds, is committed the present day care of the spiritual
flock (1 Pet. 5: 2–4). How much discernment and devotion
are requisite in order to follow the example of the Good
Shepherd, concerning the three conditions here mentioned of

those who form the flock! The Lord teaches us the need
of dealing in tender compassion and grace with those committed to our care.

This verse closes the prologue to the remainder of the book.
Having shown who it is who is about to interpose for the redemption and comfort of His people, the prophet will now testify as
to the incomparable attributes of their Creator-God, who will
undertake for them. They must be awakened to a consciousness
of His infinite greatness, His character and power. And as
idolatry has been an outstanding transgression of Israel, leading
to the sufferings they have received from the Gentile nations,
these attributes are set in contrast both to the condition of the
nations (*vv. 15-17*) and to the nature of idols and their makers
(*vv. 18-20*). All this leads up to a renewal of consolatory assurances (*vv. 29-31*).

Two comprehensive and challenging questions (what appears
as a third is really part of the second) are asked, the first (*a*)
concerning His omnipotence, the second (*b*) concerning His
omniscience:

(*a*) " **Who hath measured the waters in the hollow of his hand**
(how very small are the contents possible to a human hand!),
and meted out heaven ('the heavens') **with the span** (the verb
signifies to prove, weigh, measure out, and so to regulate—see
'directed' in *verse 13*; contrast the width and ability of a human
span), **and comprehended the dust of the earth in a measure**
(how small is human capacity, which measures with the third
part of an ephah!), **and weighed the mountains in scales, and
the hills in a balance** (how little can man weigh, whether in a
steelyard or in a pair of balances! did man adjust the equilibrium
of the earth?)? "

The questions are a magnificent way of bringing home the puny
activities and power of mere man compared with the mighty
Creator.

(*b*) The second series of questions relates to His omniscience.
a fact which forecloses all instruction from others: " **Who hath
directed** (or 'regulated'; the same word as is rendered "meted
out" in *verse 12*) **the Spirit of the Lord** (that is, who provided
Him a standard by which to act), **or being His counsellor hath
taught Him ? With whom took He counsel, and who instructed
Him** (or 'made Him understand'—see marg.) **and taught Him**

in (or 'concerning') **the path of judgment, and taught Him
knowledge, and shewed to Him the way of understanding** (or
'made known to Him prudent counsels')?" (*verse 14*).

All this combines the faculties of knowledge, wisdom and
understanding. The questions resemble, and have the same
object as, those which the Lord asked Job (chapts. 40 and 41),
whom He converted by the argument from design. Here He uses
the argument of analogy. Let Israel then consider the nature of
their Redeemer and turn away from imaginary and futile sources
of help.

From His attributes as Creator the thoughts are now directed
to His absolute control as Governor of the nations, a control
which never causes Him any difficulty or presents Him with any
problem. " **Behold, the nations are as a drop of a bucket** (i.e.,
a drop hanging on a bucket: does the drop cause the carrier any
burden?), **and are counted as the small dust of the balance** (the
merest speck of dust or sand! how much does that make a scale
descend?): **behold, He taketh up the isles as a very little thing**
(or as in the R.V. marg., 'the isles are as the fine dust that is
lifted up,' i.e., by a puff of wind), (*verse 15*).

Further, whatever can be offered to God in worship and
sacrifice must ever be far short of the glory of His Being. " **Lebanon is not sufficient to burn** " (i.e., to provide wood for the fire
of an offering), nor could its pastures provide an adequate supply
of sacrificial beasts. The privileged Jew would ever come short
in this respect. And as for the Gentiles, sacrificial offerings are
not in the question. The nations are " **as nothing before Him ;
they are counted to Him less than nothing** (their moral corruption
renders them worse than if they were non-existent) **and vanity** "
(*tohu,* a waste or chaos,—the same word as in Gen. 1: 2, R.V.,
"waste", and Isa. 45: 18, R.V.), (*verse 17*).

This being so with man, much greater are the insignificance
and worthlessness of an idol. Let Israel beware! " **To whom
then will ye liken God ? or what likeness will ye compare unto
Him ?** " (*verse 18*). Accordingly there follows the first of a series
of passages characterized by withering sarcasm poured upon the
infatuation of idol framers and worshippers, and aimed at Israel.
Here the idol makers are especially in view, both the rich man
who can afford one made of metals and adorned with gold and
silver, and the poor man who applies for the fashioning of a
wooden one (*vv. 19, 20*).

Four questions follow in *verse 21*, addressed to Israel. They are in the (*a*), (*b*), (*b*), (*a*), or chiasmic, order: (*a*) "known", (*b*) "heard", (*b*) "told you", (*a*) "understood",—a strong method of appeal or instruction.

(*a*) Failure to recognize and acknowledge God from the evidences of creation (*vv. 22 to 26*) prevents the reception of the knowledge of His will, (*b*) by preaching, and (*b*) by teaching, through (*a*) the darkening of the understanding. So had it been with Israel. They had become like the Gentiles (see Rom. 1: 20 to 32).

Let us ever beware lest the wonders of nature fail to produce in us the adoration of its Maker.

So now there follow statements of God's position, power and authority, and the prophet passes alternately from the physical universe to the inhabitants of the world: " **It is He that sitteth** (here of sitting enthroned) **upon** (or 'above') **the circle of the earth** (the vault which arches over the earth)." That is His position relatively to creation. Now for the puny diminutiveness of the inhabitants of the earth: they are " **as grasshoppers** " (i.e., in His sight; cp. Num. 13: 33). Next, again, as to creation (*verse 22*): " **that stretcheth out** (lit., 'has stretched out') **the heavens as a curtain** (a thin, transparent fabric; marg., 'gauze'), **and spreadeth** (lit., 'has spread out') **them out as a tent to dwell in.**" Further, again, as to earth-dwellers, and especially their rulers: " **that bringeth princes to nothing ; He maketh the judges of the earth as vanity** "—two classes of authorities, the former those who possess the highest distinction and greatest influence, the latter those who exercise the chief judicial and administrative power. The former are made to be as though they were non-existent; the latter are made a desolation (a *tohu*: see *verse 17*). See 1 Cor. 2: 6.

The R.V. marginal rendering of what follows depicts more accurately the suddenness with which the naturally promising great men of the earth just mentioned are brought to nought under the mighty hand of God: " **Scarce** (scarcely) **are they planted, scarce are they sown, scarce hath their stock taken root in the earth, when He bloweth upon them, and they wither, and the whirlwind taketh them away as stubble** " (*verse 24, R.V. marg.*). The breath of the Lord consumes them (cp. 11: 4;

2 Thess. 2: 8, R.V., and Rev. 2: 16); the forces of nature, which are His, blast them.

As in *verse 18*, where the prophet challengingly declared the incomparableness of God, after recording the insignificance of the nations, so here, recalling this challenge, God, after the demonstration of the finiteness of the inhabitants and the evanescence of their governors, Himself says " **To whom then will ye liken Me, that I should be equal** *to him*? **saith the Holy One** " (*verse 25*). This is a change in the distinction; it is not now between His illimitableness and their insignificance, but between His essential and absolute holiness and the self-degradation of His corrupt and idolatrous people. Alas, the folly of making and worshipping any but their true and living God!

This is pointedly followed by a third mention of the incomparable power of God as Creator. The first (*verse 12*) was given as a challenging question; the second (*vv. 21, 22*) as a number of appealing reminders of what they had been taught to recognize; the third is given as a command: " **Lift up your eyes on high, and see who hath created these** (or 'see: who hath created these?'), **that bringeth out their host by number**," causing them to come forth, so to speak, night after night, as a general brings out his armoured host to the field: " **He calleth them all by name: by** (or rather, 'because of') **the greatness of His might, and for that He is strong in power, not one is lacking.**" Not one is absent from the muster-roll (*verse 26*).

Omnipotence alone is requisite for the whole constant, glorious and orderly procedure. The heavenly host exists and moves, not simply by natural laws. The Son of God is Himself the sustaining Centre, Upholder and Controller of all: "all things have been created through Him, and unto Him: and He is before all things, and in Him all things consist" (i.e., hold together), Col. 1: 16, 17. He upholds "all things by the word of His power," Heb. 1: 3.

While what has just preceded is retrospectively a protest against idolatry in the nation, it is also introductory to a message of comfort to the remnant of the godly who are cast down and despairing? Hence they are addressed in the words "O Jacob" as well as "O Israel," to remind them of the covenant made with their ancestor. They thought that the Lord had abandoned them in His wrath, having grown weary of them: " **Why sayest thou, O Jacob, and speakest, O Israel, my way is hid from the Lord, and my judgment is passed away from** (or 'overlooked by') my God ? " (*verse 27*). Their way was one of great suffering and their judgment, their right, was withheld by their oppressors. This is prophetic of what they will yet experience in "the time of Jacob's trouble" at the hands of the Antichrist. They thought, as some of them will no doubt yet think, that God had entirely forgone the judicial vindication of His people.

The baselessness of such despair is met by a double question, recalling the same questions as in verse 21: " **Hast thou not known ? hast thou not heard ? the everlasting God, the Lord, the Creator of the ends of the earth, fainteth not, neither is weary ; there is no searching of His understanding** " (*verse 28*).

Any of us who are tempted to despondency because of the pressure of adverse circumstances should lay hold of the facts which we have accepted by faith, as well as gather from our experiences of God's merciful dealings with us, that He, the Creator of all things, is "the same yesterday and to-day, *yea*, and for ever", and therefore has the same power at our disposal as He manifested in His creative acts. He never suffers from over-exertion; and since His understanding is infinite, He knows all about us. Our most trying experiences, whether from without or within, are not only known to Him, but are under His absolute control. He appoints the time for His interposition and our deliverance.

So far from becoming faint, " **He giveth power to the faint ; and to him that hath no might He increaseth strength** (or giveth strength abundantly)," *verse 29*. What we need is faith to open our hearts to receive the strength He is ever ready to impart while we are undergoing the trial. That is His way of making our trials blessings. He aims at making us realize our utter incapability, so that we may take hold of His strength instead of despairing under the affliction.

The strongest can never be sure of freedom from weariness, and an obstacle placed in their path may easily make them stumble: " **Even the youths shall faint and be weary, and the young men shall utterly fall : but they that wait upon the Lord shall renew their strength** (marg., change, i.e., gain fresh); **they shall mount up with wings as eagles ; they shall run, and not be weary ; they shall walk** (or go forward), **and not faint** " (*vv. 30, 31*). To wait upon the Lord is not simply a matter of patience, or even of longing, it means trust and the confidence which characterizes our hope. To experience this is to go from strength to strength, drawing continually from the resources of His power. To mount up with wings is to rise above difficulties, to fly above the mists and darkness of earth into the clear sunshine of God's presence. Would that we more readily entered into this delightful experience. We shall do so, if Christ is a reality to us.

Some suggest that the meaning is that of putting forth fresh feathers, as birds do after moulting, but the rendering in our Versions seems better. The eagle is characterized by three things, rapidity of flight, power of scent, keenness of vision. So our mounting up is not only a matter of rising above difficulties, it involves a joyous and quick discernment of the will and way of God for us and the keen vision of Himself by faith.

But then we are very much on the earth, and hence the metaphor of running and walking: "I will run the way of Thy commandments, when Thou shalt enlarge my heart" (Ps. 119: 32). "I will walk at liberty; for I have sought Thy precepts" (verse 45). Running is suggestive of energetic effort, but what is also needed is the steady progress in the Christian path in the enjoyment of quiet communion with God.

CHAPTER XLI

At the beginning of chapter 41 the Lord speaks to the Gentile nations. Let them try to contend with Him (*verse 1*). The fact that He declares beforehand the raising up of a conqueror from the east is but a sign that God Himself is the supreme Controller of the world's affairs (*vv. 2–4*). The idolatry of the nations will eventually bring Divine judgments upon them, and Israel, as God's chosen people, will become His instruments in chastising them (*vv. 5–16*). There follows another challenge to the Gentiles. Let them show their ability to foretell the future, as God does. They and their objects of worship shall be brought to naught (*vv. 21–29*).

The opening challenge by the Lord to the Gentile nations is issued as follows: " **Keep silence before Me, O islands** (standing for great nations at the extremities of the continents); **and let**

the peoples (Gentiles, not Israel, as one might gather from the A.V., 'people') **renew their strength** (i.e., get fresh strength: they need it from their point of view if they are to contend with God; compare and contrast 40: 31); **let them come near; then let them speak** (that is, let them make a reply after hearing the evidence): **let us come near together to judgment."** The nations are called, not to a tribunal for God to pass a verdict of condemnation upon them, but to a tribunal of reason, to hear facts and draw conclusions.

God Himself opens the contest by way of challenging questions followed by statements of fact. The person in view is Cyrus, the raising up of whom is prophetically foretold in the past tense, which regards a future event as just as certain of accomplishment as if it had already taken place. But there is not only the power thus to predict the future with certainty (that is God's prerogative alone), but the power to raise up a man for the accomplishment of the Divine purposes. This is the meaning of *vv. 2, 3*: " **Who hath raised up one from the east** (in verse 25 he is said to be raised up from the north, and both become true of Cyrus, for he was connected both with Persia in the east and Media to the north), **whom He calleth in righteousness to His foot** (see, however, the R.V. margin)? **He giveth nations before him, and maketh him rule over kings** " : what follows describes his conquests that were to be.

The challenge is then uttered in another way: " **Who hath wrought and done it, calling the generations from the beginning?"** (*verse 4*). That is to say, who is the Author, and whose is the authority, through whom such an event derives its origin and progress? Jehovah provides His own answers: " **I the Lord, the first, and with the last, I am He."** That He is "the first" means that He is pre-existent to all history and that all things are under His control; He brings in one generation after another; that He is "with the last" means that He brings all things to their appointed end; hence the isles will be made to see and fear, and the ends of the earth will tremble. " **They drew near, and came** " (*verse 5*). That is, they would come to meet the threatening danger. So they would in regard to Cyrus. So they will at the end of this age.

And what lies behind these futile efforts? " **They helped every one his neighbour; and** *every one* **said to his brother, Be of good courage** " (*verse 6*). Accordingly they resorted to their idolatry. " So the carpenter encouraged the goldsmith, and he that smootheth with the hammer him that smiteth the anvil, saying of the soldering, It is good : and he fastened it with nails, that it should not be moved." With what scorn the description of this is given, in contrast to the statements concerning the attributes and controlling authority of God!

The Lord now continues His message of consolation to Israel, addressing them by the same twofold names as in 40: 27, but now in the opposite order; for now it is not a message to the weak and faint, but a reminder of His electing grace and the promise of restoration and deliverance, though further on the former order will be resumed (*verse 14*).

He reminds them that they are His own by choice, and children of promise. They are " The seed of Abraham My friend". Their earliest history is a guarantee of irrevocable blessing. Three times Abraham is called the friend of God: in 2 Chron. 20: 7, in the prayer of Jehoshaphat; here, in the Divine confirmation of this; and in Jas. 2: 23, which combines God's dealings with Abraham with this passage in Isaiah. The word rendered "friend" denotes one who is loving and beloved, an object of desire, and one who enjoys the utmost intimacy. So the Lord reminds His people of what they owe to the faith of their ancestor. " Thou," He says, speaking of Israel, " whom I have taken hold of from the ends of the earth, and called thee from the corners thereof." The R.V. is right in the rendering "taken hold of", and the meaning seems to be not so much that of strengthening as that of attaching firmly to oneself. From the point of view of Palestine, Ur of the Chaldeans was sufficiently remote to be called the ends and corners of the earth. God called Abraham from thence with a view to the rise of his seed as a nation, which was pre-existent in His counsels.

God's calling is always effectual. We may remind ourselves of this in our own experience in connection with the sphere of service allotted to us. If it has not been a matter simply of our choice and decision, it is ours by reason of His plan and appointment and the directing power of the Holy Spirit.

The Lord now speaks of Israel as His servant, here first in Isaiah, and this is frequently repeated, down to the 6th verse of chapter 49. He says here " Thou art My servant, I have chosen

thee and not cast thee away (or despised thee)," *verse 9.* So the servant character of Israel is the outcome of an act of pure grace and not through any merit on their part, as is intimated by the hint that He might reasonably have despised them and cast them away. But further, the nation had become, in spite of its waywardness and transgressions, the servant of Jehovah in the fulfilment of His purposes thus far, and it is destined to act in this capacity in full measure hereafter.

Accordingly His people have good reason to abstain from fearfulness and dismay. Hence the Lord says to them, as He still says to us, " **Fear thou not, for I am with thee ; be not dismayed, for I am thy God : I will strengthen thee ; yea, I will help thee ; yea, I will uphold thee with the right hand of My righteousness** " (*verse 10*).

Three reasons are given by the Lord for freedom from fear and dismay: (1) His presence: "for I am with thee"; (2) His relationship: "I am thy God"; (3) His assurances, and these are threefold, (a) of power: "I will strengthen thee," fortifying in weakness, difficulty and opposition; the word combines also the meaning of taking hold of; (b) of assistance: "yea, I will help thee," giving guidance, direction and protection; (c) of support: "yea, I will uphold thee with the right hand of My righteousness," suggestive of His faithfulness in the fulfilment of His promises; the Hebrew word for the right hand is associated with the idea of power and success, and suggests prosperity. The "yea" is cumulative, it gathers up what precedes and thus imparts added assurance to what follows.

Let us not fail to take to ourselves the comfort of these promises, whether by regarding them as applicable only to Israel, or by a self-complacent state of soul, which unfits us for the ever needed comfort and power for acting as the servants of the Lord in the realization of our own demerit and helplessness.

Israel, as the people of God, have ever had numerous and mighty foes, and their persecuting power and antagonism grow and will grow more intense as the end of this age draws near. The comforting promises which have just preceded lead now to the assurance of the overthrow of their enemies and the repeated guarantee of help.

In *vv. 11, 12*, four descriptions of the enemy are given: (1) All that " **are incensed** " against His people (indicative of the fierce heat of their Satanically instigated antagonism) are to be ashamed and confounded; (2) " **they that strive with thee** " (lit., 'the men of thy conflict'); (3) " **them that contend with thee** " ('the men of thy feuds'); (4) " **they that war against thee** " ('the men of thy warfare'). Every sort of foe is included in the doom. They are to perish, and are to become " **as nothing** ", as a nonentity.

Verse 13 follows with the comforting assurance, " **For I the Lord thy God will hold thy right hand, saying unto thee, Fear not; I will help thee.**" Not only is there the promise of the overwhelming defeat of all their foes, but likewise the promise of protection and strength. Not only is there to be deliverance, but Israel itself is to be taken up and used for the accomplishment of God's purposes. The assurance of help is repeated from verse 10.

> Our right hand is that with which we do our work, it is the emblem of our activities. That God will hold that, indicates that we can do nothing apart from Him and that it is His will for us to realize that the power we require to do anything of value must be His.

In *verse 14* the "Fear not" is repeated as an introduction to the promise that Israel is to have power over those who have opposed them. The twofold address presents different aspects of their state. Firstly, " **thou worm Jacob** ", suggesting a helpless and prostrate condition, as of a struggling creature of the dust (cp. Job 25: 6), the object of contempt and disgust. With that condition their Messiah has identified Himself in His sufferings at Calvary, by very reason of which He will be their Redeemer (Ps. 22: 6); secondly, " **Ye men of Israel** "; the Hebrew word is suggestive of a diminished condition, as in the A.V. margin, 'men few in number' (the same word as in Gen. 34: 30; Deut. 4: 27); this they will be after their great tribulation.

The Lord brings us down that He may lift us up. For the third time He says " **I will help thee,**" and guarantees it, first by His Name Jehovah, and then by the pledge " **and thy Redeemer is the Holy One of Israel** " (R.V.). He appends, so to speak, His signature to His declaration. Jehovah is the unoriginated, self-existent, ever-existent One, and again and again He announces His title as the ground of the assurance of His redemptive work: see, e.g., 43: 14; 44: 6, 24; 48: 17; 49: 26; 54: 5, 8; 60: 16; Jer. 50: 34 (cp. Isa. 29: 22; 51: 11; 62: 12; Jer. 31: 11). In each place the word rendered "Redeemer" is the verb corresponding to the noun *goel*, a kinsman-redeemer-avenger. The redemption is ever based upon His gracious fulfilment of the obligation of a kinsman (Lev. 25: 48, 49), in becoming incarnate with a view to His atoning sacrifice.

Verses 15 and 16 vividly depict the nation as the Lord's instrument in bringing their enemies to nought. Israel will be a sharp, new threshing roller with two-edged knives, like an instrument that cuts up the straw for fodder, and separates the grain from the chaff. The mountains and hills (figurative of proud and powerful foes) will be threshed to powder, and scattered and destroyed, as chaff is blown by the wind. The Lord's irresistible whirlwind will abolish the last remnant of them.

The nation will have learnt to glory, not in their own prowess and might, they will " **rejoice in the Lord** ", and " **glory in the Holy One of Israel** ". But Jehovah, looking into the assured future, thinks compassionately of " **the poor and needy** ", pining away through thirst (there is no "when" in the original), not only the exiles in Babylon, but all such among His people in their privations and sufferings at all times. The Lord promises to have regard to them and to answer their prayer. He will " **open rivers on the bare heights, and fountains in the midst of the valleys.**" He will " **make the wilderness a pool of water, and the dry land springs of water.**"

While all this depicts a change from the homeless condition of Israel to the abundant blessing they will receive in the Millennium (cp. 35: 6, 7, a passage which confirms the fact that Isaiah wrote both parts of this book), yet these promises clearly convey a spiritual significance. For the allusion is to the water supernaturally provided in the wilderness journeys from Egypt, and this is applied spiritually in 1 Cor. 10: 4. Cp. John 4: 14; 7: 37-9, and see Rev. 22: 17.

Verse 19 goes on to describe figuratively the manifold provision of refreshment and comfort for the nation in the coming day. This fullness is indicated in the mention of the seven trees which the Lord says He will plant in the wilderness, which will be turned into a veritable paradise. Beautiful branches will be provided for the Feast of Tabernacles. The trees are all fragrant as well as durable, and again this twofold character is figurative of the spiritual fragrance and permanency of the Spirit-given communion to be enjoyed.

Moreover, this planting and plenteousness will be manifest not as the outcome of mere natural production. The people will realize in a fourfold way that all this is to be the effect of the operation of "the hand of the Lord" and of His creative power. They will " see, and know, and consider, and understand together " (*verse 20*).

The progress of idea in these four verbs is noticeable and significant. They describe what should be the result of our meditations in the Scriptures, and of His dealings with us.

At the beginning of chapter 41 the Lord declared the fact of His Deity by His absolute power to raise up a potentate to subdue nations, and to overrule the rise and course of generations. Now He declares His Deity on the ground that He alone has knowledge of, and predicts, the future. Formerly He issued His challenge to idolaters; now His challenge is to the idols themselves, the gods of the nations. Jehovah and His people (for He is " **the King of Jacob** ") are on one side, the idolatrous Gentiles are on the other. Let their gods come forward, produce their " **strong reasons** " (i.e., their proofs) and thus establish their deity if they can (*verse 21*).

And, in addition, says the Challenger, " **Yea, do good, or do evil** (i.e., express yourselves in one way or another, that is to say, show some sign of life), **that we may be dismayed** (or rather, as in the R.V. margin, may look one upon another, i.e., look one another in the face so as to measure ourselves in the contest; cp. 2 Kings 14: 8, 11), **and behold it together** (i.e., see what the result of the contest will be)," *verse 23*.

Will the idols now speak to prove their deity? Of course they cannot. Hence the withering scorn Divinely poured upon them and their makers: " **Behold, ye are of nothing, and your work** (or doing) **of nought : an abomination is he that chooseth you** " (*verse 24*).

The Lord again makes clear that power and authority alone belong to Him in the supreme disposal of national affairs. Accordingly the prophecy about Cyrus is resumed. This great potentate, a follower of the religion of Zarathustra, or Zoroaster, would be taught to recognize and call upon the name of Jehovah. He would " **come upon rulers as upon mortar, and as the potter treadeth** (or kneadeth) **clay** " (*verse 25*). The Lord in foretelling this declares again His omniscience and continues His challenge. No one else could do it, nor indeed could any of the heathen deities give any utterance at all; " **there is none that heareth your words** " (*verse 26*). Had they been able to do so, their divine power would have been acknowledged.

Verse 27 should be read as in the R.V.: " **I first will say unto Zion . . .**" His alone is the prerogative to give the primary promise of blessing to His people. All others can only repeat what He has already said. And with what manifest delight in His people's lasting good He promises to give evangelists to Jerusalem (cp. 40: 1, 2, 9)! In the words " **Behold, behold them,**" He calls upon Zion to see how His promises have been fulfilled (looking on to the future time of the fulfilment).

Verse 28 brings the contest to its foreseen issue. The idols and their devotees are silent; there is no counsellor to answer a word. The matter closes with a declaration of the Lord's contempt and wrath, and the last verse might be rendered closely to the original thus: 'Look at them all! Vanity! Their productions are nothingness; wind and desolation are their molten images.'

The judicial procedure ends at verse 25; verses 25–29 review the evidence and the verdict.

CHAPTER XLII

THE way is now open for the first great revelation and prophecy, in this second part of the book, concerning Christ. All the promises of restoration and its consequent blessing are shown to centre in Him. Later on His sacrificial Death will be before us. Now we are to see the delight of God the Father in Him, and what great things will be accomplished by Him. We are given a view of His life and character in the days of His flesh, His tenderness as well as His power, and of the great deliverance He will accomplish hereafter.

The light of the glory of His Person puts Cyrus into the shade for the time being, though more remains to be said about the latter afterwards. But it is Christ who now comes into view as the Blesser of Israel and the Saviour of Gentiles.

It is Christ whom the Lord calls His Servant in *verse 1*: "**Behold My Servant, whom I uphold; My chosen, in whom My soul delighteth.**" The quotation in Matt. 12: 18 speaks of Him as "My Beloved", giving the other meaning of the Hebrew word, and harmonizing with the declaration of the Father in 3: 17. He assumed His Servant character for the fulfilment of His Father's will on earth (Phil. 2: 7). He was "chosen" in the eternal counsels of God in the past, for the purposes of propitiation.

The demonstration of the delight of the Father in Him was the coming of the Holy Spirit upon Him, in fulfilment of this prophecy (Matt. 3: 16; Mark 1: 10; Luke 3: 22; John 1: 32, 33). This statement, "**I have put My Spirit upon Him**", is the centre one of three great declarations in Isaiah concerning the Holy Spirit in connection with Christ. The first is in 11: 2, which speaks of His Incarnation. The second, here, points to His baptism. The last is in 61: 1, pointing to the beginning of His public ministry.

From this the prophecy momentarily leaps forward to the effects of Christ's Second Advent, in His Millennial reign: "**He shall bring forth** (or 'cause to go forth') **judgment to the Gentiles.**" The mode of the fulfilment of this was given in detail by the prophet in 2: 1-4.

In regard to the apparent contradiction in the statement "**He shall not cry**" (*verse 2*), and that in verse 13, "**He shall cry**", the verbs rendered "cry" are different. The first has to do with His people, the second with His enemies. The first indicates His gentleness and tenderness and the absence of self-advertising, noisy demonstration; the second is His voice as a Conqueror, "the voice of the Lord", by which the foes of God are to be overthrown at the end of this age.

Next comes (*in vv. 3, 4*) a series of promises in chiasmic (or *a, b, b, a*) order (see note on 40: 21). First there is the bruised reed, which He will not break; then the smoking, or dimly burning, flax, which He will not quench. In *verse 4*, in the statement "**He shall not fail**", the word "fail" signifies to burn dimly, and, in the next, "**nor be discouraged**", the word "dis-

couraged" signifies to be bruised or broken. So the last and first
go together; so do the second and third. He will not bruise the
broken reed, nor will He Himself be bruised. He neither will
quench the dimly burning torch, nor will He Himself burn dimly.
Thus He causes His tried ones to share His glory.

These "precious promises" have much encouragement for
us in His loving care for us now. If we sometimes feel like the
broken reed, fit only for crushing, or feel that our light is but
a poor flickering thing, let us bear in mind His desires towards
us, and present ourselves to Him for His gracious renewing and
His restoring power.

Having called upon the hearers to contemplate His Servant,
Jehovah now addresses Him Himself, but this is introduced by
a description of His Almighty power (*verse 5*). Speaking of Himself by His title GOD THE LORD, titles of omnipotence and
eternity, He declares that He is the Creator (or Arranger) of the
heavens, and of the earth and its products, and the Giver of life
and spirit to its inhabitants. This tremendous utterance is made
the basis of an assurance and promises, and of a revelation of
His purposes. The assurance is as to the call He has given; the
promises are : (1) " **I will hold Thine hand**," (2) " **will keep Thee**,"
(3) " **will give Thee for a covenant of the people, for a light of
the Gentiles**." The purposes are : (1) " **to open the blind eyes**,"
(2) " **to bring out the prisoners from the dungeon**," (3) " **and
them that sit in darkness out of the prison house**."
All this will be made true in regard to the Person of the Lord
Jesus Christ, concerning Israel, in a day to come.

Yet what a comfort it all is to us in its secondary application
to ourselves as servants of God! We are justified in applying
verses 6 and 7 to ourselves by the fact that the Lord Jesus
uses similar language to His Apostle as recorded in Acts 26: 18.
He who has called us in righteousness will still hold our hand,
and will keep us, making us ministers of His Gospel, enabling
us to bring light and liberty to those who are in spiritual
darkness and captivity.

The Lord now makes the solemn affirmation " **I am Jehovah ;
that is My Name** ", recalling His twice repeated Name in *vv. 5 and*

6. That was the Name by which He revealed Himself to Moses, as a pledge that He would fulfil His word in regard to the commission given to him. By this title He declared (1) His self-existence, Exod. 3: 14, (2) the assurance of the everlasting and unchangeable nature of His character, verse 15, (3) His power to redeem, 6: 2-6, (4) His authority as the One who, having redeemed, claims obedience to His commands, 20: 2. That His Name is the guarantee of the fulfilment of His word, is the clear intimation here in Isa. 42: 8.

How sure and steadfast is His word! What an incentive it provides for faith to lay hold of His promises, even in the darkest hour and amidst the most perplexing and distressing circumstances!

To this declaration He adds the authoritative assurance, " **My glory will I not give to another, neither My praise unto graven images.**" This is a ratification of the significance of His Name. His glory is the manifestation of His nature, attributes and power (cp. John 1: 14; 2: 11). "My glory . . . My praise!" The revelation of His glory is designed to draw forth the praise of those to whom He reveals it. His glory and praise are incommunicable. They will not be yielded to another. All idol-devotees shall acknowledge the fact. Let them recognize now the essential difference between His glory and power and the impotence of their gods. This is the great point of the twofold utterance in *verse 9*; firstly, " **Behold, the former things are come to pass,**"— that which had been predicted, as foreordained to take place up to that time, had already been fulfilled; secondly, " **and new things do I declare ; before they spring forth I tell you of them.**" The new things are those which have just been foretold in vv. 1-7, as well as others which are to follow. All this is one great indication of the significance of His title "Jehovah", a title the prerogatives of which belong to the Lord Jesus Christ equally with the Father. See John 12: 41.

This 42nd chapter presents some striking contrasts. There is, for instance, the promise of the opening of the eyes of the blind (*verse 7*); on the other hand, there is the blindness of the Lord's Servant in having his eyes closed to all that is not consistent with His will (*verse 19*). This contrast calls for a special consideration. The whole paragraph (*vv. 10-17*) is Millennial in its aspect, and contains some of the "new things" to which reference was made in *verse 9*. The first of these is the "new song" mentioned in *verse 10*, the song of praise from nations that had long been lying in spiritual darkness, and from the lips that before had sung songs of vanity and vileness, and mournful dirges in celebration of their pagan gods.

The mention of the isles in *vv. 10 and 12* suggests the uttermost parts of the earth. In *verse 11* Kedar, a stronghold of Arabia, represents the Arabs in general (cp. Ps. 120: 5). The name was that of Ishmael's second son (Gen. 25: 13). So again, in the same verse Sela (meaning a rock), R.V., is the same as *Petra* (the corresponding Greek word). It originally belonged to Edom, then to Moab, but afterwards was occupied by the Arab prince Aretas. The "wilderness", in the same verse, is the Arabian desert.

In the coming Day the Arabs will no longer be followers of the False Prophet. The Lord will overthrow the rule of Islam, together with the ten-kingdomed dominion of the Beast. Christ will *" go forth as a mighty Man ; He shall stir up jealousy (or zeal) like a Man of war ; He shall cry, He shall shout aloud "* (*verse 13*). The cry which He will raise against His foes is referred to in Joel 3: 16; cp. Isa. 63: 1, and Jer. 25: 30, and, for the same scene, Rev. 19: 11-21.

At the *14th verse* the Lord Himself again speaks, as in the earlier part of the chapter. Confirming now the effect of His victorious shout, He says " I have long time holden My peace ", indicating the longsuffering, which is so significant in these days wherein the Gospel of His grace is permitted to go forth to all nations in spite of the antagonism of His foes and "the falling away" foretold in 2 Thess. 2: 3.

There is another striking contrast in the latter part of the chapter, concerning His people's blindness. On the one side are those who are deprived of sight because of their sin and its consequent retribution. There is, however, a gracious promise for them and then an appeal to them to open their eyes. There are ways of which they are ignorant, paths that they know not. They walk in darkness with its accompanying misery and hopelessness. The Lord will yet expel all this from them and will lead them into His own paths of righteousness and peace, making darkness light before them and crooked places straight (*verse 16*). But the Lord cannot rest content with present deafness and blindness. His people are called upon to hear and to look, that they may know His voice and see His ways.

On the other hand, and in direct contrast, come questions that contain their own answer, as to blindness and deafness with which God is well pleased. This is the blindness of one who stands in His counsels and acts as His servant, one who enjoys constant communion with Him and is blind to all that would detract from this. " **Who is blind but My servant ? or deaf as My messenger that I send ? who is blind as he that is at peace with Me, and blind as the Lord's servant ? Thou seest many things, but thou observest not ; his ears are open, but he heareth not** " (*vv. 19, 20*).

This is true of the excellencies of Christ as Jehovah's Servant. It gives a cogent and instructive message to us who by grace have been called into His service. How many things come into our experience which obscure our vision of the Lord Himself, which would make us deaf to His voice, things to which our fleshly nature is all too ready to respond! In how many ways are we tempted to forgetfulness of the fact that we are here simply to do the will of Him who has called and sent us! To act according to our own will brings grievous sorrow to our hearts. Be it ours to listen to His voice and to be deaf to all that is contrary to it, to walk as those who "look not at the things which are seen, but at the things which are not seen ", whose eyes are open to behold the glory of the Lord and are blind to that which would dim the vision.

After the record of this faithful blindness, the reproof given to Israel is resumed from verse 18. They saw many things but observed not; their ears were opened but they heard not. They would not walk in His ways, neither were they obedient to His Law. Even when the judgment of God fell upon them, they laid it not to heart (*vv. 24, 25*). *Verse 21* again interposes a record of the counsels of the Lord, and now in regard to the Law, " **It pleased the Lord, for His righteousness' sake, to magnify the law and make it honourable.**" The inherent character of the Law is set in contrast to the ways of His people to whom He gave it.

There is also an indication of the way in which God has exhibited His glory in all His dispensational dealings in connection

with the Law, and particularly in its complete fulfilment in
the perfect character and life of the Lord Jesus. To this Psalm 40
bears the predictive testimony, "I delight to do Thy will, O My
God; yea, Thy Law is within My Heart." His perfect obedience
is succinctly described in Phil. 2, in the statement, "He
humbled Himself, becoming obedient even unto death" (R.V.),
that is to say, obedient from the beginning of the days of His
flesh until the climax of His obedience was reached on the
Cross.

In the Person of His Son Jehovah magnified the Law both
by His life and by His death, to which the life was preliminary,
as showing that He was the only One who could make expiation
for sin. God thus magnified the Law "for His righteousness'
sake". Christ Himself is spoken of as "Jesus Christ the
Righteous", and His work on the Cross is described in Rom.
5: 18 as "one act of righteousness" (R.V.), in contrast to
Adam's one trespass. The Law put all men under condemnation. The death of Christ brings "justification of life". Thus
the Lord has demonstrated His unswerving righteousness in
providing the ground upon which righteousness is reckoned to
the sinner through faith. The Law has been made honourable,
i.e., glorious, so that it might be "established", Rom. 3: 31,
and might be fulfilled, not as a means of life, but by those who
have life. This is the essence of the Gospel we are commissioned
to preach, and in the fellowship of this glorious ministry, we
are "ambassadors on behalf of Christ".

At *verse 23*, the beginning of the last paragraph of the chapter,
the last of the series of appealing questions is made: " **Who is
there among you that will give ear to this? that will hearken
and hear for the time to come?** " The question relates to what
has preceded, and immediately to the deplorable state of Israel,
who as a nation were yet in their hardened condition, " **robbed
and spoiled** " (*verse 22*) and given up to suffer at the hands of
Gentile nations, a suffering yet to be intensified at the close of
the "times of the Gentiles" (*vv. 24, 25*). The appeal is, again,
to godly ones in the nation, amidst which the Lord has never
ceased to possess a remnant of those who fear His Name and wait
for the consolation of Israel, those who are ready to give ear to
the voice of God.

It is possible for a believer to be robbed and spoiled, possible so to yield the inner springs of his being to the outer influences of the world, that, like Samson of old, he loses the consciousness of the Lord's approval and is robbed of his spiritual power. An irretrievable loss! For though he may be restored, the loss of a reward consequent upon the period of backsliding will be eternal. To be taken captive by our spiritual foe is to be "**snared in holes**" and "**hid in prison houses**" (*verse 22*). There are many such places in the world for the one who turns from the will and way of the Lord.

On the contrary, there are those whose ears are opened to hear the voice of God and will "**hearken and hear for the time to come**" (*verse 23*). The Scriptures are constantly pointing God's people to events determined for the future by His unthwartable counsels. Such parts of Scripture are generally termed prophecy, and this is by some counted as too deep for consideration, and as having very little practical effect upon the daily life and work of the believer. The very opposite is the case. The assembly at Thessalonica was not many months old when the Apostle reminded them how often, when he was with them in his pioneering work, he instructed them about the Man of Sin and the Day of the Lord and other matters of the future (2 Thess. 2: 5). Such instruction would not only guide their thoughts but prove a barrier against the influences of the world. To-day, then, the Lord appeals to us to hearken "for the time to come", that is, to know His mind as to what is coming on the world and as to our eternal destiny, so that our lives may be conformed to His will.

The saddest feature of the people's state, next to the fact that they had so grievously sinned against their God, was, that, in the judgment that retributively fell upon them in their being given up "for a spoil" and to the cruelty of "the robbers" (*verse 24*), they failed to discern that all this was the Lord's doing. He it was who had kindled the fire of human persecution and tyranny. A preferable rendering for "the fury of His anger and the strength of battle", is "the heat of His wrath and the violence of war" (or, as in the Septuagint, "the war that prevailed against them"). It had set His people "**on fire round about**", yet they "**knew not**": it burned them, yet they "**laid it not to heart**".

These things are written that we may not fail to discern the gracious purposes, the wisdom, the love, that lie behind the chastening hand of the Lord. If we strive not against sin with the utmost resistance, we shall forget the exhortation "which reasoneth with us as with sons". Let us, on the contrary, bow in the subjection that apprehends the motive and meaning of His dealings with us, realizing that what He does is "for our profit, that we may be partakers of His holiness". This is the very acme of blessedness, and the means of power in our service! Thus shall His ways with us produce "peaceable fruit . . . even the fruit of righteousness" (Heb. 12: 4–11).

CHAPTER XLIII

In the 43rd chapter the Lord turns from His lament over the blinded, hardened, unrepentant state of Israel to unfold His covenanted dealings of mercy, past, present and future, and bases all both upon His creative power and His redeeming grace. Doubly precious are God's irrevocable assurances and promises in this passage, to us who stand in the fulfilment of Christ's atoning sacrifice, His Person being ministered to us by His Holy Spirit.

The change from righteous indignation to loving consolation and comforting promises and assurances is deeply significant. It is designed to demonstrate that restoration could not be accomplished by any meritorious efforts on the part of His erring people. Their dire need must be met by Divine grace.

The love of God is not sentimental, it is never exercised at the expense of His holiness, it never compromises His justice. The love that chastises antedates the chastisement.

So when the Lord says, "I have loved thee" (*verse 4*), He is recalling a love that was in exercise long before the apostasy and rebellion that inevitably called forth His righteous retribution. His love was in evidence (1) in His creative and formative acts: "the Lord that created thee," a supernatural act involved in His predetermined counsel, "and He that formed thee," a

supernatural process, similarly predetermined and witnessed in
His dealing with the patriarchs and the offspring of Jacob; (2) in
His redeeming power: " **I have redeemed thee** "; how constantly
He reminds them that nothing but His immediate strength gave
them deliverance from Egypt! (3) in His call of them: " **I have
called thee by thy name, thou art Mine.**"

To call by name, in Scripture phraseology, is not simply to
give a name to anyone, it conveys a tenderness that delights in
the possession of the called: "He calleth His own sheep by name,
and leadeth them out" (John 10: 3). Hence the addition "thou
art Mine". In 48: 12 He speaks of them as "My called".

Creation, redemption, calling—these three, are all fulfilled for
each one of us—"created in Christ Jesus", redeemed "through
His blood", called "through His grace".

In *verse 1* the "fear not" is based upon the past facts of God's
mercy; the repetition in *verse 5* is based upon the fact and comfort of His presence.

When circumstances tend to cause anxiety, and the threatening attitude of things might give rise to natural apprehensions,
it is good, not only to recall the gracious dealings of our God,
but to hear His reminders of what He has wrought on our
behalf in the past, of His inalienable presence with us, and the
unthwartable fulfilment of His promises, as in the present
passage.

The first promise assures us that when we pass " **through
the waters** " the Lord will be with us, and " **through the rivers,
they will not overflow** " us (reminders of the Red Sea and the
Jordan). Spiritually He has brought us out of Egypt and into
Canaan, and His assurances that He will never leave us nor
forsake us holds good amidst all that would overwhelm us.

The next promise assures us of preservation when we walk
" **through the fire** ". If water speaks of danger that springs
from circumstances, fire speaks of that which arises from
persecution, as in the case of the three youths in Nebuchadnezzar's furnace. Both forms enter in one way or another into
the lives of God's people, but it is the design of the Lord to
banish fear from our hearts, and to strengthen our faith, by
all that is contained in the assurance " **I am the Lord thy
God,**" titles which tell first of the majesty and grandeur of
His infinite Being, and then of His almighty power (*verse 3*).

The statement " **I have given Egypt as thy ransom, Ethiopia and Seba for thee** " is in the perfect tense, putting facts which were in the near future in Isaiah's time as already completed in the unalterable purposes of God. To Him, the timeless One, future events, alike with those in the past, are as real as those in the present. It was after the return of the Jews from captivity that God rewarded Cyrus the Persian Monarch for liberating them, by permitting him and his son Cambyses to possess Egypt and the neighbouring kingdoms. Seba was the large district between the White and the Blue Nile, contiguous to Ethiopia. The possession of these lands was not merely a gift, it was a ransom price (a *kopher*, or covering), the people on whose behalf payment was made being covered by it.

This remarkable prediction, which had its fulfilment in the reign of the Persian monarchs, was but the beginning of similar events that have followed and are yet to follow. This is declared in *verse 4*, where the Lord says " **I will give men for thee, and peoples for thy life** " (R.V.), words which point not only to already accomplished facts but to the establishment of the Millennial Kingdom, as the next verses show. But all this is based upon Divine grace. In spite of all the failure of Israel the Lord regards them as precious in His sight, and honourable, and declares His immutable love for them.

Here we may see a comparison and a contrast in regard to ourselves. He views us as precious in His sight because we are "accepted in the Beloved"; the love which He has for us is of the same degree as the love which He has for His Son (John 17: 23). The contrast lies in this, that, whereas earthly nations are given for Israel's life, the life which God gives us is to be devoted to the blessing of every nation in the work of the Gospel.

The assurances in *vv. 5 and 6* are of peculiar interest in these times when the question of the Jews is occupying the attention of the world. What is taking place is surely preparatory to the fulfilment of the promises of God when Gentile nations in general (here represented by "the north" and "the south") will be compelled to restore His "sons and daughters". The phrase in *verse 7*, " **every one that is called by My Name**," resumes the comforting message in verse 1. Identification in character with Himself, and

possession by Him for the display of His glory and grace, are
the two chief thoughts suggested.

The three statements at the end of verse 7 form a progress
to a climax:

1. **" I have created him for My glory "**; that expresses the
thought of His power in bringing the nation into being;

2. **" I have formed him "**; that points to the process of His
transforming grace by which the one created is made to reflect
His glory;

3. **" Yea, I have made him "**; this points to the completion
of the Divine act. The verb rendered "I have made" signifies
more than simply to make, it conveys the thought of bringing
a work to perfection.

All this is true for every one of us, and expresses the wonders
of God's counsels and power, and the riches of His grace. He
who has (1) created us anew in Christ, (2) is transforming us
by the operating power of His Holy Spirit, and (3) will perfect
that which concerns us, at the coming of the Lord.

In *verse 8* the command **" Bring forth the blind people that
have eyes, and the deaf that have ears,"** is not issued with
regard to bringing Israel out of captivity, but is a general summons to assemble to the place appointed for the vindication of
the Being, character, authority and decisions of God. The command is thus to be distinguished from the promise, "I will
bring", in verse 5. God will indeed first restore His earthly people
to their land, but after this the summons is both to His people
and then to all the nations to attend for the purpose mentioned.
Israel, no longer in blindness and deafness, are to have eyes to
see and ears to hear, as was intimated in 42: 18, 19, but *verse 9*
states that the Gentile peoples (the word is plural and does not
refer to Israel) are to be assembled.

Before the Gentiles can be enriched in Millennial fullness, they
must be made to acknowledge the facts relating to the true God,
in contrast to their idolatry, superstition, man-worship and
rejection of the Divine claims. The challenge is issued to the
nations to bring their witnesses, that they may be justified. But
there will be no such possibility. The only alternative is **" let
them hear, and say, It is truth "**.

In *verse 10* the Lord declares that Israel are His "witnesses, and His servant whom He has chosen" (cp. 44: 8). The nation has always been a witness to His existence, but will be His combined witness and servant in a special way when restored.

Meanwhile He has taken us up in His sovereign grace and has made us His witnesses and servants, that we may declare His saving grace to the ends of the earth.

There is a special significance in the identification of Israel as God's servant with the Lord Jesus as similarly mentioned in chapter 42: 1. They could never be His servant apart from their Messiah, and it is only as we realize our identification with Christ that we can be owned as His witnesses and fulfil our service worthily of Him.

God's challenge to the nations is to "bring" their witnesses that they may justify their acknowledgment of those who are no gods (*verse 9*). The A.V. "bring forth" does not adequately express the meaning. It is a case of bringing witnesses to a court of judgment. The Gentiles would do so only to be condemned. In contrast to this Jehovah makes the twofold declaration concerning His earthly people, " **Ye are My witnesses** " (*vv. 10 and 12*).

Connected with the first of these is their witness to the un-originated and self-sustained nature of His Being. " **I am He** " is a declaration that He is God exclusively and eternally in the past and future. Since His Being has no beginning and no end, the idea that there could be any other being apart from His, possessed of the attributes of Deity, is self-contradictory: " **Before Me there was no God formed, neither shall there be after Me.** " How futile, therefore, are the efforts of the heathen to demonstrate that the objects of their worship are true gods! And not only so, but how utterly doomed to failure will be the attempt of the Man of Sin to compel the combined nations under him to venerate him as God! The doom of that blasphemous arrogance will be sealed by the Son of God Himself.

The second declaration, that His earthly people are His witnesses, is put into connection with the facts, not only that He is the one and only God, the great Jehovah, but that He alone is the "Saviour" (*verse 11*), and that, besides this, there is none that can deliver out of His hand (*verse 13*). He is not only the Eternal One but He is the Almighty One. " **I will work,** " He says, " **and who shall reverse it ?** " (R.V. marg.; A.V.

"turn it back"). Not only can no one hinder Him, but no one can change what He has established.

Since all this is so with regard to His earthly national witnesses, let us take courage and renew our strength, as those whom He has called to be His witnesses through the Gospel.

The *14th verse* begins a new section, extending to 44: 5, the subjects being Avenging, Deliverance, and the Outpouring of the Spirit. The first of these has to do with the execution of Divine judgments upon the Chaldeans, called down upon them by their maltreatment of God's people. For their sake, i.e., for the purpose of releasing them, He has " **sent to Babylon** ", that is to say, has sent there the agents of His judgments (cp. 13: 3). The Chaldeans would be driven " **as fugitives . . . in the ships of their rejoicing** " (R.V.), thus overthrowing all their proud commercial enterprises. Ancient history makes known that they navigated both the Euphrates and the Persian Gulf, using vessels built by Phœnicians, both for commerce and war. The vessels of their navy, in which the Babylonians gloried, would be degraded into becoming the means of an escape.

In view of the deliverance of Israel, God gives them (*in verse 15*) a fourfold reminder concerning Himself: (1) He is Jehovah (the ever and self-existent One), the Name of His covenant relationship with His people and His "memorial unto all generations" (Exod. 3: 15; Hos. 12: 5); (2) " **your Holy One** ", a title here set in contrast both to their unholy departure from Him and to the unholy character of their pagan captors; (3) " **the Creator of Israel,** " the One who, having brought this nation into being, having formed them for His praise, and therefore sustaining them through all their grievous circumstances and vicissitudes, would not allow them to be in permanent rejection and bondage; (4) " **your King** ", a title set in contrast both to the deplorable condition of the kings of Judah and Israel, and to the eastern despot who had temporarily been permitted to reign over them, through their rejection of God's sovereign claims upon them.

The Lord assures them now that it is He who " **maketh a way in the sea and a path in the mighty waters** " (*verse 16*).

While this holds good for Israel, it is likewise true in the experiences of all His saints. The waters of the nations "roar and are troubled", yet God has a path for His people through all this, a path not only of deliverance but of Gospel witness, which will go on its way until its appointed end.

Verse 17 affords a reminder (appropriate to the present times) of the overruling power of God in regard to the armies of the nations. Whatever the hearts of potentates may devise, it is the Lord who " **bringeth forth the chariot and horse, the army and the power** ". The calamities of war are "His judgments". By these means He designs to turn the hearts of men to repentance. He also has His national purposes to fulfil, and the day will come when the enemies of His earthly people will " **lie down together** ", and will be " **quenched as flax** " (i.e., as a wick).

Verse 18 is a command not to call to mind the former things. That does not mean that we are not to remember God's past mercies. These we are indeed to keep in memory. But here the subject is confined to what He is about to do (*verse 19*). He will " **do a new thing; now it shall spring forth** " (lit., 'even now it sprouts up'). Contrast 42: 9, where a distinction was drawn between the former things which had to come to pass and new things which God was declaring. It was there said of the latter that they 'were not yet sprouting up'. His future mercies are brought before us as if they were already beginning. He will make a way in the wilderness, and rivers in the desert.

Let us apply these promises to our own experiences, and gather together the four phrases, designed for our comfort in times of trial and difficulty; (1) " **through the waters** "—they are themselves a means of giving us to experience the presence of the Lord (*verse 2*): (2) " **through the fire** "—we are assured of preservation (*verse 2*): (3) " **in the sea** ", and " **in the mighty waters** " (*verse 16*)—here God provides a way; troublesome conditions are a means of giving us to realize the guidance of God: (4) " **in the wilderness** " and " **in the desert** " (*verse 19*) —guidance and refreshment are our portion there. If the waters speak of overwhelming trials, the wilderness and the desert speak of the condition of the world around us, with which if we are unduly occupied we shall suffer spiritual depression. But God has a way amidst such conditions, a path of fellowship with Him, a path of joy and fruitfulness.

God promises to do "**a new thing**". The whole earth is to
be blessed when God's earthly people enjoy the blessings of His
redemptive work. This subject is continued in *vv. 20 and 21.*
The termination of the sufferings of Israel will involve the termination of the sufferings of creation. Because God will give
waters in the wilderness and rivers in the desert for His people,
"**the beasts of the field**," He says, "**shall honour Me, the
jackals and the ostriches**" (see the R.V. and A.V. marg.). Contrast what is said of these animals in 13: 21, 22. God's care for
animals (about which the Lord Himself spoke when on earth)
has already been stated in 11: 6–9; 30: 23, 24; 35: 7; see also
65: 25.

But these blessings are not to be granted merely for the welfare
of the animal world and of humanity. The paramount object is
the honour of God Himself. The animals, in their unconscious
enjoyment of Millennial bliss, will thereby give "honour" to
God, and as to Israel, He speaks thus: "**My people, My chosen,
the people which I formed for Myself, that they might set forth
My praise**" (R.V.), *verse 21.* What a change from their present
condition! How greatly the Lord Himself must look forward to
the coming day!

This purpose is exactly what is designed for us in this present
period, whom God has called "out of darkness into His marvellous light", that we may 'show forth His praises' (1 Pet.
2: 9; R.V. "excellencies", or, what is more commonly the
meaning of the word, "virtues", as the A.V. marg.). Virtue
is moral excellence. When used of God it is more comprehensive,
and stands for all His attributes, His power, His grace, and all
that has been exhibited in the Person of His Son. The conduct
of our life and our whole activity are to be devoted to this
highest of all objects.

There can scarcely be found any more striking contrast in the
Old Testament than that between the remonstrance uttered by
God in *vv. 22–24* and the grace and mercy that follow in *vv. 25, 26.*
The former part records the iniquities of Israel both negative and
positive, five negative and three positive. Instead of calling upon
the Lord they had become weary of Him. Instead of presenting
their offerings to Him they had 'made Him to serve with their
sins and wearied Him with their iniquities'.

The phrase "**thou hast made Me to serve**" is very significant. The verb thus rendered denotes to impose servile labour upon a person. *Verse 23* says that God had imposed no such servile labour upon them, but their sins weighed heavily upon Him, as a burden does upon a servant.

Our minds instinctively turn to the Cross. At what a cost the Lord undertook the burden of human guilt! We shall never know how heavily it weighed upon God the Father to spare not His own Son but deliver Him up for us.

In the light of this we can the better understand the contrast in *verse 25*; "**I, even I, am He that blotteth out thy transgressions for Mine own sake, and I will not remember thy sins.**" This is love manifested, not at the expense of Divine holiness and justice, but on the very ground of it.

"**For Mine own sake** "—that expresses the free grace by which our sins are removed, for there is nothing in the sinner which merits it. By the sovereign act of God's grace in the death of Christ His justice dealt with sin; His grace and love blot it out.

When the Lord calls upon Israel in *verse 26*, saying "**Put Me in remembrance; let us plead together; set thou forth thy cause, that thou mayest be justified,**" He is summoning them to remind Him, if they can, of any merit on their part whereby they might be justified. He had just stated that He, and He alone, could and would blot out their transgressions and clear them of guilt, and further that, such had been their guilt, He would do it not for their sakes but for His own. Acquittal must be by grace alone. If they think otherwise let them state their case (as in a court of justice) and set forth their cause, as against His.

Immediately He shows the impossibility of their success. Their first father had sinned, their teachers had transgressed against Him. They were sinners from the beginning and throughout their history, and, in view of their persistent impenitence, judgment was inevitable: "**I will profane,**" He says, "**the princes of the sanctuary, and I will make Jacob a curse and Israel a reviling** " (*verse 28*).

So verse 25 is not simply a sweet promise; it is part of an argument. It anticipates what is set forth in Romans in regard to the Gospel, namely, that man has no merit, that justification is by grace, and that it is conditional upon repentance and faith (though there is, of course, a distinction between God's dealings with Israel and those now relating to the Gospel). These O.T. foreshadowings deepen our understanding of the ways of God with men.

CHAPTER XLIV

THE unbounded grace of God is marvellously demonstrated in the opening part of this chapter. Reproof and remonstrance in chapter 43 are immediately followed by assurance and promise, based upon His predetermined counsel and creative acts regarding the nation. In wrath He remembers mercy.

The Lord recalled His gracious utterances at the beginning of chapter 43, with the added fact that Israel is His "chosen". In the two passages He uses the same three words as in the record of His creation of man, "created" (Gen. 1: 27), "made" ("make", Gen. 1: 16), "formed" (Gen. 2: 7), but now with reference to the birth of the nation. All this makes His purpose and His pledge to Jacob unalterable, despite the gross apostasy of His people. He even calls them "Jeshurun" (a Hebrew word meaning "upright"; the Sept. translates it "beloved"), an appellation previously assigned through Moses (Deut. 32: 15; 33: 5, 26), and anticipative of Israel's future condition of righteousness (vv. 1, 2).

Divine delight breathes through the promises that follow: the thirsty are to be satisfied, the seed of Jacob to be blessed by the outpouring of the Spirit, with resulting national and spiritual fertility (vv. 3, 4). The time is near. Grace will triumph.

This was written for our present comfort too. Let us walk as God's Jeshurun and "be filled with the Spirit".

Verse 5 is a prediction of the effects upon Gentiles of Israel's restoration. The threefold statement is to be read in the light of Ps. 87: 4, 5, where Rahab (i.e., Egypt), Babylon, Philistia,

Tyre and Ethiopia are mentioned as coming in for the privilege of knowing God, and one and another are to be noted as having been born in Zion.

Among the Gentiles in Millennial blessing one will declare himself as belonging to Jehovah; another will "call himself by" (or rather, "will solemnly name") the name of Jacob, i.e., will make it the object of a solemn exclamation; another will declare in handwriting (not, as in the margin, "write on his hand") "unto Jehovah," witnessing that he belongs to Jehovah alone; he will add the name of Israel as a name of high honour, a two-fold joyous attestation. As Rom. 11: 12 says, "the fulness of Israel" will be still more "the riches of the Gentiles," than even is the case with the present effects of the Gospel.

There is a striking parallel between this verse in Isaiah and the results of the Gospel we preach. Just as in the coming day a Gentile will own that he belongs to Jehovah, so the convert to-day learns to acknowledge that he is the Lord's possession (1 Cor. 3: 23; Gal. 3: 29); so also does he name "the Name of the Lord" (2 Tim. 2: 29, R.V.: cp. 1 Pet. 4: 16, R.V.).

In *verse 6* the Lord renews for the third time His pledge of redemption, by His title of Redeemer (see 41: 14; 43: 14), and introduces another remonstrance against the evil and folly of idolatry by a series of further declarations concerning Himself: He says " **I am the first, and I am the last.**" This title, claimed by God three times in Isaiah, here, in 41: 4 and 48: 12, and by Christ three times, in Rev. 1: 17; 2: 8; 22: 13, indicates Their oneness in the Godhead, Their eternal pre-existence and Their absolute supremacy. It predicates that all creatures animate and inanimate owe their existence to Them, and that the beginning, course and issue of all circumstances are under Their supreme control. Israel may therefore rest assured that all the Divine promises and pledges will be fulfilled by Him who is their "King", their "Redeemer, Jehovah of Hosts".

He who has redeemed us by His blood is "the First and the Last" in all our circumstances and experiences. He who gave us being, who was the Beginner of our new life in Christ, will be with us as the Fulfiller of His purposes in and through us now and for ever. In the commencement, the course and the

completion of any circumstance in our life, as, for instance, in
the case of our special service for Him, He is "the First and
the Last". He was the Beginner of our service, as the One
who called us to it, and, when it is finished, the completion
will be His by His Holy Spirit. Has He not said "I will never
leave thee nor forsake thee"? Well may we rely upon His
grace and power and love.

In *vv. 7 and 8* the Lord repeats to a large extent what He
said in 41: 22, 23 and 43: 9, 10. Here again He issues His
challenge as to who can proclaim (that is the meaning of the
word "call", see the R.V. marg.) and declare things as He does,
setting them all in order. This He Himself has done since He
appointed **" the ancient people "**. He has raised up prophets
among them, making known **" the things that are coming "**.
Note the two predictive phrases, (1) **" the things that are coming "**, that is, future things, (2) things **" that shall come to
pass "**, that is, things that are approaching, which are more
immediately at hand. What other nation could produce prophets
like that? What other nation had been so dealt with by God?
Let the gods and the prophets of Gentile peoples declare such
things. The prophecies uttered by Jehovah reach back to the
beginning of human history. In the two preceding passages the
challenge was as to the possibility of declaring or unfolding former
things (what scorn this pours upon the philosophies of sceptics
and propagandists of mere scientific theories!). Here stress is
upon matters of the future, not upon former things.

Seeing that none of the heathen gods could answer such
challenges, well might Israel be freed from fear and be confident
that God, beside whom there is no other (*verse 6*), would, and
will, certainly accomplish what He has fortold; and since this
is made good in the history of His people, they, in contrast to
the prognosticators of the nations, are His witnesses. The utmost
ferocity and antagonism of Satan and his hosts, and of all human
foes, can never prevent Israel from being His witnesses, witnesses
to His own Being and the unthwartable character of His counsels.
" Is there a God beside Me ? " He says, **" yea, there is no Rock ;
I know not any."** The R.V. rightly has "Rock" (see the A.V.
marg.), and this is appropriate to the comforting exhortation,
"Fear ye not, neither be afraid", appropriate also to the declaration of His own character.

The Rock is representative of immovability, strength and protection. Let us whom He has raised up to be His witnesses take comfort in this. Things around us are in a state of upheaval and uncertainty. The earth (i.e., its inhabitants) is changing, and the mountains of many Governments are falling into the seas of revolution and disturbance. Let us, therefore, renew our confidence in our God and take courage to bear witness boldly and stedfastly for Him.

Verses 9–20 contain the most striking of all the Divine remonstrances against the makers of idols. In contrast to Israel as God's witnesses, the idols are " **their own witnesses** " (*verse 9, R.V.*). From that point onward withering scorn is poured upon the blindness and grotesque folly of the framers thereof. All this was a remonstrance against Israel, who had turned from their own Maker to fall into the degradation of the heathen about them.

In *verse 21* the Lord calls upon His people to bear these things in mind, basing His admonition upon the facts that they owed their very existence as a nation to His supernatural operation, and that as His people they were His "servant" —a direct contrast to the idolatrous slaves to the stock of a tree.

And now the yearning heart of the Lord breaks forth in accents of infinite grace. His people would not be forgotten of Him. He had blotted out as a thick cloud their transgressions and as a cloud their sins. Let them return to Him, in view of the fact that He had redeemed them (*verse 22*).

There is a striking element of gospel grace in this, grace that manifests itself even before conversion. But what is set immediately before us is God's gracious desire towards us as His servants, in order that fellowship with Him may be constantly maintained, for the joy of His own heart, and for the efficiency of our witness for Him and of the service we render.

In the assurance of *verse 22*, the word rendered " **I have blotted out** " is used of blotting out (*a*) a name, whether from a book or otherwise, Exod. 32: 32, 33; Deut. 9: 14; 29: 20; 2 Kings 14: 27; Ps. 69: 28; 109: 13, (*b*) curses, with the water of bitterness, Num. 5: 23, (*c*) the rememberance of a people, Deut. 25: 19,

(d) sin or sins, Neh. 4: 5; Ps. 51: 1, 9; 109: 14; Jer. 18: 23; Isa. 43: 25, and here.

As to (d), whatever the particular metaphor may be, whether of a stain or a debt from a ledger, or, as in this verse, accompanied by the simile of the removal of a dense mist ("**a thick cloud**") or any such element ("a cloud"), transgression and sin are vividly depicted as separating man from God and preventing that holy and blessed intercourse which delights His heart and that of His redeemed. Only the cleansing of His wind (Job 37: 21) and the sunshine of His grace can dispel the cloud. All removal of guilt has been made possible actually and only by the blood of Christ, whose sacrifice underlies the descriptive language of the assurance here given.

Here the subject is that of restoration, the renewal of communion: "**return unto Me.**" Here the reason assigned is that of His redeeming mercy; in 43: 25 the reason for the blotting out was "**for Mine own sake**", the vindication of His attributes and character.

Verses 21 and 22 contain most cheering assurances of past redemption, a promise of remembrance in the future, and an invitation to return to fellowship with God in the present. And now, in view of the glorious and assured issues of all this, the whole creation is called upon to exult and "**break forth into singing**" (*verse 23*). "The creation itself also shall be delivered from the bondage of corruption into the liberty of the glory of the children of God" (Rom. 8: 21, R.V.), i.e., liberty will be characteristic of the glory, and creation will have full scope for the exercise of the powers imparted to it by God.

Here the essence of the glory to be enjoyed by the nations lies in this, that Jehovah "**will glorify Himself**" in Israel (R.V.). For Israel's Redeemer, who formed His earthly people from their earliest existence, is He "**that maketh all things; that stretcheth forth** (or 'extendeth', the same word as in 40: 22, where the figure is that of stretching a curtain) **the heavens alone; that spreadeth abroad** (the same word as in Ps. 136: 6, 'spread forth', R.V., and Isa. 42: 5) **the earth by Himself**" (*verse 24*).

Verse 25 refers to the Chaldean soothsayers (cp. 47: 9). It reminds us, too, of 1 Cor. 1: 20. *Verse 26* is strikingly paralleled in 1 Cor. 1: 21, 22. God turns worldly wisdom into foolishness, and "**confirmeth the word of His servant, and performeth the counsel of His messengers**".

Let us, to whom is committed the message of the Gospel, take fresh courage in this. Amidst religious superstition and varied antagonism, we know that "His word will not return unto Him void". Be it ours to preach "Christ, and Him crucified" faithfully, perseveringly and devotedly. He will confirm the word "with signs following".

As to the primary application of the phrase "His servant" (*verse 26*), that Israel is in view seems clear from verse 21, but now as represented (according to the confirmatory statement which follows) by "His messengers". That is to say, Israel here stands for the faithful prophets, the Lord's spokesmen in the nation. His promises given through them would be fulfilled, of the restoration from captivity, the rebuilding of Jerusalem and the Temple, under the decree of Cyrus, and of the drying up of "the deep" and "the rivers" of Babylon (literally accomplished by Cyrus, in respect of the Euphrates, and figuratively portending the destruction of the power of Babylon, *verse 27*).

Rightly we who are messengers of the Gospel may apply to ourselves and our ministry the truth of the words "that confirmeth the word of His servant, and performeth the counsel of His messengers". So it was with the first heralds of the Gospel, "the Lord working with them, and confirming the word by the signs that followed" (Mark 16: 20). Our work is essentially the Lord's; it is ours only in a secondary sense. The word spoken is to be derived from Him. His servant is His mouthpiece. The counsel we take is imparted by Him if our fellowship is really with Him and with His Son Jesus Christ. "It is God which worketh in you both to will (according to His 'counsel') and to work (according to His 'word') for His good pleasure" (Phil. 2: 13, R.V.).

CHAPTER XLV

THE 45th chapter begins with a second word from the Lord as to Cyrus. The first, at the end of chapter 44, was an utterance about him; now the Lord addresses him personally. The titles assigned to him and the provision made for him are unique. Such things were never said of or to another Gentile monarch. He is called the Lord's "anointed" as well as "My shepherd". Jehovah had called him by his name, and surnamed him; the former refers to his actual name (a Persian designation of the sun: cp. vv. 6, 7); the surnaming refers to the two titles now given him as already mentioned.

By his conquests nations would be subdued and made to recognize the Person and claims of Jehovah (*verse 6*). Before him the doors would be opened. The Lord would go before him, making the **"rugged places plain "** (cp. 40: 4). He would be given the treasures of darkness (his conquest of Asia made him immensely rich; he obtained over £126,000,000 worth). And all this because he was the deliverer of Israel, releasing the Jews from captivity and restoring the remnant.

In *verse 5* the Lord reaffirms to Cyrus that He is Jehovah, and that He girded, or equipped, him when he knew Him not. Such are the predetermined counsels of God, unthwartably carried into action at their appointed times.

The object for which the title was made known to the Gentile potentate was that people might know Him as Jehovah, the only true God, **" from the rising of the sun, and from the west "** (*verse 6*), i.e., the whole habitable world. Cyrus' restoration of the Jews was designed to secure this. That restoration had a preparatory part in leading to the proclamation of a worldwide Gospel in these times.

When the Lord says, in *verse 7*, **" I form the light, and create darkness ; I make peace, and create evil "**, His words are to be understood in the light of the context. He is speaking to Cyrus, whom He had appointed and empowered **" to subdue nations "** and to give deliverance to His earthly people.

The Persians believed in two co-existent principles virtually regarded as gods. The one, Ormuzd, good, symbolized by light, the other, Ahriman, evil, symbolized by darkness, both eternally in conflict, the world being the theatre. Hence the present declaration by God addressed to Cyrus. Accordingly, the immediate reference is not to the evil of sin, which God did not create, but to the judgments of war with its consequent calamities, which, for instance, Cyrus was appointed to inflict upon Gentile powers, and to the peace which he, as God's chosen instrument, would bestow upon Israel.

In *verse 8* the statement regarding peace is expanded in the assurance of blessing hereafter, when the skies will " **pour down righteousness** ", and salvation and righteousness " **will spring up together** ".

At the *9th verse* the word of the Lord is addressed to those in Israel who were criticizing the ways of God (the message to Cyrus having been finished). The opening remonstrance should read as in the R.V. (the italicized words in the A.V. weaken the meaning). " **Woe unto him,** " says the Lord, " **that striveth with his Maker! A potsherd among the potsherds of the earth!** " He who complains of God is but a poor perishable vessel among others of the same sort. The word rendered "potsherd" signifies here the whole vessel, as in Prov. 26: 23 (R.V. "an earthen vessel overlaid with silver dross") and Jer. 19: 1, where the same word is used.

Then follows the absurdity of a clay pot challenging its fashioner as to what he is making, and sneering at him as if he had no hands. The fault-finders had better leave the matters of His people in His competent hands. He had " **made the earth and created man upon it** " (*verse 12*). His hands had " **stretched out the heavens** " and " **commanded all their host** ". Let the grumblers therefore drop their complaints and realize that everything depends absolutely upon God. He had raised up Cyrus in righteousness and would " **make straight all his ways** ", so that he could build God's city and let His exiles go free, and that without expecting price or reward. Such was the mighty work of the Spirit of God upon the heart of the eastern monarch (*verse 13*).

We have in this Scripture a passage, which, while establishing our hearts in the realization that everything is under the entire control of the Maker of Heaven and earth, and His purposes among the nations are unthwartable, may also be useful in our help to those who wonder if, after all, God is stronger than His foes, and will yet bring deliverance.

In *verse 14* the Lord's message passes from the immediate future relating to Cyrus to the then distant prospect of what will be accomplished in the coming day of Israel's restoration. This double view is a frequent feature of O.T. prophecies, either in successive passages, as here, or in the same pronouncement.

Gentile nations will submit themselves to Israel, abandoning their idolatry, and Israel will be saved for ever (*vv. 14–17*). " **The labour** (i.e., the products) **of Egypt, and the merchandise** (i.e., the riches from trading) **of Ethiopia, and the Sabeans** (the men themselves, R.V.—a race in Upper Egypt), **with their prowess and strength, shall come over unto thee,**" i.e., will voluntarily surrender (cp. the same three in 43: 3). How fully they will do so is shown in the five statements which follow. And what will lie behind it all will be their recognition of the presence of God among His people, " **Surely God is in thee ; and there is none else, there is no God** (i.e., no other)."

The lesson for us in this is contained in the parallel in 1 Cor. 14: 25, where it is probable that the Apostle had these words in Isaiah in mind. What will be true of Israel in the day to come is the will of the Lord for us now. The purpose of our testimony is edification, or building up. It is God's good pleasure for us to attract the souls of the ignorant and unconverted to Christ. The Spirit of God designs to operate in and through us collectively, that such may realize the presence of the Lord and become true worshippers.

In the *15th verse* Israel is the speaker, and not the Gentiles, as in the preceding verse. This verse is not a continuation of the future acknowledgment by the Gentile nations. To understand this verse we must observe that the statement " **Thou art a God that hidest Thyself** " is not a mournful utterance as if they thought that God had turned away His face from them in anger (as in 57: 17). The meaning is that God is mysterious in His dealings and guides the affairs of nations in a way contrary to natural expectations and in a manner impossible to be discerned by mere human intelligence. Israel will be utterly astonished to find nations who have walked in heathen darkness and in alienation making supplication to them, acknowledging that God is among them and recognizing that He is the only God. It is as if they will say 'Truly Thou hast acted in a marvellous way, passing our utmost comprehension.' That is why they will address God as "Saviour". He will be seen to be the Saviour of the Gentiles as well as Israel universally in the establishment of the Millennial Kingdom.

This reminds us of the Apostle's outburst of marvel at the

depth of the riches of God's wisdom and knowledge, the unsearchable character of His judgments and the untraceable nature of His ways (Rom. 11: 33). The theme of universal blessing is the same in both passages.

Have there not been times in our experience when, owing to circumstances of extreme disappointment and trial, God has seemed to hide His face? However dark our path may be from the earthly point of view, it can be ours so to live as to enjoy the light of His countenance and the smile of His approval, and all as a result of the work of grace accomplished for us on the Cross.

After this parenthetic verse 15 there follows a contrast between the doom of idol-makers and the unending blessedness of Israel. The former shall be ashamed, confounded and " **go into confusion** ", but Israel, " **saved with an everlasting salvation** ", shall " **not be ashamed nor confounded** " to everlasting ages (*verse 16*). The restored nation will never apostatize again, and so will never know captivity and penal judgment.

The phrase " **world without end** " is not a happy rendering. Corresponding to that in the original (lit., 'for ages') is the N.T. phrase rightly rendered "for ever" (e.g., Rom. 11: 36, lit., 'unto the ages'). The literalizing of this and similar phrases is to be avoided.

The *17th verse* brings to a close this section (which began at 44: 6) and brings to a consummation the prophecies therein contained giving promise of deliverance, glory and rejoicing to Israel. It gathers up much that has preceded. And firstly by way of the reaffirmation of God as the Creator of heaven and earth, and as being the only true God. The *18th verse* first introduces God as the Speaker and then gives His own words: " **For thus saith the Lord that created the heavens ; He is God** (the correct R.V. should be noted; it declares His absolute and exclusive Deity) **that formed** (same word as in 37: 26; 43: 7, 21; 44: 10, 21) **the earth and made it** (same word as in 37: 16; 41: 4; 43: 7; the two words convey respectively the ideas of fashioning and finishing); **He established it** (a word combining the ideas of establishing and maintaining); **He created it not a waste** (a *tohu*, i.e., not as a desert or desolate place; the same word as in Gen. 1: 2, R.V., "waste"), **He formed it to be inhabited.**"

The earth was not formed for its own sake. God had the creation of man in view.

What follows, to the end of the chapter, is again in the Lord's own words; He begins by confirming what had just been stated as to His exclusive Deity, making, however, the change from "He is God" to "**I am Jehovah**", and adding "and there is none else" (cp. 44: 8). "**I have not spoken in secret,**" He says, "**in a place of the land of darkness**"; that is to say, His utterances are not like those of soothsayers, nor do they issue from the lower regions, like the mutterings of spiritists and necromancers. "**I said not unto the seed of Jacob, Seek ye Me in vain.**" The word rendered "in vain" is *tohu*, the same as in *verse 18* (R.V., "a waste"). Hence the meaning is that God did not say 'Seek ye Me in a desert,' i.e., without the prospect of deriving any benefit from the search. On the contrary He 'speaks righteousness'.

He gives promises to those who seek Him, which are fulfilled consistently with His righteous character; 'He declares things that are right'; that is to say, His word is sure, and the blessing promised to His earthly people will verily be granted in His appointed time. See the N.T. parallel to this in 2 Cor. 1: 20; "For how many soever be the promises of God, in Him is the Yea: wherefore also through Him is the Amen, unto the glory of God through us."

Now again, just as in *vv. 14–17*, the restoration of Israel will be followed by the enlightenment and deliverance of the Gentile nations. The Lord, having renewed His assurance to Israel, addresses a summons to those Gentiles who have escaped from the judgments upon the world and are brought into the blessing of the Millennial Kingdom. "**Assemble yourselves,**" He says, "**and come; draw near together, ye that are escaped of the nations.**" None of these will have been worshippers of the Beast, for all such will be removed from the earth by Divine judgment through angelic ministry (Rev. 14: 9–11; cp. Matt. 13: 49).

In view of this the protest against their idolatry is renewed (*verse 20, as in verse 16*), as also is the challenge issued to erstwhile idolaters to do what God alone can do, foretell the future; cp. 41: 22, 26; 43: 9 (*verse 21*). Jehovah alone has done this, and now, declaring the salvation He is about to impart to the whole world, He says **"And there is no God else beside Me; a just God and a Saviour; there is none beside Me."** This repeated statement stresses its tremendous import in view of the circumstances. Now follows the commanding invitation, **" Look unto Me, and be ye saved, all the ends of the earth,"** and a third time He declares **" for I am God, and there is none else "** (*verse 22*).

Deliverance from the period of Divine wrath upon the world (which will be coincidental with the great tribulation) and from pagan idolatry, will be followed by the worldwide acknowledgment of God. The prophecy of this is introduced by a Divine oath by which God, swearing by Himself, pledges the unthwartable accomplishment of His purpose: **" By Myself have I sworn, the word is gone forth from My mouth in** (or 'of': see R.V. marg.) **righteousness** (cp. *verse 19*), **and shall not return, that unto Me every knee shall bow, every tongue shall swear "** (*verse 23*). This, which speaks of earthly Millennial conditions, is quoted (from the Septuagint Version) in Rom. 14: 11, which there, though of universal application, is used to refer to the fact that all believers will stand before the Judgment-Seat of Christ. In the Romans passage the Divine oath is put in the form "as I live" (cp. Num. 14: 21, 28; Deut. 32: 40, R.V.), expressing God's power and authority. The bowing of the knee signifies the recognition of, and subjection to, the Lord's authority; the confession of the tongue indicates the acknowledgment of the inerrancy and rightfulness of His judgment.

After God's word has gone forth it never returns without fulfilling its purpose; that is the meaning of "shall not return" (see the extended assurance in 55: 11).

The R.V. of *verse 24* is important. The bending of the knee and acknowledgment of the name of Jehovah in homage to God will be voluntary in the Millennial day: **" Only in the Lord, shall one say unto** (or 'of') **Me, is righteousness and strength "** (lit., "fulness of righteousness", i.e., righteousness completely fulfilled). The foes of God will be compelled to bow (see Phil. 2: 10, 'things under the earth'), but that is not in view in this passage. "In the Lord" signifies voluntary acceptance and recognition of Jehovah in all His attributes, power and dealings. There is repeated emphasis on God's righteousness as the basis of His dealings—**" a just God and a Saviour ":** in *verse 21*,

righteousness and salvation; here righteousness and strength.
Strength comes to us only as we walk in righteousness before
Him.

Men will come to Him from every part of the world: antagonists
will be put to shame. The seed of Israel will be justified (made
righteous), not by works of the Law but "in the Lord", in a
joyous acknowledgment of their Messiah by virtue of their
relationship to Him. In Him they "shall glory", not in their
superiority and prowess. And Israel will have a spiritual seed,
all being justified on the ground of the atoning sacrifice of
Calvary. That which is now being wrought out among Jew and
Gentile in this day of gospel grace for the formation of the
Church, will have its counterpart in the redeemed on earth in
the Millennial Kingdom.

CHAPTER XLVI

Introductory Note

AT this chapter there is a change in the subject. There are now
three prophecies relating to Babylon. Yet there is a connection
with what has preceded. For the prophet has been foretelling
what was to be expected by Israel through the raising up and
the administration of Cyrus. He is now going to show what
Cyrus will carry out regarding Babylon. This potentate would
be the instrument of the judgment of the Lord upon the gods of
Babylon. At the same time the three prophecies contain matters
relating to what is yet future in connection with Israel, and
admonitions continue to God's people. The first prophecy
occupies this chapter; the second is in chapter 47, the third in
chapter 48. The first deals with the gods, the second with
Babylon itself, the third with deliverance from Babylon.

Bel was the Jupiter of the Babylonians and was their tutelar
deity. Nebo corresponded to the Roman Mercury and was the
tutelar deity of the later Chaldean royal household.

Bel would 'fall headlong'; Nebo would stoop till he shared the
same fate. Instead of being carried in procession, their images
would be a burden to the "beasts" (camels, dromedaries and

elephants), and "cattle" (horses, oxen and asses). But even so the burdens would not arrive at their destination, they would not be delivered; in their flight from the conqueror they would be overtaken, and go into captivity (*vv. 1, 2*).

The rest of chapter 46 consists of three admonitions: the first is to all Israel (*vv. 3–7*); the second to apostates in the nation, associates with idolaters (*vv. 8–11*); the third to the rebellious (*vv. 12, 13*). The first and third are a call to "hearken", the second to "remember". God desires the ready ear to hear, the ready mind to recollect.

In the first admonition His people are reminded of their unique origin and support. Divinely formed as the seed of Abraham, they had been borne and cared for from their earliest existence onward. So much for the past. As to the future, He, the unchanging One (" I am He "), promises to bear them on His shoulder (a contrast to the Chaldean burdens in *vv. 1 and 2*), and to carry them to old age and hoar hairs, a figurative way of assuring the remnant that throughout their experiences His care would never fail them.

The statement in *verse 4*, " I have made " (or rather, 'I have done it'), speaks not so much of His creative power, as of the fact that as He has acted in the past so will He in the future. He is "the great, unchangeable I AM."

In accordance with this He immediately asks to whom they will liken and compare Him, putting another god side by side with Him so that they may be equal. Let them consider, and contrast the egregious and crass absurdity of fashioning, worshipping and appealing to images (*vv. 6, 7*).

The second admonition begins with a call, based upon the preceding, to those who are turning to idolatry, 'to shew themselves men,' i.e., to be firm instead of faltering. Let them call to mind " **the former things** ", the great truths relating to His Person and His dealings of old in the history of the nation, His absolute Deity, evoking adoration, His sole power to declare " **the end from the beginning, and from ancient times things that are not yet done** " (*verse 10*). Cp. 41: 22, 26; 44: 7; 45: 21. He alone can say " **My counsel shall stand, and I will do all My pleasure.**"

It is good for the believer to call to mind the former things, to remember the way the Lord has led and helped and delivered.

It stirs the soul to renewed praise, and stimulates faith and hope as to the future.

In *verse 11* this power to predict with absolute inerrancy is again illustrated in regard to Cyrus, as in 41: 2–4. He is called the **" ravenous bird from the east "** (Persia), **" the man of My counsel from a far country "** (Media, as in 13: 5, 17). The potentates of earth, summoned on to the arena of history, are God's instruments to fulfil His counsel, whether for judgment or for deliverance; and Cyrus combined the two, judgment on Gentile nations, deliverance for the captives of Israel.

God's words are duly carried into action: **" I have spoken, I will also bring it to pass "**; so with His purposes: **" I have purposed, I will also do it."**

The third admonition addresses those who resist God's will in their ignorant obduracy. They are the **" stouthearted "**, not courageous, but stiffnecked. They are **" far from righteousness "**; their unbelief has produced despair of the fulfilment of God's word, and banished desire for knowledge of it. Consequently they are without the salvation He grants on the basis of righteousness (*verse 12*).

There is, however, promise of salvation for those who accept His conditions. **" I bring near,"** He says, **" My righteousness, it shall not be far off, and My salvation shall not tarry "** (*verse 13*; cp. Deut. 30: 13, with Rom. 10: 6–10, which quotes from the Septuagint with certain modifications, and speaks of the same subjects of righteousness and salvation as in this Isaiah passage).

On the basis of His righteousness, established for Israel, as for us, on the ground of the Death of Christ, God will **" place (or give) salvation in Zion for Israel My glory,"** or "My glory to Israel" (R.V. marg.). The glory of God which has departed from the nation (cp. Ezek. 9: 3 and 11: 23) will return to it, and that in full measure, so that Israel, shining in the Divine splendour, will worthily reflect His glory.

CHAPTER XLVII

THE 46th chapter pronounced judgment upon the gods of Babylon, the 47th declares the doom of Babylon itself. Her pride would be humbled in the dust. For the phrase "**sit on the ground**," see 3: 26. She had been noted for her luxury and debauchery, and called "**tender and delicate** " (*verse 1*). Now she who was mistress must do the menial work of grinding at the mill. As a prisoner of war she would be compelled to abandon modesty and wade through her rivers.

All this Babylon would bring upon herself through her treatment of God's people. He is their "Redeemer", the Conqueror of their foes. He is " **Jehovah of hosts** ", possessed of absolute authority. He is "**the Holy One of Israel** ", signifying their character as it should be in relation to Himself, and the unholy character of their oppressors (*verse 4*).

Babylon had been looked upon as an Empress, "the lady of kingdoms" (the king of Babylon called himself "king of kings", Ezek. 26: 7; cp. Dan. 2: 37). Now she must go into darkness, hiding herself for shame. When the Lord used her as His instrument for the chastisement of His people (*verse 6*), she exceeded her authority, mercilessly treating the aged and helpless.

This has been the case with all the potentates who have been permitted to occupy the land of Palestine and hold His people in captivity, and the same thing will obtain in regard to the Antichrist in the future.

Verses 8–10 depict further the character of the guilty city, her voluptuousness, her self-exaltation, as well as her self-deification in adopting the title " **I AM** ", which alone belongs to God, her false sense of security, her sorceries and enchantments (astrology had its origin in Babylonia), her seared conscience in declaring that no eye saw her wickedness, and so virtually denying the existence and omnipresence of God. Possessed of natural wisdom and knowledge, she had used these to pervert her ways.

Hence evil would come upon her, of which she would not "**know the dawning** " (*verse 11*, R.V.), or rather, as in the margin, 'know how to charm away'. Mischief would fall upon her which she could not expiate (see A.V. marg.).

Enchantments and sorceries had been practised there 'from her youth' (*verse 12*), i.e., from the time of the re-establishment of Babel by Nimrod (Gen. 10: 10, which is historically subsequent to 11: 9).[1] The practice of the black art would not deliver her

---

[1] See Hislop's " *Two Babylons.*"

from her doom. Her traffickers would wander each in his own way (*verse 15*, R.V. marg.; cp. Rev. 18); they would flee to their own localities, leaving Babylon to its doom.

CHAPTER XLVIII

THIS chapter is addressed especially to the Judæan captives who have " **Come forth** (or flowed) **out of the waters of Judah** "; that is, they had their source in Judah. They make great profession, but their ways do not conform thereto. They swear by the Name of Jehovah, and extol Him as the God of Israel, but " **not in truth, nor in righteousness** ". " **They call themselves of the holy city,**" but its holiness placed them under an obligation to be holy themselves. They profess to rely upon God; but His name was " **the Lord of Sabaoth** ", a Name demanding reverence and submission, not external religion (*vv. 1, 2*).

Now comes a renewal regarding God's sole power to predict with inerrancy. But there is a difference from similar previous statements. Those in 41: 22; 42: 9; 43: 9 were contrasted with pagan idols and idolaters. That in 46: 9, 10 was in contrast to Israelitic idolaters, but had special reference to Cyrus. Here *vv. 3 to 5* speak of the Divine predictions of the apostasy and obstinacy of Israel. Further, the Lord would show them things which He was now creating, not those of long ago, though all were foreknown by Him, as were their treacherous dealings; they were transgressors from their earliest days (*vv. 6–8*).

But the " **new things** " of *verse 6* include Israel's redemption. Had they their desert they would be cut off entirely. His mercy is ever consistent with His character; accordingly He says " **For My Name's sake** (His Name expresses His nature) **will I defer Mine anger, and for My praise will I refrain for** (i.e., hold back towards) **thee, that I cut thee not off** " (*verse 9*).

This dire captivity, like the coming time of their great tribulation, and like their present bitter experiences, constitute a refining process: " **Behold, I have refined hee** (this looks to the issue), **but not as silver** (the smelting was a higher character); **I have chosen thee in the furnace of affliction** " (*verse 10*). The primary meaning of the verb rendered " **I have chosen** " is to prove

with the object of approving, and hence the meaning of choice
—not chosen for the purpose of affliction, but chosen in it with
a view to approval as a result of it (some would render it 'I
have proved thee').

This is the gracious design of the Lord in our trials and
afflictions. This will enable us to appreciate, and praise Him
for, His grace and love therein, and will keep us from despondency. He only designs 'our dross to consume, and our
gold to refine' (see Zech. 13: 9 and cp. 1 Pet. 1: 7). This will
have an end and a blessed issue, and will be accomplished for
His own glory: " **For Mine own sake, for Mine own sake** (the
repetition stresses the solemn importance of the fact), **will
I do it** (i.e., bring about salvation); **for how should My Name
be profaned ? and My glory will I not give to another** " (verse
11). The adversaries of the Lord and His people will never
be afforded a ground for scoffing at God and His doings. His
ways and acts constitute His glory, and this will never be
relinquished.

A second time His people are called to hearken (see verse 1
and, for the third and fourth, vv. 14, 16); and now for the following reasons: (1) His absolute Deity—" **I am He** (cp. 43: 10);
I am the first, I also am the last "—the eternal, the unchangeable (see 41: 4; 44: 6; Rev. 1: 8, 17; 22: 13): (2) His power as
Creator (verse 13): (3) His power as the Director of events (vv. 14,
15): it is He who has appointed the destroyer of Babylon and
the Chaldeans. Of Cyrus, again, the Lord says He has loved,
called and brought him, and " **he shall make his way prosperous** ":
(4) His power as the God of prophecy and its fulfilment (verse 16).
The close of verse 16 brings before us a striking instance of
the work of the Trinity: " **and now the Lord God hath sent Me
and His Spirit.**" That Christ is the Speaker, and not the prophet,
is to be gathered from a comparison with 61: 1 (cp. 11: 2; 42: 1).
His words are undoubtedly a prelude to what He is about to
declare of Himself in chapter 49: 5, 6. Jehovah, having prepared
for the deliverance of His people by Cyrus, has sent His Servant
acting by His Holy Spirit to accomplish a great deliverance for
the nation and meanwhile to instruct and lead them. This is
His message to His people: " **Thus saith the Lord, thy Redeemer,
the Holy One of Israel ; I am the Lord thy God, which teacheth**

thee to profit (to do that which profiteth), **which leadeth thee by the way that thou shouldest go** " (*verse 17*).

This was the purpose of the trials and bitter experiences of captivity. This is the gracious design of the chastening given us by God: "He for our profit, that we may be partakers of His holiness" (Heb. 12: 10). How often we fail to do "that which profiteth!" It is not mere guidance that is here spoken of, it is the disciplinary dealing that gives us instruction to cease from that which profiteth not, and brings our wandering feet into the path of conformity to His will.

Hence the ensuing appeal, " **Oh that thou wouldest hearken** (the R.V. margin gives this true rendering) **to My commandments! then should thy peace be as a river, and thy righteousness as the waves of the sea** " (*verse 18*). This is an appeal for the listening and obedient ear. Peace and true prosperity are conditional upon the contrition of heart and the responsive faith that accept and carry out the Word of God.

Peace is likened to the tranquil flowing of a river, *righteousness* to the power of the billows of the sea, *offspring* to the abundance of the grains (R.V.) of sand. What Israel might enjoy nationally, we may enjoy spiritually. Spiritual fruitfulness is dependent upon peace and righteousness.

To this end separation from evil is essential: " **Go ye forth of Babylon.**" This is very significant. Suggestive also is the injunction to accompany the separation and deliverance with the voice of singing and with a joyful testimony. Israel was instructed to bear the news of their redemption " **even to the end of the earth** ". This the godly remnant will do in a day to come. Meanwhile the worldwide testimony of the Gospel is committed to us. The blessings described at the end of *verse 20* and in *verse 21* suggest the very elements of the gospel messages.

This portion of the prophecy ends with the solemn statement, " **There is no peace, saith the Lord, unto the wicked.**" This refers to the godless in Israel, and the word rendered "wicked" literally signifies "loose", indicating a careless moral condition which prevents the experience of peace and excludes such from blessings promised to the righteous.

This statement is repeated with one variation at the end of chapter 57. Here it marks the close of the testimony concerning Babylon, which began at 46: 1. There is no further mention in the book either of Cyrus or Chaldea, or of the idolatry which had formed the subject of expostulation and remonstrance.

PART III (b)

JEHOVAH'S SERVANT, HIS SUFFERINGS AND GLORY
(*Chapters XLIX–LVII*)

CHAPTER XLIX

FROM this chapter to the end of chapter 57 consists of nine prophecies. Chapter 49 contains the first and its subject is twofold:

The Self-witness of Jehovah's Servant (vv. 1–13), and a Comforting Promise in Zion's Despondency.

There is a renewed association of Israel as the servant of Jehovah with Christ in the same relation. While Israel is directly addressed in this way in *verse 3* in its restored condition, yet in *vv. 5 and 6* the Servant of the Lord is marked as in distinction from the nation itself, and the statement there, "**that thou shouldest be My Servant to raise up the tribes of Jacob, and to restore the preserved of Israel**", shows that Christ Himself is in view and not here the remnant of the nation. Moreover, *verse 6* is quoted in Acts 13: 47 as directly applying to Christ, though there in connection with the Gospel. All this is entirely appropriate, inasmuch as Israel could not in its restored state act as the Lord's servant in the earth apart from identification with Christ Himself as their Messiah on the ground of His sacrificial and redemptive work at Calvary.

Since the evangelization of the Gentiles is in view, the message goes forth, "**Listen, O isles, unto Me ; and hearken, ye peoples, from far**" (*verse 1*), that is, the far distant nations (cp. 42: 4, 10, 12 and see 5: 26). The twofold statement, "**the Lord hath called Me from the womb ; from the bowels of My mother hath He made mention of My Name**", is specifically true of the Lord Jesus (see Matt. 1: 21). Moreover, it is noticeable that everywhere else where Israel is thus spoken of, the phrase "from the womb" is used without the addition of the word "mother" (51: 2 is not an exception).

The Speaker, as the Servant of Jehovah, now applies a simile and a metaphor to Himself as His Agent in this relationship. The Lord has made His mouth " **like a sharp sword** ", hid in the shadow of His hand, just as a sword is kept in the sheath, ready for use at the appointed time for the purpose of overcoming the enemy. He has made Him " **a polished shaft** ", keeping Him close in His quiver, so that in due time He may pierce the heart. That Christ Himself is in view and that the time is yet future is indicated in chapter 11: 4 and 30: 30–33; cp. Hos. 6: 5 and Heb. 4: 12. The latter passage, together with these, and Rev. 1: 16, show how closely identified are the Personal Word and the spoken word. See also Joel 2: 10, 11; 3: 16; 2 Thess. 2: 8; Ps. 2: 5.

In *verse 3* Christ identifies Himself with His people Israel, for it is in close association with Him that the restored nation is to become His servant, and it is in Israel that the Lord will yet be glorified on the earth.

In this relationship, and in view of the bitter experiences which will have preceded that time of glory, *verse 4* strikes a note almost of despondency, though it is only of a momentary character, and in a certain way it may be referred to Christ in the time of His suffering and rejection by Israel: " **But** (*R.V.*) **I said, I have laboured in vain, I have spent My strength for nought and vanity** (i.e., to no purpose)"; but this is not an utterance of unbelief or despair, for immediately the heart expresses the assurance of the truth, " **yet surely My judgment is with the Lord, and My recompense with My God** ".

The service we seek to render often seems to produce little or no result. In addition to ineffectiveness there come circumstances of extreme difficulty and trial, which tend to weigh down the heart. And if Satan could accomplish his purpose, he would use all this to cast us down into despair and if possible cause us to cease from the work and turn back through perplexity and distress. Here then is a passage designed by the Spirit of God to give us to consider all such circumstances in the light of God's all wise counsels, so that while in the midst of conflict we may be encouraged to share His vision and know that our judgment is with Him, and that with Him is the recompense for our seemingly fruitless work.

The language of *verse 5* and what follows is clearly that of the Messiah, who here bears testimony to the object for which He is the Servant of Jehovah, namely, " **to bring Jacob again to Him, and that Israel be gathered unto Him** " (R.V.). It is Christ alone who will do this, and a still wider purpose is in view in *verse 6*.

The parenthesis between (note the R.V. brackets) expresses the delight of the Lord Jesus in the Father's approval. His statement " **I am honourable in the eyes of the Lord, and My God is become My strength** " is introduced by the word "for", which expresses the fact that His work in the restoration of Israel is especially pleasing to the Father. It is clear, too, that His resurrection is in view. In the darkness of Calvary He said "My God, My God, why hast Thou forsaken Me?" He was "crucified through weakness". Now He declares that His God has become His strength. This is to be taken with chapter 52: 13, which predicts that the Lord's Servant would be "exalted and extolled and be very high".

The " **Yea** " at the beginning of *verse 6* introduces an extension of the scope of Christ's work of salvation, as well as a confirmation of what has just been stated as to the salvation of Israel. The delighted heart of Jehovah looks on to the worldwide fullness of blessing: " **It is too light a thing** (or rather it is only a small thing) **that Thou shouldest be My Servant to raise up the tribes of Jacob, and to restore the preserved of Israel: I will also give Thee** (more expressive than 'make Thee') **for a light to the Gentiles, that Thou mayest be My salvation unto the end of the earth.**"

This has a present application to the work of the Gospel in fulfilment of the command of the Lord Himself to go into all the world and preach the gospel, and to be His witnesses "unto the uttermost part of the earth". The complete fulfilment will take place in the Millennial age. Both are comprehended in Rom. 11: 12, where the present application is described as "the riches of the world" and "the riches of the Gentiles", and this is followed by the exclamatory prediction of what the restoration or "fulness" of Israel will mean for the world.

In *verse 7*, in the continuation of His utterance to His Servant (for it is still Christ who is primarily in view), we are reminded again of the time of His humiliation. That was a necessary basis for the carrying out of the work of saving grace. So He is called the One " **whom man despiseth** " (see 53: 3 and cp. 50: 6, 7),

and " **whom the nation abhorreth** ", referring to His treatment
by the Jews, and, thirdly, in a very suggestive phrase, " **a
Servant of rulers** ".

This provides an instance of the very real way in which the
Lord Jesus identified Himself with the nation of Israel. That
nation had become a servant of rulers. This was the result of
its departure from God. At the same time there were men such
as Daniel, Ezra and Nehemiah who, while they were suffering
with their people, served Gentile rulers in the fear of the Lord.
So Christ, in the days of His flesh, made Himself subject to
Roman rulers, handing Himself over to their will that He might
fulfil the great purposes for which He had come. Included also
are such beneficent deeds of mercy as that which He wrought
for a centurion. In these many ways the verse points to His
Self-humbling.

The outcome of it all will be seen in the coming day of glory,
when " **Kings shall see and arise ; princes, and they shall worship ;
because of the LORD that is faithful,** *even* **the Holy One of Israel,
who hath chosen Thee** ". Cp. 52: 15, which foretells that kings
shall shut their mouths because of Him (R.V. marg.). How
great the change of attitude from that of the present time!
How startling will be the revelation of the Lord of glory in a
world that has lain in darkness, superstition and alienation from
God!

Verse 8 tells how Jehovah heard the prayer of His Servant
when, in the lowly condition which He shared with His people,
He "offered up prayers and supplications with strong crying and
tears unto Him that was able to save Him from death" (Heb.
5: 7). Here He says to Him: " **Thus saith the Lord, In an acceptable time** (in a time of favour) **have I answered Thee, and in a
day of salvation have I helped Thee : and I will preserve Thee,
and give Thee** (or set Thee) **for a covenant of the people, to raise
up the land, to make them inherit the desolate heritages ; saying
to them that are bound, Go forth ; to them that are in darkness,
Shew yourselves.** " It was an acceptable time when God raised
Him from the dead, and since Christ identifies Himself with
Israel the words will become true of the nation in fellowship
with Him in its restored condition.

That Christ Himself is made "a covenant of the people"
indicates the Personal bond which will hereafter unite the nation
to Him as the result of His having been heard and helped. The

exiled prisoners will be freed and, being restored to their land, will manifest themselves as His people.

The verses which follow give one of the most glorious descriptions of the effects of Christ's Second Advent. The promises far exceed anything that took place in the return from captivity under Cyrus. The people are depicted as a flock returning home: **" They shall feed in the ways,"** that is to say, they will be able to have sufficient supplies of food on their journeys home without going long distances to get food. **" On all bare heights shall be their pasture."**

They will know neither hunger nor thirst, nor will they suffer from the heat of the sun. And all this will be due to the fact that the Lord **" that hath mercy on them "** will lead them in Person; **" even by the springs of water shall He guide them "** (*verse 10*).

In their return from all parts of the world their journeys will be characterized by entire freedom from obstacles and difficulties. **"And,"** He says, **" I will make all My mountains a way, and My high ways shall be exalted "** (*verse 11*). Comfortingly He speaks of "My mountains" and "My ways". They are His by creation and therefore He can order for their alteration so as to make everything favourable for the return of His people.

All this is applicable to our present experiences. The mountains of difficulty which face us in our pilgrim path can become highways of communion with God and of joyous fellowship with His people, if we trust in the Lord with all our heart and present to Him our whole being for the fulfilment of His will.

In the coming day Israel will be gathered to their appointed earthly centre from all parts of the world: **" Lo, these shall come from far : and, lo, these from the north and from the west ; and these from the land of Sinim "** (*verse 12*). The west seems to be a comprehensive term, and would include districts in Africa as well as Western Europe and the Americas. Some regard Sinim as referring to the near east. The Sinite is mentioned in Gen. 10: 17. But there can be little doubt that the geographical scope is far wider, and that, as several Orientalists have maintained, the reference is to the land of China. In very ancient times Tsin was the name of a feudal kingdom in Shen-si, the first king of which began to reign in 897 B.C., and it is not at all improbable that the existence of the Chinese was well known in Palestine and Western Asia generally. Accordingly the prophecy has in view the gathering of Jews from the uttermost parts of the world (cp. *verse 6*).

Such a prospect calls forth the jubilant summons to the heavens, the earth and the mountains to rejoice and to break forth into singing, " **for the Lord hath comforted** (a prophetic perfect tense) **His people, and will have compassion upon His afflicted** " (*verse 13*). *Verse 14* records the grievous lament of the nation in its long period of suffering. The tribulation has been judicial indeed, but unbelief, instead of repentance towards God, complains of being forsaken by Jehovah and forgotten by the Lord.

The complaint elicits an expostulation and an assurance, to the effect that His love not only is as inalienable as a mother's love but exceeds it. So far from forgetting Zion (which again stands for its inhabitants), He says " **I have graven thee upon the palms of My hands : thy walls are continually before Me** " (*verse 16*). Jews had a custom of marking on their hands, or elsewhere, a delineation of the city and the temple, as a sign of their devotion to, and perpetual remembrance of, them. The Lord graciously adopts the figure to confirm His assurance. However great the devastation wrought by Gentile powers might be, the walls are ever before Him in their restored and perfected condition in the future.

To be graven on the palms of His hands is suggestive of the closest identification with Himself, of His unchanging love, and of His constant mindfulness of us in all His emotions and activities. Often, in our unbelief, remissness and forgetfulness, we lose sight of our preciousness in His sight in Christ. What is here conveyed in figure finds its fulness of expression in the outflowing of the Lord's heart to the disciples in the upper room, "Even as the Father hath loved Me, I also have loved you: abide ye in My love" (John 15: 9).

Verses 17 to 21 reaffirm the promise of the eventual gathering of the scattered outcasts of the nation back to their land. " **Thy children make haste** " (a variant reading is "thy builders"). The exiles enter: the destroyers and wasters go out. The children whom Zion thought she had lost come in crowds (*verse 18*). With a confirming oath Jehovah assures her that her people will be like the ornaments with which a woman decks herself and like the beautiful girdle which a bride fastens round her bridal attire (R.V.).

And the reason is (note the "For" of *verse 19*) that, notwithstanding the recovery and productiveness of the districts which had been desolated and rendered untenable and the removal of those that had swallowed her up, there will not be room for all her inhabitants. Her children will say in her hearing (i.e., will call to one another) that the place is too narrow, and room must be provided.

Her people had been exiles and wanderers and she had been left "solitary" (or "barren"). Now she finds herself surrounded by a multitude of her children. How, she wonders, had they been "borne" to her (R.V., margin—not "begotten")? Who had brought them up? " **Where were they?** " (R.V.). The answer is about to be given.

Sometimes the Lord refrains from manifesting His dealings and, in testing our faith, keeps us waiting till the appointed time for the disclosure of His actings and significance. Far greater the joy when the unfolding comes than if there had been no mystery, no darksome circumstances, and far greater the glory of His grace.

> " *God moves in a mysterious way*
> *His wonders to perform*
>
> .   .   .
>
> *Behind a frowning providence*
> *He hides a smiling face*
>
> .   .   .
>
> *Blind unbelief is sure to err,*
> *And scan His work in vain;*
> *God is His own interpreter,*
> *And He will make it plain.*"

The close of the 49th chapter, from *verse 22*, gives the Lord's answer to the surprised questions arising from Zion in verse 21. He shows how the multitude of scattered Israelites will be delivered from their exile and those who oppressed them, and be gathered to their own land. He will employ the Gentile nations to take their part in accomplishing this gathering. " Behold," He says, " I will lift up Mine hand to the nations, and set up My ensign to the peoples." The lifting up of His hand suggests that some marked sign or indication will be given to all the nations as to what is to be done. The setting up of a standard is a frequent figure in Isaiah: see 5: 26; 11: 10, 12; 18: 3; 62: 10 (one of the many indications that there was only one author of this book). The military metaphor may point to some connection with the Lord's interposition in the warfare of Armageddon (see the end of the chapter).

Other metaphors follow. The nations will bring Zion's sons " in their bosom ", and her daughters " shall be carried upon their shoulders ". Just as foster-fathers give diligence to care for those committed to them, and nurses give their best in caring for the children they nourish, so will kings and princesses devote themselves to the welfare of God's ancient people. They will pay homage to them to the utmost, and subject themselves to them, doing them the most lowly and menial service. The statement that they shall " lick the dust of Thy feet " points to the submission of those who before had taken part in oppressing them (see Ps. 72: 9; Mic. 7: 17).

By all this Zion will recognize Jehovah and His ways: " thou shalt know that I am the Lord." Then follows the comforting promise, " and they that wait for Me shall not be ashamed." In 40: 31 the promise is that "they that wait upon the Lord shall renew their strength." In the present passage the promise is negative: they will not be put to shame. Here too the exercise of patience is in view, in the endurance of all that is difficult and adverse until the Lord's time for deliverance comes.

We wait *upon* Him in prayer. We wait *for* Him in the confident assurance that present conditions of trial and sorrow will have a future of joy and peace such as can come only by the direct and manifest intervention of the Lord Himself.

In the next verses the tyrants with all their power and malign intentions are in view. The rhetorical question in *verse 24* is divided into two distinct parts: " Shall the prey be taken from the mighty " (it certainly will, and not merely the Chaldeans

are in view, but the Beasts of Rev. 13); 'or the captive host
of the righteous be delivered?' (margin). The captives are not
lawful captives, as the text seems to indicate, though that would
be true of those who had been taken into captivity by the
Chaldeans under God's ordering; but the time in view is far
beyond the return from captivity under Cyrus, and is yet future.
Hence the marginal reading is to be preferred, which shows that
the captives are the righteous ones whom the Lord will snatch
from the hands of the Antichrist, whom Satan will instigate to
endeavour to exterminate the Jews.

The assurance is given that the Lord Himself will contend with
those that contend with His people. The passage again points to
the time of Armageddon (Har-Magedon) and the Second Advent.
With the statement "**I will feed them that oppress thee with
their own flesh ; and they shall be drunken with their own blood,"**
cp. Rev. 14: 20. All the world will discover and recognize that
Jehovah is Israel's Saviour and Redeemer, " **the mighty One of
Jacob."**

All the efforts of the combined nations to establish "peace and
safety" in the earth, however sincere the motive, however good
the intention may be, are foredoomed to failure. The world's
last great conflict, in which the Jewish question will be upper-
most, will see the fulfilment of the Scriptures which make known
that righteousness can be established in the earth only by the
Personal Advent of Christ in judgment upon the foes of God
and in the deliverance of His people.

CHAPTER L

Two facts stand out prominently in this chapter: (1) the
responsibility attaching to Israel for her state of rejection,
(2) the stedfastness and faithfulness of the Servant of Jehovah.

In *verse 1* the Lord asks two questions by way of protest, each
repudiating the idea that the evils which had befallen the nation
were the result of arbitrary dealings on His part. Nay, their
state was due to their transgressions.

" **Where,**" He says, " **is the bill of your mother's divorcement,
wherewith I have put her away ?** " (R.V.). This is a denial by

the Lord that He had broken off the relation in which He stood
to Zion (Israel's mother). He had betrothed Zion to Himself,
and she had no bill of divorce to show, by means of which He
had put her away, thus removing the possibility of receiving her
back in case she should have married another (see Deut. 24: 1-4,
and especially verse 4). Her sad condition of being put away was
not caused by any such proceedings.

Further, He asks " **or which of My creditors is it to whom I
have sold you ?** " That Israel was sold and exiled was true,
but Jehovah had not been in the position of being indebted to
creditors. In other words, His having given her into the hands
of Gentile powers was not through His giving way to their
constraint, as if He was discharging a debt by so doing. Nay,
they were sold for their iniquities, and Zion, their mother, was
put away for their transgression. The mother suffered through
the perverseness of her children. Sinners often put down the
evils that come upon them to any cause except their own
transgressions.

But there are further questions, questions in a different manner
of Divine protestations, telling of Jehovah's power in the exercise of
mercy, and all leading to a Personal testimony by Messiah Himself.

" **Wherefore, when I came, was there no man ?** " (*verse 2*).
The past tense is prophetic. He "came", not merely by His
prophets, nor would He come simply by deliverance from
captivity. He would come in the Person of His Servant, the
Messiah-Redeemer Himself. But how was it that there was no
man, none willing to receive the message? (cp. 53: 1). How was
it that 'when He called, there was none to answer'? His hand
was not shortened (an emblem of weakness) that it could not
redeem (cp. 59: 1). He who could dry up the sea, make rivers
a wilderness, clothe the heavens with blackness and make sackcloth their covering (telling especially of His retributive judgments
upon Babylon), had power to deliver. And with this in view,
He would send His Servant. Eventually He came, and declared
at the outset of His ministry, that He had been sent "to proclaim release to the captives . . . to proclaim the acceptable
year of the Lord" (Luke 4: 18). Instead of receiving Him and
His message, they cast Him forth to destroy Him.

So now there follows, in *verse 4*, in the words of Christ Himself,
a description of His testimony as the Sent One, His obedience
to Him who sent Him, His sufferings and His vindication.

God spake to prophets by special and periodic revelations, by visions and dreams. With the Servant of Jehovah it was different. Here He discloses the secret of His inner life in the days of His flesh, and the secret source of His ministry and ways: "**The Lord God hath given Me the tongue of them that are taught, that I should know how to sustain with words him that is weary : He wakeneth morning by morning, He wakeneth Mine ear to hear as they that are taught.**" A joyous lowliness and condescension breathe through His illustration taken from discipleship. In the days of the fulfilment of this prophecy He says "My teaching is not Mine, but His that sent Me" (John 7: 16); again, "as the Father hath taught Me, I speak these things" (8: 28), and "I speak the things which I have seen with My Father" (8: 38); and again, "the Father which sent Me, He hath given Me a commandment, what I should say, and what I should speak" (12: 49; cp. 14: 10, 24).

How He 'sustained with words' the weary is told out in the Gospel narratives, both in His public ministry (e.g., Matt. 11: 28) and in the comfort He gave to the widow, the diseased, the distressed and the tempest-tossed.

The Lord daily listened to His Heavenly Father's voice. In this He sets us an example. It was His joy to say "I do always the things that are pleasing to Him" (John 8: 29), and it is only as we are attentive to His voice day by day that we can fulfil His will, enabling us to say with the Apostle, "we make it our aim . . . to be well-pleasing unto Him."

He says " **The Lord God hath opened Mine ear, and I was not rebellious, neither turned away backward** " (*verse 5*). This was the very perfection of obedience. Cp. Psalm 40: 6, where, however, the word rendered to open signifies to dig, which may either refer to the custom of boring a servant's ear, in token of perpetual service (Exodus 21: 6), or be figurative simply of devotion to God's will. Here in Isaiah a different word is used, with the latter meaning. The Lord Jesus knew all the suffering that lay before Him, and with undeviating stedfastness He pursued His pathway to the Cross.

To that consummating act *verse 6* points: " **I gave My back to the smiters, and My cheeks to them that plucked off the hair : I hid not My face from shame and spitting.**" With striking detail this prophecy predicts what the Lord actually endured as recorded in the Gospel. He set His face to His persecutors without faltering, knowing that the words that follow would be fulfilled, that the Lord God would help Him and that He would not be ashamed.

His example is an incentive to us, when called to suffer the pressure of fierce antagonism, so that with fixity of purpose we may fulfil that which the Lord has committed to us. We can never suffer as He did, but our life and testimony can be marked by the same characteristics as those which marked His. "We must through much tribulation enter the Kingdom," but to suffer for His sake makes it all a glory and joy.

He looked to the future with confidence, and so may we. He says, " **For the Lord God will help Me ; therefore have I not been confounded** (He had not suffered Himself to be overcome by mockery and opposition): **therefore have I set My face like a flint, and I know that I shall not be ashamed** " (*verse 7, R.V.*).

The design of our Father is to give us such confidence in Him and in the assurance of His help, that we may be free from every tendency to despair under the weight of trouble. If we are walking in the path of obedience we can ever be assured of His present help and of deliverance and victory in His own way and time.

The Lord knew that, in spite of every accusation both by man and by the spiritual foe, He would be triumphantly vindicated. He says " **He is near that justifieth Me ; who will contend with Me ? let us stand up together** (i.e., let the foe draw towards Me): **who is Mine adversary ? let him come near to Me** " (*verse 8*). He does not say 'He will justify Me' but "He is near" that will do so, which declares His consciousness of the presence of His Father, as, for instance, when standing before Caiaphas and his associates and before Pilate and his men of war.

His justification took place in His resurrection. He was "declared to be the Son of God with power, according to the spirit of holiness (that is the sinlessness which marked Him as the Holy One of God), by the resurrection of the dead " (Rom. 1: 4). This is further borne out by the clause in

1 Tim. 3: 16, "justified in the spirit" (referring directly to
His resurrection).

A second time He says " Behold, the Lord God will help
Me." Such repeated expressions are characteristic of Isaiah's
prophecies.

As for God's accusers and foes they shall all " wax old ", or
rather, fall to pieces like a worn-out garment, a prey to the moth,
an insect which, working slowly and imperceptibly, accomplishes
thoroughly its deadly destruction (*verse 9*).

That finishes the testimony of Messiah Himself. Just as the
chapter opened with the declaration of Jehovah, so it closes.
Here it is addressed first to the believer who fears the Lord and
obeys the voice of His Servant, a title which looks back to what
has been stated concerning Him in verses 4, 5, that is, to the
one who follows in His steps (*verse 10*).

A believer may be walking in darkness circumstantially and
have no light, and in such conditions may be tempted to
despondency. Sometimes a situation seems hopeless. A variety
of trials and adverse circumstances may crowd upon him.
Here then is the message, uplifting and soul-stirring. " Let
him trust in the Name of the Lord, and stay upon His God."
True faith is tested faith, and proves its reality by standing
the test. God is "a very present help in trouble". Faith not
only accepts this as a fact, but learns to lean upon God Himself and to prove the power and love of His almighty arm.
That turns our darkness into light. The heart is cheered and,
more still, is empowered to rise victorious over all that opposes,
rejoicing in the light of His countenance.

The next words (*verse 11*) are addressed to unbelievers and to
their presumptuous self-confidence. They kindle a fire and gird
themselves about with firebrands, and walk proudly in the
flickering flame which they have kindled. Not only so, their
fire is kindled against the Lord and against His Christ. For this
the Divine retribution is inevitable. They must suffer from the
effects of the burnings which they have kindled. It comes from
the hand of Jehovah Himself. Their activities, with all their
malice and hardheartedness are brought to a terrible end and
they " lie down in sorrow ", a contrast to the joyous restfulness
of the believer who stays himself upon His God!

CHAPTER LI

THE subject of this chapter is the promise of salvation for Israel on a righteous basis and the removal of the cup of wrath. The Lord now addresses those among His people who are faithful and, following after righteousness, long for salvation and the fulfilment of the promise to Abraham. They share his spirit of faith in refraining from making mere earthly things and pursuits the objects of their ambition. Abraham was himself the rock from which the stones, of which the house of Jacob was built, had been hewn, and Sarah was the hollow of the pit from which they had been digged. For the reference here is to the fact that, in the advanced and barren condition of the married life of Abraham and Sarah, the Lord wrought by His own supernatural power in response to Abraham's faith (*vv. 1, 2*).

In this connection the R.V. of Rom. 4: 19-21 should be noted. Its correct rendering brings out more forcibly than the A.V. the character of Abraham's faith: "And without being weakened in faith he considered his own body now as good as dead (he being about a hundred years old), and the deadness of Sarah's womb: yea, looking unto the promise of God, he wavered not through unbelief, but waxed strong through faith, giving glory to God and being fully assured that, what He had promised, He was able also to perform."

All this was the origin of the nation of Israel and the Lord calls them, in the figurative language of the rock and the pit, to remember this, and further reminds them that " **when he was but one I called him (R.V.), and I blessed him and made him many.**" Hence the strengthening assurance of comfort for Zion and her waste places and the blossoming out of her wilderness " **like Eden, and her desert like the garden of the Lord ; joy and gladness shall be found therein, thanksgiving and the voice of melody** " (*verse 3*). Just as joy came to Sarah after a long period of unfruitfulness, so Israel, after its long time of trouble and desolation, shall yet be made to rejoice.

The paragraph beginning at *verse 4* speaks of the times when the restoration of Israel will issue in blessing for all the world, and then later in the passing away of the whole of the old creation.

The present message of the Gospel is not here in view. The Lord makes the promise, " **a law shall go forth from Me, and I will make My judgment to rest for a light of the peoples** (i.e., the Gentiles)" (*verse 4*). The law is not that of Sinai but stands for instruction which God will give through the instrumentality of Israel. That He will make His judgment to rest is, more literally, 'I will make a place for My right.' Hence the Lord declares that His righteousness is near, that His salvation is gone forth, and that His arms will judge the nations, that is, they will come under the judgment which His arms will inflict.

But the result of the judgment is that the remaining nations who survive it, even the far distant isles, will rely upon His arm. For that which ministered judgment will subsequently act in mercy and salvation. Thus the might of God's power, represented by His arm, will be exercised in two great contrasting ways (*verse 5*).

Not only will sin exist during the Millennial age, the whole of the old creation has been defiled by it. The heavens are to vanish like smoke, the earth is to fall to pieces like a garment, and its inhabitants are to die out as if they were nothing (this seems to be the meaning of the phrase rendered " **in like manner** ") (*verse 6*). Cp. 2 Pet. 3: 13.

Those who are saved (these are comprehended in the phrase "My salvation") will never perish, and God's righteousness will stand for ever. And now, in a striking parallel between this passage and the one in 2 Peter, there follows an appeal to those who know God's righteousness and share it, " **the people in whose heart is My law** " (*verse 7*). In the Isaiah passage they are exhorted not to fear the reproach of mortals or to be alarmed at their revilings. The persecutors are to perish just as a garment is consumed by a moth and wool by a worm (*verse 8*). A Jewish proverb says that "the worm is brother to the moth." God uses little things to accomplish great ends, whether by way of judgment or for purposes of grace.

The order here is salvation and righteousness; in the preceding verse it was righteousness and salvation. The whole is in the chiasmic order; the order is reversed again in *verse 8*.

These promises must have aroused in the hearts of the faithful a longing for the promised salvation (*verse 9*). They knew that the arm of the Lord could bring it about. Was it not His arm that overthrew Pharaoh and his hosts? The mention of Rahab has reference to Egypt, and the dragon to Pharaoh himself, with an allusion doubtless to the power of Satan acting through him (*verse 10*). The Egyptians are vividly described as having been cut into pieces. Pharaoh himself was not drowned in the waters but was "pierced". The memory of past deliverance and the assurance of future deliverance call forth the vivid appeal, uttered three times, for the arm of the Lord to awake.

It is good for the soul to recall the mercies of God in days gone by, but it is needful not to be occupied merely with a retrospect, but to let the power of the hope do its purifying work. The double view strengthens the power of prayer, prayer not merely for deliverance but for what will accomplish the glory of God. This meets with a response on His part far exceeding the mere expectation of deliverance.

What follows is scarcely exceeded anywhere in Scripture in the beauty of its language and in the sweetness of the assurance given to God's people as to their future. It begins not with the word "Therefore", but with "And", connecting the promise with the appeal, not by way of conclusion but with the closer combination, expressing the assurance more directly and decisively: **"And the ransomed of the Lord shall return and come with singing unto Zion ; and everlasting joy shall be upon their heads : they shall obtain gladness and joy, and sorrow and sighing shall flee away "** (*verse 11*). All this speaks gloriously of the Millennial blessedness to be enjoyed by Israel. The prospect is enhanced and strengthened by the retrospect of past trials and sufferings.

So it is with the still brighter prospect that we enjoy who are members of the Church. Our present experiences of sore trial and affliction are brightened by the hope, a hope that "sweetens every bitter cup".

Verses 12–15 continue in a different way the comfort ministered by the Lord. Many of His people were in fear because of the oppressor, and doubtless in the coming day, in the time of

"Jacob's trouble", the oppression of the man of sin will tend to have a similar effect. To this time the present passage seems to point. The Lord speaks of Himself as their Comforter. This being so, what had they to fear? " **Who art thou,**" He says, **" that thou art afraid of man that shall die, and of the son of man which shall be made as grass** (lit., 'made a blade of grass')? " The tyranny of the Antichrist will be shortlived. The Lord has ever had His own way and time for delivering His earthly people.

Fear is the offspring of forgetfulness of God. The realization of the presence and power of the Lord is the all-sufficient antidote. Again and again the Lord reminds Israel that He was their Maker and that His power had stretched forth the heavens and laid the foundations of the earth. Why then should they continually stand in dread of the fury of the oppressor even when he was preparing to destroy?

The *14th verse* is rightly put in the R.V. as a promise: " **The captive exile** (lit., he that is bowed down, i.e., bound in fetters in prison) **shall speedily be loosed ; and he shall not die and go down into the pit, neither shall his bread fail.**" While the conquest of Babylon by Cyrus is probably immediately in view here, the prophecy will ultimately have its fulfilment in the coming time when Jews, suffering privation in exile among the nations under the Antichrist, will be set at liberty to come back to their land in recognition of their Redeemer Messiah.

The Lord pledges His all-sufficiency for this, in that He terrifies the sea when its waves roar, by putting His restraint upon it. That is probably the true meaning in *verse 15*. The Hebrew verb is the same as that rendered "rest" in verse 4. The reference here does not seem to be to the dividing of the sea when Israel was delivered from Egypt, but to the roaring of the waves which by His word are frightened into stillness. That is what the Lord did on Lake Galilee. The waters of the sea are interpreted in Scripture as symbolizing the restlessness and tossings of the nations. See Ps. 65: 7; 98: 7; Isa. 17: 12, 13; Ezek. 26: 3; Luke 21: 25, 26 and Rev. 17: 15. The greatest turmoil among the nations will prevail during the latter part of the rule of the man of sin, and especially at the time of the warfare of Armageddon. But the Lord will still that tempest by His Personal intervention.

Verse 16 tells how the Jews will become His messengers. He will put His words in their mouth (the perfect tense is prophetic).

He will cover them in the shadow of His hand, not only protecting them but equipping them for His purpose in view. This purpose is stated as follows: " **that I may plant the heavens and lay the foundations of the earth, and say unto Zion, Thou art My people.**" The last clause refers to Millennial conditions and accordingly the planting of the heavens and the founding of the earth may point to changed conditions in the universe when the Kingdom of righteousness and peace is established. For the forces of nature both in the heavens and the earth will not be used any more for the exercise of Divine judgments, as has often been the case and must again be so before the Lord comes in glory. There is doubtless also a reference to the new heavens and earth which are to be created hereafter.

The messenger of the Gospel may apply to himself the comfort of the assurance "I have put My words in thy mouth". He is "the Lord's messenger in the Lord's message"; his testimony is effectual only as he adheres to the truth of Scripture. Again, as His messenger he is under His protecting care, covered by the shadow of His hand, indicating the pleasure the Lord has in one who rightly ministers His truth.

The last paragraph of this chapter, beginning at *verse 17*, describes in vivid language the effects of the judgments inflicted upon the nation as a result of its persistent rebellion against God. Jerusalem is depicted as a woman lying on the ground in a state of helpless stupefaction through having drained to the dregs the cup of staggering, the cup of the fury of the Lord. Not one among all her sons was able to guide her or, taking her by the hand, to lift her up. Devastation, ruin, famine and the sword had come upon her, and the prophet himself, like Jeremiah in his lamentations, could not find how to comfort her. Her sons, instead of assisting her, were lying helpless at the corners of all the streets, like an antelope taken in a hunter's net and exhausted by vain struggles to be free (*vv. 18–20*).

Deliverance could come only from God, and in His pity and mercy He promises to bring it (*vv. 21–23*). He remembers that they are His people, and describes Himself as the One who pleads, or, rather, conducts, their cause as their Advocate or Defender. And inasmuch as the nations whom He has used, and

will yet use for the punishment of His people, overstep the limits
of the power committed to them, and, acting as the agents of
the evil one and priding themselves in their despotism, wreak
their vengeance upon His people, God will take " **the cup of
staggering, even the bowl of the cup of His fury** ", and will make
their tormentors drink it. They thought they would trample
upon the nation just as foes tread upon a street. God
reverses the position and brings human pride down to utter
degradation.

All this will yet be enacted in the coming time of "Jacob's
trouble", when Satan's efforts to destroy Israel reach their
height.

CHAPTER LII

AGAIN the call of the Lord comes to Zion to awake and put on
her strength and to Jerusalem to put on her beautiful garments.
Here, as in the two preceding instances, the call is the result of
what precedes. She has been in a state of utter prostration and
covered with dust, powerless under the fury of her enemies and
robbed of her royal and priestly robes, wearing instead the
chains of captivity around her neck. From all those who had
defiled and degraded her she would be delivered.

But she was not only to arise but was to take her seat in a
position of restful dignity and authority. Strangers will not be
allowed to pass through her any more (cp. Joel 3: 17; see also
Nahum 1: 15, where the R.V. rightly translates "the wicked
one", i.e., the Antichrist). Babylon has sat as a queen but would
be brought down to the dust; Jerusalem would be raised from
her dust and sit upon her throne of glory (*vv. 1, 2*).

The promises which follow in *vv. 3 to 6* are set, with their
comfort, in the background of past misery. The Lord's people
are reminded that they " **were sold for nought** " (R.V.), they
were handed over to Gentile powers; not that the Lord might
gain any advantage from that; His sole purpose was to bring
them to repentance under His chastening rod. No money would
be paid for their redemption. That would be accomplished by
His sovereign grace and almighty power. Their deliverance would
emanate from Himself solely and absolutely.

So with redemption from the power of sin and Satan.
Man can do nothing to effect it. It must be "according
to the riches of His grace" (Eph. 1: 7; Col. 1: 14; 1
Pet. 1: 18, 19).

As illustrations, the oppression of two Gentile powers is mentioned, Egypt and Assyria. For though the actual oppression is
recorded only of the latter, it is evidently intimated in regard
to the former, according to the principle of parallelism. Israel
went down to Egypt "at the first" (R.V.) simply to sojourn
there until the famine in Canaan was over. After their bondage,
their deliverance was wrought by the outstretched arm of the
Lord. They are reminded of this again and again throughout
their history. On the other hand, the Assyrians invaded their
territory and drove them into captivity as the instruments of
God's disciplinary dealings. Let them remember each case, now
that similar trouble had come upon them by Babylonian
aggression.

The rhetorical question asked by the Lord Himself in *verse 5*,
" What do I here ? ", has been interpreted in several ways.
The right meaning seems to be 'What advantage do I gain in
the midst of My people?', as is indicated by the next clause,
" seeing that My people is taken away for nought ". And then
as to the enemy themselves, "they that rule over them do howl".
This is not the howling of misery (that idea seems to have led
to the A.V. rendering "make them to howl"); here the verb
is used of the blustering war-cry of the oppressors and it was in
that spirit that the Name of the Lord was blasphemed continually
by them.

The shrieking and the blaspheming would be made to cease by
the direct power of God. The Name so despised by the Gentiles
will be made known to His people. His nature, character and
power as represented by His Name will be revealed to them in
the day of their redemption. His self-manifestation will cause
them to know the voice of their Redeemer; see 63: 1, where, in
answer to the astonished question of His people as to who He
is, He replies "I that speak in righteousness, mighty to save".
Here in *verse 6*, in view of that assured event, He says " Behold,
it is I", or, as in the margin, "Here I am". He will make known
not only the character of His Person and attributes, but His
very presence as their Deliverer.

This is how the Lord reveals Himself in our times of tribulation and difficulty. He uses such circumstances by way of increasing our knowledge of Himself, His character, His power and His grace. It is when we come to an end of ourselves that He makes Himself known to us. Wits' end corner provides the turning at which the Lord manifests to us not only our own helplessness but His almightiness. We may be like Peter, who, finding himself going down to a watery grave, cried out "Lord, save me". Christ planned the whole circumstance so that His ardent follower might know the strength of His arm and His power to do more than deliver. How often in the midst of the troubles of His disciples He said (that with which this passage in Isaiah ends) "It is I!"

Verses 7 to 10 consist of a triumphant exultation consequent upon the news of the great deliverance wrought for the Lord's people in the eyes of all nations. Wars will have been made to cease to the ends of the earth. Peace will prevail because God reigns and Jehovah is returning to Zion.

"**How beautiful upon the mountains are the feet of him** (or 'them'—the pronoun is collective) **that bringeth good tidings, that publisheth peace!**" The feet of the messengers are lovely to behold (not the sound of the footsteps but the appearance of their feet), beautiful not only because of their buoyant rapidity, but because of the rapture of heart which lends character to their movement, and the very nature of their errand.

The mountains are those of the Land, and especially those north of Jerusalem. What are natural obstacles are made highways for God's heralds. He has declared "I will make all My mountains a way". The world will cry "peace and safety" (1 Thess. 5: 3)—the old delusion, that man is his own saviour! Destruction will come upon them, confounding their politics and chasing away their cherished dreams. God's Christ alone can bring deliverance, and at His Coming the messengers publish "peace and salvation". Not the "safety" of an imagined security, but the salvation wrought by the arm of the Saviour Himself!

So it will be. But so it is now in respect of the messengers of the Gospel and its good news; and for this we have the confirmatory quotation in Rom. 10: 15, where "the mountains" is omitted, for the emblematic becomes the actual in the Gospel. The Apostle exults in that in which he was himself such an assiduous messenger! And it is ours to share in the activity and the joy. The feet of one who goes forth with the evangel, at home or abroad, are lovely in the sight of Him who died to provide both the message and the messengers.

There are three blessings pronounced in the message, *peace, good,* and *salvation; peace* with God through the blood of Christ, instead of alienation; *good,* that which benefits and profits, instead of evil, the blighting effect of sin; *salvation,* which not only saves from death and judgment, but ministers continual preservation, with its eternal realization, instead of doom and eternal perdition.

The "watchmen" (or watchers) in *verse 8,* who " **lift up the voice together** ", rejoicing with singing, are the prophets (Isaiah himself being one), like those who look out into the distance as from a watch-tower. They are distinct from the messengers just mentioned, who will bear the news of the Kingdom when Christ's Millennial reign is ushered in. Contrast the blind watchmen, the false prophets, in 56: 10. These faithful watchers, who saw future events from afar, are described in 1 Pet. 1: 10–12. Cp. Isa. 21: 8, 11 and Hab. 2: 1–3.

The day is coming when they will " **see, eye to eye, when** (or, rather, 'how') **Jehovah returns to Zion** ", lit., 'makes Zion to return' (the same construction as in Ps. 85: 4). They will see the Lord restoring Zion, as vividly as one person is to another when he looks straight into his eyes (see Num. 14: 14, R.V. marg.). No wonder they will join in a chorus of praise. Those who foretold these things apart from one another during the course of many centuries will, in one great company and in bodily presence, utter their joy before Him who has been the great Subject of these prophecies.

In *verse 9* the ruins of Jerusalem are called upon to do the same. The language is vivid, it visualizes and depicts the glory of restoration after the long periods of desolation: " **Break forth into jubilation, join in singing, ye ruins of Jerusalem.**" And the reason is twofold, God's word and work: the word of consolation, " **The Lord hath comforted His people** "; the work of delivering power, " **He hath redeemed Jerusalem** ". His word has been carried out in act. "Jesus . . . was mighty in deed and word" (Luke 24: 19). Moses "was mighty in his words and works" (Acts 7: 22). Cp. 2 Thess. 2: 17.

Comfort and deliverance, these are the constant ministration of the Holy Spirit in our sorrows and distresses, our trials and dangers: comfort *amidst* them, deliverance *from* them! We may rejoice in the consolation, and be confident of the deliverance.

Verse 10 first looks back from future fulfilment. " **Jehovah hath made bare His holy arm in the eyes of all the nations.**" The metaphor is that of a warrior, removing all coverings and accoutrements from his arm so as to exert his power to the utmost. The foolish misconceptions the nations have had about God will be mightily dispelled. Their refusal to acknowledge the Person, facts and claims of His Son will meet the force of His direct interposition. "**All the ends of the earth shall see the salvation of our God.**"

Verses 11 and 12 deal with another side of the circumstances, and give a view of the setting free of the exiles. They are bidden to go out from the scene of their captivity. The language of the command bears reference to Babylon, but Babylon here stands for more than the city itself, it speaks of world conditions, as the preceding context shows. They are commanded to touch no unclean thing. They are not to take with them the Babylonish gods, as they did when they took of the spoils of Egypt. The vessels they are to carry home are "**the vessels of the Lord**". This points to the return under the decree of Cyrus, when the vessels taken by Nebuchadnezzar were to be restored (Ezra 1: 7–11). Again, unlike the exodus from Egypt, they would not go out in haste nor by flight. Their attitude, instead of that of fugitives, was to be one of complete preparedness for the resumption of the worship of the Lord in His Temple. For this the requisite is absolute purity.

Yet they would need His guidance and protection, and of this they are assured: "**for Jehovah will go before you ; and the God of Israel will be your rearward.**"

All this has its direct messages for those who, themselves vessels, set apart to the Lord for His use (2 Tim. 2: 21), have a holy responsibility to keep themselves unspotted from the world, and to cleanse themselves "from all defilement of flesh and spirit, perfecting holiness in the fear of the Lord". And as to the promises, all that is here assured and much more, is gathered up in the pledge, "I will be to you a Father, and ye shall be to Me sons and daughters, saith the Lord Almighty." The relationship Divinely established at the new birth finds its practical expression on His part in our experiences and circumstances in a manner impossible if the condition is not fulfilled.

CHAPTER LII 13-15 and CHAPTER LIII

THE division into chapters requires that what is marked as chapter 53 should begin here. These three verses and the twelve which are marked as chapter 53 comprise one great theme of the suffering, rejected, atoning and exalted Servant of Jehovah. The opening words " Behold, My Servant " speak not of Israel but of Messiah, as in 50: 10.

The connection with what has just preceded is significant. Deliverance from captivity has just been in view, deliverance from Babylon, and deliverance yet future and final. Babylon itself was not actually mentioned and is not spoken of again in Isaiah.

Deliverance can be wrought alone by Jehovah's Servant, whether for Jew or Gentile. So the Lord calls attention to Him, first to His prosperous dealing, then to His exalted position itself (*verse 13*). There follows a brief mention of His humiliation as antecedent to the coming manifestation of His power and glory (*vv. 14, 15*). And all this, in its condensed form, is the very theme which, having been thus introduced, is expanded in the twelve following verses.

" Behold, My Servant shall deal wisely." Two meanings are contained in this word, wisdom (one feature of which is prudence) and prosperity. These might be combined in a fuller rendering, 'shall deal wisely, with consequent prosperity.' Strikingly this describes His life on earth, in all that He said and did, with its prosperous effects, and in maintaining His testimony without surrendering His life till the appointed hour. No greater

prosperity ever accrued from any act than from the giving up
of that life in His voluntary and atoning sacrifice.

"**He shall be exalted and lifted up, and shall be very high.**"
Three stages are in view, His Resurrection (the word rendered
"exalted" signifies to rise up in exaltation), His Ascension (the
thought is that of a glorious ascent), and His position at the
right hand of God (see Acts 2: 33; Phil. 2: 9; Heb. 1: 3 and 13).

"**Like as many were astonied at Thee** (with the change from
a statement of fact concerning Him to an utterance addressed
to Him; cp. ch. 49, vv. 7, 8) . . . **so shall He startle** (R.V. marg.)
many nations." The similarity of the verbs in these corresponding statements is to be noted. In the degradation and disfigure-
ment which man inflicted on Him many were astonished; in the
coming manifestation of His glory He will astonish (cause to
leap and tremble in astonishment) many nations; "startle" is
the meaning here, not "sprinkle" (as the grammatical phraseology
makes clear).

The fact that "**His visage was so marred more than any man,
and His form more than the sons of men**" was the cause of the
astonishment of those who beheld Him. The soldiers hit Him
with a mock sceptre one after another on his face and His thorn-
crowned brow, till His features were unrecognizable. The form
of scourging administered was that by means of which the flesh
was cut away from breast as well as back. So Psalm 22: 17 foretold: "I may tell all My bones; they look and stare upon Me."

In the coming Day the astonishment at His power and glory
will be so great that kings will be overpowered into speechlessness,
struck dumb at the sight of what they had never heard of. More
still, they will be made to grasp the reality and significance of
the stupendous manifestation: "**that which they had not heard
shall they understand.**"

There follows immediately the reason why they had not heard.
The cause lay with Israel. They (not the prophet) are the mourning and repentant speakers in the next verse. They acknowledge
with lamentation their unbelief. As a nation they had refused
to believe the message proclaimed to them. That is the meaning
of the rhetorical question rendered in our Versions, "**Who hath
believed our report?**" (*verse 1*). See the R.V. margin. The word
rendered "report", means that which was heard, that which was
declared, and the reference is to the Gospel preached at Pentecost
and afterwards, which was persistently rejected by the nation.

Witness Paul's protests and lament, Acts 13: 46; 18: 6; 28: 28; Rom. 9: 1; 11: 7, 8; 1 Thess. 2: 14–18.

So with the manifestation of God's power in Christ: " **to whom hath the arm of the Lord been revealed ?** " is a prophetic question expressing the confession to be made in the coming day of repentance, that Israel had in its unbelief failed to recognize what God had wrought in raising Christ from the dead. All that follows is a full acknowledgment to be made of the great facts concerning Him when the nation is restored.

They did not realize that " **He grew up before Him** (Jehovah) **as a tender plant, and as a root** (a sprouting root) **out of a dry ground** " (*verse 2*).

The pleasantness of Christ in the eyes of Jehovah, in the days of His childhood and growth into manhood, as a tender twig and the verdant shoot, is set in contrast with the barren and enslaved condition of the nation.

They saw nothing in His appearance to make them feel naturally attracted to Him, nothing of comeliness or beauty to delight their natural senses. On the contrary, " **He was despised and rejected of men ; a man of sorrows, and acquainted with grief** " (*verse 3*). The special meaning of the word rendered "grief" is sickness, or disease. The former clause marks His life as one characterized by the inward smart of experiencing the effects of the sins and sorrows of those around Him; the latter clause marks Him as One uniquely capable of complete acquaintance with various forms of illness.

The latter part of the verse expresses still more strongly the attitude of the people as a whole. It shows the character of their despisings: " **and as one from whom men hide their face He was despised, and we esteemed Him not.**" Men hide the face from, or turn away from, that which is considered unbearable to behold. Their estimate of Him is put very strongly; they regarded Him as nothing. All this records the depths of remorse with which the nation hereafter will recall their attitude shown Him in the days of His flesh.

In *verses 4 to 6*, they enter into the subject more deeply, confessing that His sufferings were of quite a different nature from what they had supposed them to be. The sufferings of the Cross are now in view.

The change of their ideas is marked by the opening word " **Surely** " or " **Verily** ". The statement " **He hath borne our** griefs, and carried our sorrows," expresses more fully what was mentioned in the preceding verse as to His being a man of sorrows and acquainted with grief. It tells how the Lord bore in His own Person sufferings which were other than His own. Matthew quotes this in connection with His deeds of healing and deliverance (Matt. 8: 16, 17). Yet that statement does not speak of His making a substitutionary atonement.

Verse 4 takes us directly to the Cross, for only to that could the statement apply, " **yet we did esteem Him stricken, smitten of God, and afflicted.**" In their blindness they looked upon His sufferings as the punishment of His own sins, which they must have regarded as especially great.

But now, under the power of the revelation of the great facts, there comes an entire reversal of their opinions. This is marked in a special way by the series of emphatic personal pronouns in the plural in what follows. " **But He was wounded for our transgressions, He was bruised for our iniquities: the chastisement of our peace was upon Him** " (*verse 5*).

The words rendered "wounded" (or pierced) and "bruised" are the strongest terms to describe a violent and agonizing death. There is stress on the "our" in both statements. The chastisement which was administered to Him by God was that which makes for our peace (the word *shalom* is comprehensive and describes not simply a peaceful state, but well-being in general); " **and with His stripes we are healed** "—not the Roman scourging; the margin gives the literal rendering, "bruise". So in the Sept., and see 1 Pet. 2: 24, margin. The expression conveys in condensed form the stroke of Divine judgment inflicted upon Him. The healing, the spiritual soundness which we receive, is expressly set in direct contrast to the bruising or Divine stroke to which He submitted.

Now comes the climax of conscience-stricken admission on the part of the penitent nation: "**All we like sheep have gone astray, we have turned every one to his own way,**" and then the grateful realization and recognition of the tremendous fact, " **and Jehovah hath laid on Him the iniquity of us all** " (*verse 6*).

What the nation will hereafter acknowledge is true of the whole human race. Man has substituted his own will for God's will. Being granted the power of self-determination, a feature which, among others, marks him as made in the image of God.

he has used that power to go "his own way" and make himself
ego-centric instead of God-centric.

In this universal condition of guilt and misery the grace of
God has interposed. Sending His own Son "in the likeness of
sinful flesh and as an offering for sin" (Rom. 8: 3, R.V.), He
made to meet upon Him the whole weight of our iniquity and
the righteous wrath due to it.

The third paragraph, *verses 7 to 9*, describes His sufferings,
death and burial. "**He was oppressed** ('treated unsparingly'),
yet He humbled Himself (i.e., He suffered voluntarily) **and opened
not His mouth; as a lamb that is led to the slaughter, and as
a sheep that before her shearers is dumb; yea, He opened not
His mouth.**" This all expresses His voluntary endurance and is
apparently set in striking antithesis to the straying away, in
the first part of verse 6.

The scene passes next to the unrighteous judicial verdict passed
upon Him, and from thence direct to Calvary. "**By oppression
and judgment** (a hendiadys, i.e., one sentiment conveyed by two
expressions, here signifying 'by an oppressive judicial sentence')
He was taken away (Matt. 26: 66; 27: 22-31, and see Acts 8: 33,
which translates the Sept.), **and as for His generation, who**
among them **considered that He was cut off out of the land of
the living? for the transgression of my people was He stricken,**"
or 'was the stroke upon Him.' This is preferable to the R.V.
margin, "to whom the stroke was due." The stress of the
passage is what Christ endured.

This section, which has described the character of His sufferings
and the manner of His death, closes with a statement as to His
burial: "**And they** (R.V.; i.e., 'His generation') **made His grave
with the wicked** ('with sinners'), **and with the rich** ('a rich man')
in His death." The first part of this would seem to refer to the
intention of the rulers, who would have had Him ignominiously
buried with the two robbers. The Roman authorities, however,
granted the body to Joseph of Arimathæa, the "rich man"
(Matt. 27: 57).

The Hebrew word rendered "death" is in the plural; this is
expressive of the violent character, not to say the comprehensive
nature, of His death.

In what follows, the A.V. rendering "**because He had done
no violence, neither was any deceit in His mouth**" is probably

correct, rather than the R.V., "although. . . ." The clause is to be connected with what immediately precedes. The fact of His freedom from sin made it fitting that He should receive an honourable burial, instead of being cast into a criminal's grave, to which his enemies would have committed Him.

The last section of the chapter gives a threefold testimony concerning the experiences of His soul. We are taken into the inner sanctuary of His Being. Again, *verses 10 and 12* speak of the dealings of Jehovah with Him, judicially in respect of His death and compensatingly in respect of His reward. *Verse 11* speaks of the outcome of His Sacrifice in His own satisfaction therein and the justifying grace He ministers to others.

The statement " **Yet it pleased the Lord to bruise Him** " speaks of the determinate counsel of Jehovah in causing man's sin to be subservient to the actings of His grace, in the suffering inflicted upon His sinless Servant on the Cross. That He " **put Him to grief** " speaks of the extreme distress brought upon Him.

What follows is probably rightly rendered as in the margin: " **When His soul shall make an offering for sin,** " i.e., a trespass offering, a sacrifice offered to God with the effect of clearing the sinner from his guilt. The sin-offering was presented by the priest from the point of view of the offerer, but the trespass-offering had especially in view the demands of God's justice. That is what is indicated here. This is the first of the three statements as to His soul.

This voluntary act of surrendering His life (a life with which God was ineffably pleased) to meet God's righteous demands concerning man's guilt, is shown to have the following results (*in verses 10–12*) relating to Christ Himself:

(1) " **He shall see His seed** ". An Israelite was regarded as conspicuously blessed if he had a numerous posterity, and especially if he lived to see them (Gen. 48: 11; Ps. 128; 6). Here then we have an intimation of the exceeding joy of. Christ in seeing the results of His sacrifice in the countless multitude of His spiritual posterity from among Jew and Gentile.

(2) " **He shall prolong His days,** " another blessing regarded as a high favour among Israelites (cp. Ps. 91: 16; Prov. 3: 2, 16). Here, however, the reference is to the unending resurrection life of the Lord, and to the joy that breathes through His

words "I was dead, and behold I am alive for evermore"
(Rev. 1: 18).

(3) " The pleasure of the Lord shall prosper in His hand."
That is to say, the predeterminate counsels of God shall have
their joyous realization. The phrase "in His hand" points to
His Mediatorial and High Priestly work, as well as to the exercise
of His authority and power in His Kingdom.

(4) " He shall see of the travail of His soul, and shall be
satisfied." This is the second mention of the soul of Christ in
the passage. All the glory that follows and will follow will be
viewed by Him as the outcome of His atoning sufferings, which
will never cease to be present to His mind as the all necessary
and all sufficient means by which His heart is satisfied in the
redemption of those that have become His own possession. This
is true both in the progressive work of saving grace and in its
entire fulfilment when the Church is complete and Israel is
saved.

(5) " By His knowledge shall My righteous Servant justify
many." There is stress upon the word "righteous". There
could be no justification for others, no reckoning of righteousness,
were it not for His flawless righteousness, by which alone He was
competent to render Himself voluntarily as a propitiatory
Sacrifice.

The phrase translated "by His knowledge" may be rendered
in two ways, either "by knowledge of Him" or "by His own
knowledge". Regarding the former, to know Him is life eternal
(John 17: 3; 1 John 5: 20; cp. 2 Pet. 1: 3); this is the objective
sense. The other is the subjective. In chapter 11: 2, one of
the seven spirits which were foretold as resting upon Christ is
"the spirit of knowledge". Again, one of the qualifications of a
priest is that his lips keep knowledge (Mal. 2: 7), so that people
may seek the law at his mouth. Further, in Matt. 11: 27 the
Lord says that knowledge of the Father belongs only to Himself
and "to whomsoever the Son willeth to reveal Him". In the
whole passage both the priestly and the mediatorial work of
Christ is unfolded as well as the prospect of His regal glory
(see 52: 15 and 53: 12). Because of what He is in His own Person
as well as in this threefold office, and because of His absolute
knowledge as the Son of God, He would effect the justification
of many. That is to say, He would make righteous all that come
unto God by Him. But only on the ground of His vicarious

sacrifice, and this is why the statement **"And He shall bear their iniquities "** immediately follows. By reason of this He is an eternal Priest, qualified to dispense all that accrues from His offering.

There yet remains another glorious effect of His sacrificial death. Jehovah will **" divide Him a portion with the great, and He shall divide the spoil with the strong."** The Sept. renders it, "I will give Him the mighty for a portion." The thought is not that of dividing into portions, but of assigning. "The great" and "the strong" are general terms, and do not specify particular individuals; they do not refer to specially prominent persons or those who are mightier than others, but to all who by reason of faithful adherence to His will are to be made sharers in His regal authority when His Kingdom is established.

The Father and the Son co-operate, and the Son will "divide the spoil with the strong". The latter are mentioned in Ps. 110: 3 as volunteers in the day of His power, partaking with Him of the spoils of His triumph. The Sept. renders this second statement, "He shall divide the spoils of the mighty" suggesting His triumph over His foes, and this meaning is accepted by many.

Again we are directed to the foundation work of His atoning sacrifice. The very establishment of His sovereign power in the earth will rest upon that finished work. It is here finally set forth in four statements. All the future glory, all that will accrue by way of reward to the faithful is because (1) **" He poured out His soul unto death "**; (2) **" He was numbered with the transgressors "**; (3) **" He bare the sin of many "**; (4) **" He made intercession for the transgressors."** The last two of these are set in striking contrast to the fact that He was numbered with the transgressors, and this is accurately set forth by the R.V. "yet" instead of "and". The former points to the unrighteous opinion of those who pronounced sentence upon Him and handed Him over to execution. Little did they realize that in what He endured on the Cross He was Himself the sin-bearer, and the closing statement refers especially to His intercessory prayer while He was being nailed to the tree. Then it was that He made intercession for the transgressors.

For the third time mention is made of His soul, and now in connection with His own act in pouring out His soul unto death. Concerning this He Himself said "I lay down My life for the sheep" and "I lay down My life that I may take it again. No one taketh it away from Me, but I lay it down of Myself. I have power to lay it down, and I have power to take it again" (John 10: 15, 17, 18).

The details of this prophecy in chapter 53 grow in vividness and reach a climax in these last three verses.

CHAPTER LIV

CHAPTER 54 bursts out in exultation after the prophecies of the sufferings, sin-bearing and glory of the Servant of Jehovah in chapter 53. Israel is called upon to rejoice with singing and shouting, as her state of barrenness would yield place to fruitfulness. The experiences of their ancestress Sarah had been a foreshadowing of this. The desolate condition of the people and their land was not to last indefinitely. Jehovah had not divorced her. The time will come when she will no more be termed "Forsaken" neither will the land be termed "Desolate", for " **as the bridegroom rejoiceth over the bride** ", so will God rejoice over her (62: 4, 5) and her children will be more numerous than they were before she became desolate (*verse 1*).

She is therefore bidden to broaden out her tent and stretch out the curtains of her habitations, to lengthen her cords and strengthen her stakes, language metaphorically setting forth the extension of her territory so that there may be room for the increased population.

Accordingly the promise is given her, " **thou shalt spread abroad on the right hand and on the left; and thy seed shall possess the nations, and make the desolate cities to be inhabited** " (*verse 3*). The right hand and the left stands for both the south and the north, as in Gen. 15: 18, Egypt and the Euphrates; also for the east and the west (see Gen. 28: 14). There will be much more in the coming time than what was enjoyed in the reign of Solomon. They are to become the head of the nations, ruling over those who oppressed them (see Micah 4: 1-3). Cities desolated by war and pillage will become populous. Israel, repentant and converted, will then be the meek who shall inherit the earth.

Such are the Lord's ways. Enlargement follows curtailment when His chastening hand has done its work. When the disciplined soul learns to realize more fully what was accomplished at Calvary and bows in self-judgment before Him, spiritual enlargement is sure to result. Fruitfulness, which has suffered through impoverishment of soul, bursts forth in abundance, for the glory of the Lord and for the enrichment and blessing of others.

The passage that follows from *verse 4* onwards is full of the tenderest promises and comfort, telling out the lovingkindness of the Lord, His covenant mercies, and the glorious future in store for the nation. Israel is no longer to fear, for she will not be put to shame. She is exhorted not to be confounded (or rather, as it may be rendered, 'to bid defiance to reproach'). Her future will be so delightful that she will 'forget the shame of her youth', the time when she was in bondage in Egypt. There she was like a virgin, but Jehovah who redeemed her betrothed her to Himself with a covenant of love (see Jer. 2: 2 and Ezek. 16: 60). She shall no more remember the reproach of her widowhood, the time when she endured Babylonian captivity, and was like a widow. She was not really so (cp. Jer. 51: 5), for her Husband was none other than her Maker (*verse 5*). He who had become her Husband was the One who brought her into existence, and He is " **the Lord of hosts** ", the One whose bidding the hosts above fulfil. In the Hebrew the words for Maker and Husband are plural, alike with *Elohim*, "God", the last Divine title in the verse; they are thus expressive of the fulness of the relation and of His creatorial power.

Again, her Redeemer, the Holy One of Israel, is described as " **the God of the whole earth** ", indicating that the power to assist her belongs to Him and will be exercised because of the relation of love in which she stands to Him.

The relation had suffered a kind of disillusion, but Jehovah will yet call her back to Himself, " **as a wife forsaken and grieved in spirit, even a wife of youth, when she is cast off** " (*verse 6*). Wonderful is the restoring grace of God. He calls Israel back to Himself as a husband receives back the wife he loved in his youth. She has displeased Him, but she was not as one hated. On the contrary, the Lord regards the time in which He had forsaken her, the time of her captivity, as " a small moment " (verse 7).

The time of her captivity in the east had seemed long to the captives, and this is especially evinced in the intercessory prayer and supplications made by Daniel, who realized the terrible nature of God's disciplinary dealings in the time of the forsaking. See Daniel 9 and Jeremiah's Lamentations. Jeremiah says, "Wherefore dost Thou forget us forever, and forsake us so long time?" (Lam. 5: 20). Viewing the still longer period from the unalterable character of His mercy, God speaks of it as a moment. He says " with great mercies will I gather thee " (vv. 7, 8).

At the beginning of verse 8 the R.V. rightly renders the phrase " In overflowing wrath," that is, in the gushing forth of indignation. It is with this that His " everlasting kindness " is set in contrast. The Lord then gives a pledge that He will never again be wroth with Israel or rebuke her. Similarly, He says, He pledged Himself to Noah and His descendants that He would never cut off all the flesh again by the waters of a flood. Just as the already existent rainbow was then set as a token of a covenant between Himself and the earth and every living creature, so now He speaks of His "covenant of peace" as that which will never be removed, and conveys the assurance that likewise, even when the mountains have departed and the hills have been removed, His kindness shall never depart from Israel. For He is " the Lord that hath mercy on thee " (verse 10).

Just as Noah and his family came forth into a new world after the deluge, so after "the great tribulation" will God's redeemed earthly people come forth to Millennial blessedness. "Weeping may tarry (or come in to lodge) for the night, but joy cometh in the morning" (Ps. 30: 5, where God's anger is said to last "but for a moment", just as here in Isa. 54: 7, 8; cp. 2 Cor. 4: 17).

Thus does the Lord, while administering the necessary unjoyous chastening of His people, fix His heart and keep His eye upon the "peaceable fruit of righteousness". Never does He cease to have our highest and best interests in view.

From verse 11 to the end of the chapter the future glory and happiness of God's earthly people is described in a beautiful

variety of ways, which serve to set forth the coming deliverance
and its issues in contrast to their present woes. This latter
condition He describes in tender terms: " **O thou afflicted,
tossed with tempest, and not comforted** " (*verse 11*). The tempest expresses the fury of Gentile powers in their Satanically
inspired determination to crush Israel to the uttermost. Of
Jerusalem, which at the height of the storm will become the
centre of the world's last great war, He says " **I will set thy
stones in fair colours, and lay thy foundations with sapphires.
And I will make thy pinnacles** (or minarets, not 'windows', A.V.)
of rubies, and thy gates of carbuncles, and all thy border (R.V.)
of pleasant stones." All this represents the reflection of the
glory of God Himself. The jewels which God has hidden in the
earth, and which man has unearthed for purposes of his own
avarice and self-glorification, have been designed for the purpose
of setting forth the glory of Christ's attributes and character,
and while they will be literally used to beautify the earthly
Jerusalem, they will thereby be a continuous reminder and token
to God's people of the glories and grace of Christ their Redeemer.

So the twelve precious stones, set in the breastplate of the
high priest of old, set forth the glory and grace of Christ in His
High Priestly ministry. And as from that breastplate the words
of light and instruction were given for the impartation of the
mind of the Lord to His people, so in the coming day the natural
glory of Jerusalem, instead of ministering to human pride, will
convey the mind and will of God as revealed in the Messiah.

This is what is immediately promised, for *verse 13* says: "**And
all thy children shall be taught of the Lord ; and great shall be
the peace of thy children.**" That is to say, they will all be
disciples (see the R.V. margin). They will not need human
instruction. This promise Christ Himself quoted when He said
to the murmuring Jews: "Every one that hath heard from the
Father, and hath learned, cometh unto Me," John 6: 45. The
two words in that verse in the original, "taught of God", are
combined into one adjective in 1 Thess. 4: 9, lit., 'God-taught'.
Just as believers are taught of God to love one another, so in
Israel, as those who will be 'taught of the Lord', love will
characterize them all. It naturally follows that peace will prevail. For where love is in exercise joy and peace inevitably
exist (cp. Col. 3: 14, 15).

All this is the outcome of the knowledge of the Lord. Israel will not need to teach every man his neighbour and every man his brother, saying, "know the Lord": for they will all know Him "from the least to the greatest" (Jer. 31: 34). But all this happiness will be enjoyed on the basis of Divine righteousness: **" in righteousness shalt thou be established,"** *verse 14* (see chapt. 11: 5).

No longer will foes oppress them. They will be far from oppression. They are not to fear a repetition of their troubles. They are to be far from terror; it will not come near them again. Their enemies may gather together, but all who dare to do so will fall because of them. Jerusalem will be invincible (*verse 15*). God has created the smith who blows the coal fire and produces a weapon for his work (or 'according to his trade'); He has also created the waster (or destroyer) to destroy (*verse 16*). The very creative power of Jehovah is to be used to defend His people. Accordingly no weapon formed against them shall prosper. And then, just as every hostile weapon fails, so Jerusalem, quickened into the knowledge of the Lord, and therefore conscious of its Divine right, will convict every accuser as guilty and therefore subject to punishment. **" Every tongue that shall rise against thee in judgment thou shalt condemn "** (*verse 17*).

The closing statement of the chapter sums up all the preceding promises, and describes them as **" the heritage of the servants of Jehovah "**. What is the rightful reward of the great Servant of Jehovah in His exaltation, is differently described in respect of His servants, for their heritage is of grace. And whereas He is Himself "Jesus Christ the righteous", the righteousness granted to His people is likewise a matter of grace: **" their righteousness is of Me, saith Jehovah."** That is how Jerusalem is to be established. Israel will not be able to claim anything of this by their own merit, any more than we can who are "justified freely by His grace through the redemption that is in Christ Jesus".

CHAPTER LV

THE prophet now issues an invitation to come and partake of the spiritual provision made by the Lord for those who are willing to turn from their own devices and activities and listen diligently to His voice. The invitation is to "**every one that thirsteth**", and the provision made consists not of the material benefits of water, wine and milk. These are metaphorically used of higher things than the natural products. The spiritual significance of water has been mentioned in 44: 3, where the reference is to the Holy Spirit, as in John 7: 38. Similarly in regard to wine (see 25: 6, 7). So we must understand the mention of milk (see 1 Pet. 2: 2, where the reference is to the Word of God). In Scripture the Spirit of God and the Word of God are often associated.

Moreover, the purchase is to be made "**without money and without price**" (*verse 1*). This is all of Divine grace. The possession of the spiritual blessings is, from the point of view of the recipients, dependent solely upon a sense of need and a readiness to accept them.

With this invitation we may compare the words of the parable in Matt. 22: 4, and the contrast, expressed in *verse 2* of this fifty-fifth chapter, reminds us of the contrast between grace and works in Rom. 11: 6. The paradox of buying without money is suggestive of spiritual bankruptcy. Israel was spending money and labour upon idols. Hence the solemn appeal of the opening word of the chapter; for the exclamation "Ho" is not simply a matter of invitation, it casts a reflection upon the state of those who are adopting their own devices instead of listening to the voice of the Lord.

The Lord follows His remonstrance with the gracious words "**hearken diligently unto Me, and eat ye that which is good, and let your soul delight itself in fatness**" (*verse 2*). Often in Scripture where two commands are given the second suggests the good result of obeying the first (cp. Gen. 42: 18).

The satisfaction of the soul can be obtained only in the path of the obedience of faith. By diligently listening to the voice of God and fulfilling His will we can enjoy real spiritual delight. Moreover, what the Lord here holds out is something more than meeting our need. He designs to give us an overflowing satisfaction. This is indicated by the word "fatness"; see, for instance, Pss. 36: 8 and 63: 5. This is "the riches of His grace".

He now bids His people to incline their ear and come unto Him, to hear, that their soul may live (*verse 3*) or revive (cp.

John 14: 6). Much the same thing was said later to the church in Laodicea. In such conditions the Lord calls upon the individual to hear His voice (Rev. 3: 20), and the provision He makes for the responsive heart is to find in Him the very life and sustenance of the soul.

There is much in these first three verses of the chapter that affords matter for a Gospel message, but the appeal is directly to the backslider, whose soul needs the reviving that can be effected only by returning to the Lord.

"And I will make," He says, " an everlasting covenant with you, even the sure mercies of David." In human affairs a covenant is made and ratified by each of the parties to it. Here the Lord undertakes the obligations Himself, and the covenant is virtually a promise. So in Gal 3: 17, 18, where "covenant" and "promise" are used interchangeably. Moreover, the Greek word there used, *diathēkē*, does not in itself contain the idea of joint obligation, it denotes that which is undertaken by one alone. The sole condition for the recipient is that he shall incline his ear and come. He will not thereby be putting his signature to a covenant; his acceptance of the invitation ensures the fulfilment of the "covenant of promise".

The phrase "the sure mercies of David" receives its interpretation in Acts 13: 34, which quotes from the Septuagint: "I will give you the holy and sure *blessings* (lit., things) of David." Paul uses this as the second of three quotations from the O.T. to prove that they were fulfilled in the Person of Christ, the first foretelling His birth (verse 33, see the R.V.; there the raising up of Jesus speaks of His being raised up in the nation, in His life on earth, cp. verse 23), the second foretelling His resurrection, the third His incorruptibility. What God promised to David (e.g., in 2 Sam. 7: 16), and will yet be fulfilled to him in the future earthly Kingdom, can be established in that day only in and through the Person of Christ Himself, by reason of His resurrection and exaltation, and in the glory of His Millennial reign.

David was, and yet will be, God's appointed " witness to the peoples " (the nations), and their " leader and commander " (see Ezek. 34: 24; 37: 24). Israel, possessed of worldwide dominion, will 'call a nation that they knew not' (referring to

Gentile peoples in general), and the nation that knew not Israel
will run to them (indicative of swift means of travel), 'because
of Jehovah their God', and " for the Holy One of Israel ".
Now there is no such reciprocal recognition; the opposite is the
case. But in the day of Messiah's reign, Israel will be glorified
by Him (*vv. 4, 5*). In *verse 6* there is a general appeal: " Seek
ye the Lord while He may be found, call ye upon Him while
He is near."

What follows is an appeal to the backslider; he is called upon
to forsake his way and his thoughts, and to return unto the
Lord. A return implies the retracing of one's steps to that
which was formerly enjoyed. The unregenerate man can turn,
but a return is for him who has gone back from that fellowship
with God which he once experienced. He waits to have mercy
upon him and to 'pardon abundantly' (lit., 'He will multiply
to pardon'), *verse 7*.

The foregoing appeal to forsake their own way and thoughts,
and, by returning to God, to yield themselves to Him, is urged
by reason of the fact of the utter difference between the ways
and thoughts of God and the self-willed and foolish ways and
thoughts of men (*vv. 8, 9*). Cp. 40: 27; 49: 14.

The waywardness of the backslider plunges him into unbelief and misery. He finds that his purposes are frustrated by
a mightier power than his, and the thorny path that he has
chosen brings him into spiritual gloom and uncertainty.

To all this God sets His actings and decrees in striking contrast.
Just as He has absolute control over the rain and the snow and
the produce of the earth, and man can do nothing to alter that
which God has established by His creative power, " so shall
My word be," He says, " that goeth forth out of My mouth:
it shall not return unto Me void (or, fruitless), but it shall accomplish (or, 'till it has accomplished') that which I please, and it
shall prosper in (or, 'has prosperously carried out') the thing
whereto I sent it". That is to say, it will not return without
having achieved the purpose for which the Lord sent it (*vv.
10, 11*).

His Word is His messenger (see 9: 8; Pss. 107: 20; 147:
15–19). His Word is here personified. It runs like a swift

messenger, accomplishing God's will with its vital power both in nature and amidst humanity. A word is the expression of thought. It is part of the person himself. So Christ is called the Word of God. He has declared Him (told Him out), John 1: 18. "Every thing that proceedeth out of the mouth of the Lord" provides spiritual food by which man lives (Deut. 8: 3). Just as what comes from the soil of the earth is produced by the rain and the snow, so with the soil of the human heart and the Word of God.

How great a responsibility therefore devolves upon one who is God's messenger! If the messenger's heart is in full communion with the One who sends him, his message will accomplish God's pleasure and prosper in the object for which it is sent.

In *verse 12* the Lord graciously applies the principles relating to His Word to the promise of unspeakable blessing for Israel in the coming day. " **For ye shall go out with joy**", that is to say, life's activities will be carried on without the haste of fear (cp. 52: 12), " **and be led forth with peace** " : they will never again have to fight their way through foes or flee from them: " **the mountains and the hills shall break forth before you into singing, and all the trees of 'the field shall clap their hands.**" Nature will be brought into unison with God's purposes of grace towards His people. Cp. Ps. 98: 8, where the clapping of the hands is applied to streams and billows of water. There will be a sympathy, so to speak, between nature and the joyous hearts of God's redeemed. No longer will the natural creation be subjected to vanity. The creation itself "shall be delivered from the bondage of corruption into the liberty of the glory of the children of God" (Rom. 8: 21, R.V.).

" **Instead of the thorn shall come up the fir tree** (or cypress), **and instead of the brier shall come up the myrtle tree,**" a humble, sweet-smelling, beautiful evergreen; from the Hebrew word for it comes the name Hadassah, the original name of Esther (Esth. 2: 7): " **and it shall be to the Lord for a name, for an everlasting sign** (or memorial) **that shall not be cut off** " (*verse 13*). What God will bring about in the blessedness of the Millennial Kingdom will have a twofold effect: it will tell forth His glory and will be a constant reminder to His people of His attributes and actings of grace and power.

CHAPTER LVI

THE opening words of this chapter, " **Keep ye judgment and do righteousness,**" recall the admonition in verses 6 and 7 of the preceding chapter. The thoughts and the ways of Israel were not those of the Lord (verse 8). The glorious promises which followed in that chapter were incentives to the wicked to forsake his way and the unrighteous man his thoughts; they were also preparatory to the present injunctions. Let them fulfil practical righteousness and they would thus become conformed to the righteousness of God's character and dealings. And the reason why they should do so is twofold: " **for My salvation,**" He says, " **is near to come** (the salvation expressed in the preceding promises), **and My righteousness to be revealed.**" Righteous dealing has as its basis the relationship into which God brings His people. It was a covenanted relation with Israel, involving the fulfilment of righteousness on each side. God fulfilled His part and He was ready to manifest it if they turned from their unrighteous ways and fell into line with His. If they only realized how near His salvation and His righteous dealings were in their manifestation, this itself should have impelled them to respond to His promise and command.

A special blessing is held out to him who keeps God's command, and to the son of man " **that holdeth fast by it, that keepeth the sabbath from polluting it, and keepeth his hand from doing any evil** " (*verse 2*).

As to the sabbath, ours is a perpetual sabbath keeping; "there remaineth (i.e., continueth perpetually) a sabbath rest for the people of God," Heb. 4: 9. We ourselves can only enjoy this rest in Christ if we keep our hand from doing evil.

The stranger who had joined himself to the Lord (and there were not a few who, professing the religion of Jehovah, had joined His people) might be tempted to fear that after Israel was restored to their land the Lord would separate him from them, depriving him of the privileges he had enjoyed. The fear was ill-founded, for if they 'held fast by His covenant', God would bring them to His Holy mountain, and make them joyful in His house of prayer; their burnt offerings and sacrifices would be accepted upon His altar: for His house 'would be called a house of prayer for all peoples'. And He who will gather the outcasts of Israel, will gather others to him beside "his own" that were gathered (*vv. 6–8*, R.V.).

There were others who might be tempted to despair, considering their condition and all that was taking place. There were the eunuchs, concerning whom a prohibition was given in Deut. 23: 1. But even to these a promise is given of a " **memorial** (A.V., place) **and a name better than of sons, and of daughters** ", an everlasting name that would not be cut off (*vv. 4, 5*), on condition that they refrained from profaning the sabbath and held fast by the Lord's covenant. The party wall would be pulled down, which separated the eunuchs from fellowship with the congregation of Israel. All humanly erected barriers to fellowship are destined to be removed in the coming day.

Verse 9, which the R.V. marks as the beginning of a paragraph, probably commences a new subject and forms the beginning of chapter 57. The watchman and the shepherds in Israel had given way to selfishness and debauchery. They had abandoned their responsibilities towards God's people and, instead of giving warning, they were blind to the impending danger. They were " **dumb dogs** ", unable to bark. Instead of watching they were " **dreaming, lying down, loving to slumber** ". Accordingly the Lord gives an invitation to the beasts of the field and the forest, metaphorically representing Gentile powers, to come and devour (*vv. 9–12*).

All whom the Lord makes responsible to act as shepherds over His flock need to guard themselves against gradual decline from their duty and against either lording it over the charge allotted to them, or becoming possessed of sordid aims to acquire filthy lucre (1 Pet. 5: 2, 3).

CHAPTER LVII

In contrast to the evil watchmen and shepherds and rulers, who were simply engaged in debauchery and self-indulgence, there were the righteous, who stand out conspicuously by reason of the fact that they are taken away from the coming evil, that is to say, from the impending Divine judgments. Their removal is unheeded. They are characterized as " **merciful** " (or rather, godly, R.V. margin). They " **enter into peace; they rest in their beds, each one that walketh in his uprightness** " (or 'straight before him'), *vv. 1, 2*. While the godly suffer by oppression, and by distress at what is going on around them, they do not lose their blessedness in the sight of God or their reward hereafter. They die in faith and go to enjoy the eternal peace of the spirits of the just made perfect (Heb. 12: 23).

Far better it is to suffer death for righteousness' sake than to endeavour to enjoy ease and freedom from trouble by making compromises with the world.

A striking change in the prophet's utterances follows. There is first a warning to the evil-doers to draw near to listen to the voice of God (*verse 3*). Frequently in Scripture a man's moral character is indicated by a reference to his father (2 Kings 6: 32), or his mother (1 Sam. 20: 30), or both parents (Job 30: 8). Accordingly those who were in captivity and continued the idolatry which had brought upon their fathers the judgment of their overthrow by the Chaldeans, are called " **sons of the sorceress, the seed of the adulterer and the whore.**"
All that follows, in *vv. 4 to 11*, is addressed to those who had gone into captivity. The reference to the oaks and the green trees (*verse 5*) points to those forms of tree-worship by which different trees were regarded as the special abodes of different deities. Abominable orgies were associated therewith. The slaughter of the children "in the valleys and under the clefts of the rocks" was not that carried out in sacrifice to Moloch in the valley of Hinnom, but that connected with the worship of Baal (Jer. 19: 5; Ezek. 16: 21). In *verse 6* the reference is to

stone-worship, and the libations poured out thereon. In *vv.*
7 to 9 the idolatrous worship is further described in the metaphorical phraseology of adultery, in its faithlessness towards God.

All this wickedness involved much toil and weariness (*verse 10*);
yet the people were so far gone in their alienation from the Lord,
that instead of realizing the hopelessness of their condition they
found " **a quickening of their strength** " (R.V.), and continued
to make alliances with the heathen. The longsuffering of God
did not produce repentance, but His silence by way of helping
His faithful ones would not be indefinitely postponed.

There are dangers in forming associations with those who
do not adhere to the Word of God, under the pretext of being
regarded as charitable, and, on the other hand, as a result of
urgent advice that we must all make common cause against
powerful adverse forces. Faithfulness to the Lord demands our
maintaining the honour of His Name at whatever cost. And
as the Lord came to the help of His faithful ones in captivity,
so he will in these times of laxity and apostasy.

The alliances the people were making were the outcome of
fear. They took refuge in lies and did not remember God; nor
did they lay it to their heart (*verse 11*). Forgetfulness of God
and a seared conscience go together. The fact that God does
not intervene by way of judgment leads the hardened heart to
be void of the fear of the Lord: " **Have not I held My peace
even of long time, and thou fearest Me not ?** " He says.

In *verse 12* the statement " **I will declare thy righteousness** "
does not indicate that those with whom God was remonstrating
were themselves righteous. The very opposite was the case. It
was what Israel in its blind condition regarded as their own
righteousness. It was a lying righteousness and its true character
would be declared, i.e., exposed and judged by the Lord. This
is confirmed by what follows: " **and as for thy works, they shall
not profit thee. When thou criest, let them which thou hast
gathered deliver thee ; but the wind shall take them, a breath
shall carry them all away** " (*verse 13*).

The Lord now addresses His faithful ones among His people
in captivity, and gives the assurance, " **he that putteth his trust
in Me shall possess the land, and shall inherit My holy mountain.**"
The way is to be made for the return of the captives, and the

message to be given is, "Cast ye up, Cast ye up, prepare the way, take up the stumblingblock out of the way of My people." This receives light from 62: 10, which looks on to the final gathering of Israel from among the nations. Cp. 40: 3, 4. The stumblingblock speaks of any and every obstruction standing in the way of the return (*verse 14*).

In the last paragraph of the chapter the Lord gives a message of combined glory and grace, concerning His twofold dwelling-place, the high and holy place in Heaven and the contrite and humble spirit on earth. The latter will be the condition of His earthly people after the restoration.

If we humble ourselves under the mighty hand of God, 1 Pet. 5, 6. He will exalt us, or, as He says here in Isaiah, He will revive our spirit and our heart. Contrition and humility are as cause and effect. As one has said, "The selfish egotism which repentance breaks has its root in the heart; and the self-consciousness, from whose false elevation repentance brings down, has its seat in the spirit."

If the Lord were to contend continually and always be wroth, the spirit of the object of His righteous anger would fail before Him "and the souls which He has made" (*verse 16*). Here significantly the Lord gives a reminder that the very existence of the soul is due to His creative power, and this is His touching appeal for contrition and humility before Him. In spite of His creative mercy, it became a necessity for Him to destroy the whole human race, save for eight souls, at the time of the Flood. The spread of the physical corruption consequent upon the un-licenced moral depravity of the race, and their persistent lack of repentance, would have terminated in a more terrible way than even by the Flood. The present statement seems to have a connection with the promise made after judgment had been inflicted, that God would not utterly destroy the race again.

Perhaps in fulfilling that promise, and certainly by reason of His covenant with Abraham and his seed, the Lord now makes a promise to Israel that, having smitten him for his covetousness (or rather, selfishness) and for the turning away of his own heart (marg.), He would heal him, and lead him, and restore comforts unto him, and particularly to those who mourned by reason of their wanderings (*vv. 17, 18*).

Verse 19 shows that the effects of God's dealings will divide the nation in twain. For those who became contrite and humble there would be "peace, peace", in all their scattered condition, those who were far off and those who were near. The doubling of the word conveys its perfection and perpetuity, i.e., "perfect peace", as in 26: 3. This will produce worship and songs of praise; hence the Lord introduces the promise of peace by the statement, " **I create the fruit of the lips.**"

On the other hand there will be the impenitent, the wicked, for whom there is no peace, who " **are like the troubled sea; for it cannot rest, and its waters cast up mire and dirt** " (*vv. 20, 21*).

PART III (c)

THE GODLY AND UNGODLY IN ISRAEL
(*Chapters LVIII–LXVI*)

CHAPTER LVIII

THIS chapter begins a new section of the prophecies, and in the first part the main features resemble those in what has preceded, namely, rebuke, warning, and promise. The prophet is commanded to cry aloud (lit., 'with full throat'), to lift up his voice like a trumpet, in order to declare to Israel their transgression, and the sins of the house of Jacob. *Verse 2* exposes their self-righteousness. They were at all events outwardly conformed to the ways and ordinances of God; they even delighted in approaching Him in their external religion; but they made their professed conformity to His regulations a ground of complaint that God seemed to take no notice of them. As a matter of fact, there was no real exercise of heart before Him, no contrition and humility and true communion with the Lord. Even in the day of their fast, their external ritual (cp. Zech. 7: 3; 8: 19), they found their own pleasure instead of His. They oppressed their labourers, they engaged in strife and contention, smiting with the fist of wickedness. That was not the kind of fast which would make their voice to be heard on high; it was not the kind of fast which God had chosen, not the kind of fast by which a man would really afflict his soul, bow down his head as a rush, and spread sackcloth and ashes under him. The fast that God chose should lead to the loosing of the bonds of wickedness, the undoing of the bands of the yoke, letting the oppressed go free, breaking every yoke, dealing bread to the hungry, taking in the poor and homeless, clothing the naked, and not turning away from kith and kin.

If they were in fellowship with the Lord in these respects their light would break forth as the morning and their healing would spring forth speedily; their true righteousness would go before them as the precursor of blessing, and the glory of the Lord would be their rearward. Their prayer would receive an answer and their cry to God would meet with His reply, "Here I am." Let them draw out their soul to the hungry (or bestow on the hungry what their soul desired); let them satisfy the afflicted. Then their light would rise in darkness, and their obscurity would be as the noonday (vv. 6-10).

Mere external religion and outward conformity to ritual are easy. Moreover they tend to produce a spirit of self-satisfaction. What meets with God's approval is that obedience to His word which firstly keeps the soul in true exercise of heart before Him and then leads to the fulfilment of all righteousness in our ways and relationships with others. We may seek strictly to attend certain spiritual duties, while all the time the heart is not right with God, and there is sin in the life which His all-seeing eye does not fail to discern. This is the message and lesson of this passage.

Verse 11 resumes from verse 8 the promises of abundant blessings if the conditions are fulfilled. What is promised here is (1) uninterrupted guidance, (2) soul-satisfaction even in extreme drought or barrenness, (3) the impartation of strength, so that the very physical frame becomes an instrument of the fulfilment of His will, (4) the verdant beauty of a watered garden, setting forth the beauteous effects of the indwelling Spirit of God, (5) the outflowing of blessing by the Holy Spirit, represented as a spring or fountain of water, whose waters do not deceive (A.V. margin). While all this is promised to Israel the Lord graciously designs to make it good in the present life of the believer.

In *verse 12* there is promise of national revival. The phrase " **they that shall be of thee** " is another way of saying "thy people". These, returning from exile, will build up the old ruins and raise up what had been laid as foundations generations ago, so that the people shall receive the title " **The repairer of the breach, The restorer of paths to dwell in,**" or of streets, formerly places of habitation.

But again, there are conditions. The Israelite must hold back his foot from the sabbath and from doing his pleasure or business on God's holy day, calling the sabbath a delight, " **and the holy of the Lord honourable** ", honouring it by not doing his own will, or finding his own pleasure or business, or "speaking words" (that is, words of no value, a multitude of vain utterances such as boastings and mere gossip). The one who abstained from all this would delight himself in the Lord. So it was not merely a matter of keeping a commandment. The Lord Himself is inseparable from His Law. His commandment is but the expression of His own character.

As has been pointed out, our sabbath in this day of the indwelling Holy Spirit and His ministry, is not one day in the week; "there remaineth (i.e., abideth continually) a sabbath rest (a *sabbatismos*, a sabbath-keeping) for the people of God. Our rest is in the living and glorified Christ on the ground of His finished work at Calvary. This rest does not depend on special days, it is not intermittent. If kept uninterruptedly as God designs it for us, then our delight is in the Lord and we may enjoy constant fellowship with Him. We are ever to refrain from doing our pleasure, pursuing our own ways and engaging in any business as if it was our own. If we do so we cannot enjoy the privilege of rest in Christ. We are ever to abstain from useless talk of the lips, which "tendeth only to penury" (Prov. 14: 23).

Delighting oneself in the Lord is the highest possible occupation. It is the privilege of the believer, whether in seasons of communion and worship or in the activity of service. But it is possible only as the admonitions which have preceded in this passage are fulfilled.

There are yet further promises: **" and I will make thee to ride upon the high places of the earth "** (*verse 14*). This refers especially to Palestine for the restored people and conveys the thought of their sovereign rights and dominant position, and that not only over the land but over the nations as well.

For us it speaks of our possessions with Christ in the Heavenly places (Eph. 1: 3). These spiritual blessings are our present possession and are realizable according as we renounce worldly advantages, taking up our cross daily and following Christ.

The next promise is **" I will feed thee with the heritage of Jacob thy father."** Israel has never yet been able to experience this. Their apostasy has prevented it. But it holds good for the godly remnant in the future, and its fulfilment is unthwartable, **" for the mouth of the Lord hath spoken it "** (cp. 1: 20; 24: 3; 40: 5).

CHAPTER LIX

THIS chapter continues and expands the subject of the perverseness and transgressions which have hindered the blessings promised, and which raise a barrier between God and His people. The Lord's hand was not shortened that it could not save; His power was ever ready to be put at their disposal. His ear was not heavy that it could not hear; He was only too willing to respond to their cry if they had hearkened to His word. But their iniquities had effected a separation from Him and had caused His face to be hid from them (*vv. 1, 2*).

The Lord cannot hold communion with the wilful heart. He cannot look down on sin with complacency. Perverseness of the will prevents the enjoyment of the light of His countenance.

The prophet now exposes their evil ways, their murders, lies and unrighteousness, and their trust in *tohu*, that is, in what is worthless (*vv. 3, 4*). He then employs the twofold metaphor of the hatching of basilisks' eggs and weaving the spider's web (cp. Job 8: 14). The former indicates the injurious character of all that they do. There is a twofold result; whoever eats of their eggs dies, and if an egg is trodden upon, it splits into an adder, which attacks the heel of the one who has disturbed it (*verse 5*). The second metaphor signifies the valuelessness and injurious character of their activities. No garment is produced by their weaving and their works are characterized by iniquity and violence.

The next description of their evil doings (*vv. 7, 8*) is used by Paul in Rom. 3: 15–17, in a free rendering of the passage, to describe the universal guilt of mankind. Isaiah contrasts their ways of desolation and destruction with the way of peace, firstly in relation to God and then to their fellow-men, for whoever follows their paths does not know peace. He who loves peace makes it his aim to produce it both by example and effort.

From *v. 9 to v. 15* the prophet changes from the third person plural to the first, and includes himself with his people, both in acknowledging transgression and in stating the effects of the judgments of God upon them. He says " **Therefore is judgment far from us, neither doth righteousness overtake us.**" God was not dealing with Israel's enemies in the exercise of His righteous judgment upon the foe; hence His people were left undefended, though His salvation was ever near to come and His righteousness to be revealed (56: 1). They looked for light, but behold darkness; for brightness, but they walked in obscurity (or rather, thick darkness). The words are the same as in 8: 22 (see the R.V.), which, by the way, is one of the many testimonies to the unity of Isaiah. Those in exile hoped for release, but matters grew worse for them instead of better. They groped like blind men along a wall without finding an exit. They stumbled as if they were in the twilight, although God had given them the light of noonday.

Those who persist in error find no help from the light of God's truth, although it is there for them. Christ Himself and the very Scriptures have become a stumblingblock to the Jews. So it is in Christendom: the Scriptures are read but not understood. The blinding power of ecclesiastical traditions obscures the light of God's word, and people who have the Bible remain in religious bondage, unable to enjoy the truth which would set them free if they faithfully listened to its voice instead of adhering to the systems of men.

The first part of *verse 11* depicts two conditions. Roaring like bears suggests impatience; mourning like doves suggests despondency; both are the very opposite to that peace of soul which arises from contrition of heart and submission to God's will. All this befell them because their transgressions were multiplied before the Lord and their sins bore witness against them. Moreover, it was not as if they sinned in ignorance. They knew that they were doing wrong (*verse 12*), that they were denying the Lord, and turning away from following their God, and at the same time " **speaking oppression and revolt** ", or rather, untruth the same word as in Deut. 19: 16, rendered "wrong doing" (R.V.), margin, "rebellion", where the evil referred to is that of false accusation.

In *verse 14* the statements " **judgment is turned away back-ward and righteousness standeth afar off** " do not speak of God's retributive dealings, they continue the description of the evil condition of the people. Truth had fallen in the market-place. Where righteous dealing should have been in evidence, not only was truth lacking, but anyone who departed from evil rendered himself the subject of plunder (the verb is usually rendered 'to spoil'), *verse 15*.

The latter part of verse 15 should really begin verse 16, and from this to the end of verse 18 forms the third part of the chapter. We are now given to see the attitude of the Lord towards such a condition of things and the manner of His judicial inter-vention. " **The Lord saw it, and it displeased Him that there was no judgment** (or right). **And He saw that there was no man,**" that is, that there was no man possessed of either the character or the ability to stem the tide of evil (*verse 16*). For this use of the word "man" see Jer. 5: 1. There is an old Jewish saying, "Where there is no man, I strive to be a man."

God " **wondered** (or was astonished, expressing His displeasure rather than anything like human wonder) **that there was no intercessor,**" no one acting on the side of God on behalf of His people as against their abominations and the inevitable conse-quences (*verse 16*).

In consequence of this God prepared Himself for judicial intervention. The description is vivid and striking. Different forms of expression are used: (1) direct statement, (2) similes and metaphors: (1) " **His own arm brought salvation unto Him; and His righteousness it upheld Him.**" No one could be found to co-operate with Him in that form of salvation by which His cause would be vindicated; so His own arm brought it about. No one could be found to act in righteousness in fellowship with Him; so the self-sustaining power of His own righteousness wrought for the requisite end.

God uses sanctified human agents to engage in His work and fulfil His will towards others. Witness the testimony of the prophets, "messengers in the Lord's message" (Hag. 1: 13; cp. Isa. 44: 26), and the employment by Christ of His disciples. Paul describes those who preach the gospel as "God's fellow-workers" (2 Cor. 6: 1).

Next are similes and metaphors: " **And He put on righteousness as a breastplate, and a helmet of salvation upon His head ;
and He put on garments of vengeance for clothing, and was
clad with zeal as a cloke** " (*verse 17*). There is nothing actually
physical about this. The armour and the vesture depict the
various manifestations of His character and power, the actings
of His justice and His mercy (just as in Eph. 6 the believer's
panoply describes the spiritual powers at our disposal to meet
the foe).

In explanation of this there follows a prophecy unfolding in
order the great events of the future in relation to Israel. Firstly,
the Lord will deal with the rebellious in Israel, inflicting punishment upon those in the nation who will persistently associate
themselves with the Antichrist. These are the adversaries referred
to in the first part of *verse 18*. That seems clear from what has
preceded in this chapter, especially verses 14 and 15. It is to
these apostates that the statement refers, "**According to their
deeds, accordingly He will repay, fury to his adversaries, recompence to His enemies.**"

Secondly, judgments must fall upon the foes of God in the
world of Gentiles. These are indicated by the term "the islands",
or coastlands. This is an inclusive word, embracing the furthest
nations of the Gentiles. They will be gathered together at the
end of this age, "against the Lord and against His Christ".
Similarly the isles and their inhabitants, in Isa. 42: 10, and the
isles of Kittim, in Jer. 2: 10, are joined with Kedar, to indicate
all lands from west to east. This rebellion against the Lord on
the part of the federated nations is described in the next verse:
" **for he shall come as a rushing stream, which the breath of
the Lord driveth** " (R.V.). How the Lord will intervene for the
overthrow of His foes, how " **the Spirit of the Lord shall lift up
a standard against him** ", is described further in chapter 63: 1–6.

Thirdly, following these judgments, they that are left of the
nations will " **fear the Name of the Lord from the west, and
His glory from the rising of the sun** " (*verse 19*). This will be
compulsory subjection and recognition of the claims of God and
of His Son. Fourthly, there will come the deliverance of God's
earthly people, the remnant in the nation, who (unlike their
godless fellow-nationals, who will have perished with the Beast
and the false prophet and their associates) will remain faithful
to the Lord, multitudes of them having been converted to their

coming Messiah through the testimony of the witnesses mentioned in Rev. 11: 3–12 (see also 12: 17). **"And a Redeemer shall come to Zion, and unto them that turn from transgression in Jacob, saith the Lord "** (*verse 20*).

The chapter closes with the promise of the new covenant (*verse 21*). It is based upon God's words to Abraham in Gen. 17: 4. The message **" My Spirit that is upon thee . . . "** is addressed to the restored nation, who will testify for the Lord continually. They will never cease to declare His word and bear witness for Him. The terms of the covenant are fully given in Jer. 31: 31–4, and Heb. 8: 10–12 and 10: 16, 17.

CHAPTER LX

As a result of what has just preceded a rousing message comes at once to Zion. Long has it remained in darkness and desolation, but the Millennial glory is coming, and the command "Arise" (*verse 1*) is a word imparting power in the very command. She is to rise out of the dust and to shine, for her light, or Light-giver, is come, causing the glory of the Lord to rise upon her, a contrast to the condition in 59: 10! Cp. ch. 2: 5.

Verse 2 reveals the condition of the Gentiles in their gross darkness which will exist especially under the Antichrist and which will linger until the Lord 'arises upon Israel and His glory will be seen upon them'. Then 'nations shall come to their light, and kings to the brightness of their rising'.

Until the Lord comes to receive His Church to Himself the light of Gospel testimony shines into individual hearts, while nations still lie in darkness. At the time of the removal of the Church, the deceptive power of the Devil and the rule of the Man of Sin will plunge them into gross darkness. Scripture does not justify the idea that the Gospel will spread through the world until whole nations receive the light. Only when Israel is restored will whole nations receive the light of Divine testimony and acknowledge the truth relating to the living God and His Christ. All earthly might will yield subjection by sheer compulsion, to the Lord and His glorified people.

Not only will the nations come up to Jerusalem as their centre, but they will bring God's people from all the countries where they have been scattered. "**Thy sons shall come from far, and thy daughters shall be carried in the arms,**" probably as little ones cling to the side of those who are carrying them (*verse 4*). Thus the passage recalls 49: 22, 23. The statement is metaphorical of the care and security to be provided by Gentile powers.

Verse 5 describes the awestruck joy with which God's earthly people will find themselves delivered and so abundantly blessed. The prophecy "**Then thou shalt see and be lightened (R.V.), and thine heart shall tremble and be enlarged,**" is not suggestive of fear, but of a trembling for joy, as the following passage makes clear.

The tremendous change in the circumstances of the nation will produce not only a joyous thrill but an enlargement of heart to apprehend the infinite goodness of God. The Gentile nations will devote their energies to the enrichment of God's people, and above all the Lord will thereby glorify and beautify the House of His glory, and upon the altar raised in connection with it commemorative sacrifices will be offered continually (*verse 7*).

The question in *verse 8*, "**Who are these that fly as a cloud, and as the doves to their windows ?** " can well be realized in view of the enormous development of passenger aviation in our times. The transference of the scattered Jews to their own territory could be accomplished in the course of a few days by this means.

"**Surely the isles shall wait for Me** " (*verse 9*). This indicates that the far off nations of the world will act under God's decree and direction and Gentile activity will be exercised in these matters, not by way merely of a political scheme, but with the definite object of honouring the Lord. They will minister of their wealth and substance, "**for the Name of the LORD thy God, and for the Holy One of Israel, because He hath glorified thee.**"

In *verse 10* the promise "**strangers shall build up thy walls, and their kings shall minister unto thee** " does not refer to the post-captivity decrees of Cyrus, Darius and others, but to the beginning of the Millennium and the activity on the part of Gentile nations in rendering assistance to Israel. That such assistance will be voluntary rather than by way of subjection is indicated in verse 6.

The Lord then contrasts His mercy with His wrath, as in several other places in Scripture; see, e.g., 54: 7, 8 and cp. 63: 4.

In a special sense mercy will glory against judgment (Jas. 2: 13, R.V.).

That the gates of the city will be open continually (*verse 11*) implies a state of peace, of freedom from attack, so that the wealth of the nations (R.V.) may have free entrance, and that their kings may come in triumphal procession (cp. Rev. 21: 25, 26).

Verse 12 shows that God's judgments will be exercised during the Millennium upon nations that manifest a spirit of rebellion and refuse to render help to Israel. See also Zech. 14: 17–19.

The promise of this ministry of the Gentiles is resumed in *verse 14*. There is, however, an interlude in *verse 13*, in which the Lord delights to foretell the glory of His sanctuary, the beautiful Millennial Temple, and to indicate His presence there by speaking of it as " **the place of My feet** ".

That the glory of Lebanon, with its splendid trees (cp. 41: 19) will be brought to beautify the place of the sanctuary, would seem to indicate that these trees will be planted in the environment of the Temple, perhaps by way of avenues. What is referred to here is not timber for the structure itself, but "the place", that is, the vicinity.

Verse 14 briefly looks back to the time of the great tribulation, to those who afflicted God's people. Now it will be their sons that come bending to them. Their fathers will have perished in the judgments of the day of the Lord. There will be a multitude of people who, while not having gathered themselves together against the Lord, will yet have despised God's people during the time of hostility. These will bow themselves down at the feet of Israel and will call Jerusalem " **The city of the Lord, the Zion of the Holy One of Israel.**" Instead of being forsaken and hated like a slighted wife (cp. Deut. 21: 15), the Lord will make the city " **an eternal excellency, a joy of many generations** " (*verse 15*). The nations and their kings will bestow their vital energy upon God's people, just as a mother gives her milk to a child. And above all, instead of being in a state of blind ignorance of God, they will recognize Jehovah as " **thy Saviour and thy Redeemer, the Mighty One of Jacob** ".

We may gather from *verse 17* that (instead of wood and stone) gold, silver, bronze, and iron will be used for the building of the city, so that it will be indestructible by the elements of nature and by every sort of foe. Peace, here personified, will act as magistrates, and righteousness will act as bailiffs. Violence, desolation and destruction will be absent. The walls of the city will be called "Salvation", for the city will be impregnable; the gates will be called "Praise", for God will glorify His name there continually (*verse 18*).

The sun and the moon will still exist, but will not be needed, owing to the effulgence radiating from the presence of the Lord and the Church, with His uncreated Shekinah glory (*verse 20 : cp. Rev. 22: 5*). This will be verily the triumph of light over darkness.

Under such conditions there could be no such thing as mourning; "**sorrow and sighing shall flee away**," and will give place to everlasting joy (see 35: 10). Joy is always intensified by the fact of the preceding sorrow and trial from which deliverance has come. The trusting believer can ever say of his trials "I was brought low, and He helped me."

In the Millennial state the fruitfulness and glory of nature will be accompanied by the moral excellence of the nation. The people will be "**all righteous**" (*verse 21*). The word "Jew" will never again be a term of national and moral reproach. Israel will be in permanent possession of the land, and that by what is here metaphorically described as "**the Lord's planting**". It will be by reason of this that they are righteous. They will be like a green shoot or sprout (Eng. text, "branch"). The same word is used of Christ in 11: 1. God's grace will do the planting, and that for His glory.

The nation will become abundantly fruitful from the point of view of population; "**The little one** (perhaps the one with few children) **shall become a thousand, and the small one** (perhaps one in humble position) **a strong nation**" (*verse 22*). That means not only numerical increase in population but the extension of joyous fellowship. Moreover all this blessedness will be accomplished with great rapidity: "**I the LORD will hasten it in its time**."

CHAPTER LXI

UP to the end of the last chapter the speaker was Jehovah. In the first verse of this chapter there comes a change; the speaker is not Isaiah but Christ the Messiah. In confirmation of this, what He says about Himself is identical with what has already been said about the Servant of Jehovah. He says " **the Spirit of the Lord God is upon Me** " (see 42: 1); " **the Lord hath anointed Me to preach good tidings unto the meek. He hath sent Me** (see 48: 16) **to bind up the broken-hearted** (cp. 50: 4), **to proclaim liberty to the captives, and the opening of the prison to them that are bound** " (see 42: 7; 49: 9). When the Lord Jesus was in the synagogue at Nazareth, having read this very passage, He closed the roll and said "To-day hath this Scripture been fulfilled in your ears" (Luke 4: 17-21).

This passage speaks of the Trinity. The Three in One are mentioned in the very first words uttered by the Lord. The title "the Lord God", Adonai Jehovah, is the same as is mentioned four times in 50: 4-9. Some manuscripts omit "the Lord" here.

The anointing was probably what took place when, at His baptism, "the Holy Ghost descended in a bodily form, as a dove, upon Him" (Luke 3: 22, together with 4: 1, 18).

The word rendered "the meek" primarily signifies suffering ones. The binding up of the broken-hearted is that of applying a relieving bandage to heart wounds. The Gospel of Luke almost immediately records the Lord's tender acts in this respect: see 4: 40; also the case of the widow of Nain, 7: 13-15, the woman with the issue of blood, and the daughter of Jairus, 8: 43-56, the woman with the spirit of infirmity 13: 11-13, and the lepers in Samaria 17: 11-19.

So with the proclamation of liberty to the captive, those who were bound with the fetters of sin and of the Devil. The phrase rendered " **the opening of the prison** " should probably read as in the R.V. margin, "the opening of the eyes" (as in 35: 5; 42: 7). There were many who were spiritually imprisoned and blinded by the religions of the Pharisees, Scribes and Sadducees (the Lord remarks upon their blindness in Matt. 23: 24).

Great the joy when the blinding film of human tradition and religion is removed by the power of the ascended Lord through the Spirit! great the gladness and gratitude in the possession of liberty and spiritual sight!

He was sent " **to proclaim the acceptable year of the LORD** ", lit., 'the year of the LORD'S good pleasure' (*verse 2*). The year stands not for a particular date but for a season. That

season lasted during the days of the Lord's testimony and subsequently in the proclamation of the Gospel to Israel; it applies
in a wider sense to the whole period of Gospel grace. In contrast
to the year is " the day of vengeance ". God in mercy will
shorten the period of the exercise of His wrath. The Lord, in
quoting this passage in the synagogue, finished His quotation at
the preceding clause. He had not come to earth to usher in the
day of vengeance. Later He foretold that the days of vengeance
would come upon the nation, and that Jerusalem would be
"trodden down of the Gentiles, until the times of the Gentiles
be fulfilled" (Luke 21: 22–24).

The objects next mentioned, " to comfort all that mourn ;
to appoint unto them that mourn in Zion " (verse 3) will be
fulfilled after the time of "Jacob's trouble", when the godly
remnant in Israel will have passed through their time of unprecedented sorrow. The Lord, coming as their Deliverer at His
Second Advent, will delight to minister His comfort, giving them
(what follows is the object of the verb "appoint", lit., to put
upon, resumed in the verb to give) " a garland for ashes ",
lit., a diadem, to adorn the head. For the sprinkling of ashes
on the head of those in sorrow see, e.g., 2 Sam. 13: 19.

The oil of joy is emblematic of that which refreshes and cheers
(see Ps. 45: 7). This is to be imparted in the day when the Lord
sets up His Kingdom over the world in the midst of His earthly
people. He will clothe them with " the garment of praise for
(i.e., instead of) the spirit of heaviness " (the word describes a
condition burdensome enough to cause one's death). As a garment upon the body so will be the praise of the redeemed as
the expression of inward jubilation.

The Lord who makes all things work together for good to
them that love Him, turns our very sorrows into joy. There
could be no such joy if there were no preceding sorrow. The
dark cloud makes the following sunshine all the brighter.

The change wrought by the Lord in Israel will likewise be of
a moral character. They will be called " trees of righteousness ".
Trees suggest firmness, fulness, verdure and fruit. So with the
righteousness which will characterize the nation. This will not
be their own doing, it will be " the planting of the LORD,
that He might be glorified ". Cp. 60: 21.

Verses 4 to 9 foretell the restoration of Palestine and the exaltation of Israel to their appointed position of dignity and honour and authority over the Gentile nations. Places that were waste and desolate will be fertile and thickly populated. Those who belonged to nations that afflicted them in their time of trouble will now minister to them as shepherds of their flocks, farm labourers and cultivators.

They themselves will be what the Lord designed them to be from the beginning, "a kingdom of priests" (Exod. 19: 6). Accordingly in this high service they will be, from the earthly point of view, associated with the Church in its priestly ministry. Not only so, the Gentile nations will recognize them as acting in this capacity and will acknowledge the God of Israel as the true God. All the Gentile powers who have in past periods used the world for their self-enrichment, will become the possession of His people, who will " **eat the wealth of the nations** ". All that the Gentiles boasted in, glorying in their development and prowess and in the objects to which they devoted the products and deposits of the earth, will be bestowed upon Israel under the benign and firm administration of Christ.

This whole subject is described by the Apostle Paul in Rom. 11: 12 to 32. If their fall and their present loss has meant the riches of the Gentiles through gospel grace and ministry, still greater will be the effect of their fulness, that is, the full national prosperity of Israel. "As touching the gospel, they are enemies for your sake: but as touching the election (the predestining counsel of God concerning them), they are beloved for the fathers' sake."

" **For their shame they shall have double** " (*verse 7*). They will have, so to speak, a double possession in their land, which will be extended far beyond its former confines. Whereas formerly they were in confusion, the objects of reproach and contempt, they will be filled with exceeding and unending joy. There will be altogether a double compensation for their former sufferings.

In *verse 8* the Lord makes known that in all this blessing His own character will be vindicated. He declares that He loves judgment and hates robbery with iniquity (R.V.), referring to the cruel treatment which Israel had sustained from their adversaries. In direct contrast to this He will give them their recompense in truth and make an everlasting covenant with them, with the result that they will be recognized among the nations as those whom the Lord has blessed—a complete reversal of present conditions.

What follows in *vv. 10 and 11* has been regarded by some as the utterance of the redeemed nation. It seems, however, almost certain that the Speaker is the same Person as in the beginning of the chapter. It is surely Christ, speaking in identification with His people and declaring His joy in Jehovah on their behalf. He is regarding what will have been accomplished in the coming day as if it were already fulfilled. The garments of salvation with which the godly ones in Israel will be clothed are His own garments. Just as a bridegroom " **decketh himself with a garland, and as a bride adorneth herself with her jewels** ", so will the Lord manifest Himself in His glory and beauty in His relation to His redeemed people.

The word rendered "decketh" signifies to deck as a priest, and it is in that capacity that the Lord will act in the day when His righteousness is manifested in the earth. He will then be the revealed antitype of Melchizedek. He will act in the three-fold capacity of a King, Priest and a Bridegroom. The picture of the bride adorning herself with her jewels especially portrays His earthly Kingdom as wedded to Himself. So with regard to the Church, He acts, and ever will act, as a royal Priest (Heb. 7: 17; 9: 11), and as her Heavenly Bridegroom (Eph. 5: 25–32).

Just as the earth brings forth its sprouts and as the garden causes the things that are sown in it to sprout up, so the Lord GOD will cause righteousness and praise (or renown) to spring forth (or sprout up) before all the nations. It is God that causes the seed to germinate, and the Bearer of the seed is Jehovah's Servant. All these processes are at work through the Gospel among all nations, but the immediate application here is the Millennial state of Israel.

CHAPTER LXII

THE Speaker here is not Isaiah but the LORD, as is clear from verse 6. He says He will not retain silence nor will He rest until Zion's righteousness shall go forth as the brightness of the morning and her salvation as a blazing torch. These are the actual comparisons in *verse 1*.

Verse 2 resumes what was said at the end of the preceding chapter concerning the righteousness and renown of the people as manifest to all the Gentiles. Again, the completely new position of the people will be marked by His bestowal of a new name, to correspond with their changed character. In Jer. 33: 16 the name is mentioned as "Jehovah is our righteousness". Just as now in the case of the believer righteousness is reckoned by grace and manifested in character and conduct, so with redeemed Israel. This is what the whole passage from 61: 10 to 62: 2 sets forth.

The figurative language of *verse 3* is intensely beautiful. The metaphor which describes the condition of Zion is that of " **a crown** (or coronet) **of beauty in the hand of the Lord, and a royal diadem in the hand of thy God** ". The word rendered "diadem" is used of the mitre, or rather, turban, of the High Priest, Exod. 28: 4, 39; Zech. 3: 5. Two different Hebrew words are used for the "hand" here, the first signifying the open hand, but indicating power, the second denoting the palm of the hand, indicating that which is held out for display. The two together set forth the intense delight in the heart of the Lord in manifesting the effects of His grace and redeeming power.

Again the two descriptions mark the combination of royal authority and priesthood, and in this twofold capacity Israel will share the authority of Christ. At various times in the world's history from that of Nimrod (Gen. 10: 9) to that of the Antichrist (Rev. 13), men of renown have sought to exercise this double function, so as to have authority over both the religious and the civil life of those under them. The whole history is one of dismal failure and catastrophe.

In the day to come Jerusalem will no more be called "The Forsaken one" and the land will no longer be called "Desolate". The city will be known as " **Hephzi-bah** " (My delight in her) and the land " **Beulah** " (married); His love will be as strong and as full of joy as the love of the newly married. The thought in each part of the verse is that of winning an inalienable right by a bridegroom "to have and to hold" (*vv. 4, 5*).

The same figure is used of what the believer should be in spiritual union with Christ. See Rom. 7: 4. We are married (R.V., joined) "to Him who was raised from the dead, that we might bring forth fruit unto God". We are to live therefore as those in whom He can delight.

With a view to all this God has stationed watchmen upon the walls of Jerusalem who day and night intercede with Him until His purposes concerning His earthly people are accomplished. The watchmen symbolize those who pray for the peace of Jerusalem. That especial intercession should be our constant occupation. The language is vivid: " **Ye that are the Lord's remembrancers, take ye no rest, and give Him no rest, till He establish, and till He make Jerusalem a praise in the earth** " (*vv. 6, 7*). The word rendered "establish" signifies to make ready, to prepare for oneself (cp. 51: 13, marg.).

That such intercession is the will of God is confirmed by the statement of the Lord's oath in *vv. 8 and 9*: " **The LORD hath sworn by His right hand and by the arm of His strength** " (i.e., His strong arm). With this cp. Heb. 6: 13. He declares that Gentile powers shall never again pillage the land and rob its rightful owners of that which they have produced. On the contrary, His people who have garnered their grain " **shall eat it, and praise the LORD** ".

Forcibly this reminds us that for all which the Lord bestows upon us by way of material benefits such as food and raiment, we should be in the habit of praising Him day by day. Our thanks at meal times should never become formal. It should be given out of the heart which ever recognizes the goodness of God. The food we eat is "sanctified by the Word of God and prayer" (1 Tim. 4: 5).

Further, in the coming day these who have gathered in their wine " **shall drink it in the courts of My sanctuary** ". They will delight to go up to the house of the Lord with hearts overwhelmed with gratitude.

This constant going up to the House of the Lord receives a vivid anticipation in the command in *verse 10* yet to be issued: " **Go through, go through the gates; prepare ye the way** (or clear the way) **of the people.** " Obstacles in the way of ready entrance are to be removed: " **cast up, cast up the high way; gather out the stones.** " The way of the people will be the way of the Lord (see 40: 3). This has a spiritual application as well as a physical. Everything that is an obstacle to spiritual blessing will be removed from the hearts of Israel.

All that presents a stumblingblock, all that hinders our enjoyment of free and constant access to the Throne of Grace, everything that stands in the way of our communion with God, is to be removed. Often there is much rubbish to be cleared out, such as worldly associations and fleshly desires.

Verses 11 and 12 depict the fulfilment of these promises to Israel, a banner is to be lifted up to all the Gentile nations (the word at the end of verse 10 is plural, "peoples"). For the Lord will sound out tidings to the end of the earth. There is to be a general acknowledgment of the manifestation of God's power towards His people in that their salvation has come, that " **His reward is with Him, and His recompence before Him** ". The nations will recognize Israel as " **The holy people, The redeemed of the Lord.** " The city which no one cared for will be called " **Sought out, A city not forsaken.** " That is to say, men will resort to Jerusalem. They will go there to see its glory and beauty. The wonders of God's grace and power will be manifest to them. The city will be full of people, and the streets will be filled with boys and girls enjoying their play there (Zech. 8: 4, 5).

CHAPTER LXIII

THE first six verses of this chapter consist of a dialogue between the redeemed remnant of Israel, delivered from their great tribulation, and the Lord. The time is that of Christ's Personal intervention for the overthrow of the Gentile foes gathered under the Antichrist in Palestine. Accordingly the passage follows appropriately after the Divine promises given in chapter 62.

The Jewish people, delivered from their enemies, ask, with astonishment at the power and glory of their great Deliverer, " **Who is this that cometh from Edom, with dyed garments from Bozrah ? this that is glorious in His apparel, marching** (R.V.) **in the greatness of His strength ?** " (*verse 1*). He comes not as a traveller (as in the A.V.), but as a Conqueror at the head of His armies (see Rev. 19: 14).

But why does He come from Edom and Bozrah? The answer is to be found in a comparison of Ps. 29 with Dan. 11: 45, in the latter of which the word rendered "palace" should be "encampment", the military base of the king of the North after his return from conquering Egypt, with a view to the overthrow of his national Gentile foes gathered under the ten-kingdomed confederacy of the Roman powers. All the Gentile nations are thus assembled at the warfare of Har-Magedon (Rev. 16: 16). Psalm 29 describes poetically the complete overthrow of all the nations by the power of the voice of the Lord. The geography of that Psalm is interesting and significant. The overthrow begins in Lebanon (vv. 5 and 6) and sweeps down to the wilderness of Kadesh (verse 8), the centre of which is Bozrah (cp. Num. 13: 26). The destruction is swift and complete. The distance from Sirion in Lebanon to Bozrah in Edom is 200 miles, or 1600 furlongs, which is the very distance foretold in Rev. 14: 20 in a passage parallel to Isa. 63, concerning the winepress of the wrath of God. The harmony of Scripture in its various parts is thus strikingly illustrated.

In reply to the question of the delivered nation, the Lord answers "**I that speak in righteousness, mighty to save.**" The "I that speak" corresponds to "the voice of the Lord" in Ps. 29 (see also Ps. 2: 5) and to the sword which comes forth out of His mouth, as mentioned in Rev. 19: 21. His righteousness will then be manifested in the deliverance of His earthly people.

In *verse 2* a second question is asked by them: "**Wherefore art Thou red in Thine apparel, and Thy garments like him that treadeth in the winefat** (or rather, winevat)?" The Lord's response to this in *vv. 3, 4* makes clear the time of the event, namely, the final destruction of Gentile powers before the Millennial reign. He says "**I have trodden the winepress alone; and of the peoples** (plural) **there was no man with Me: yea, I trod them in Mine anger, and trampled them in My fury; and their lifeblood is sprinkled upon My garments, and I have stained all My raiment. For the day of vengeance was in Mine heart, and the year of My redeemed is come.**" With this vividly metaphorical description of the treading of the winepress cp. Joel 3: 9–16; Rev. 14: 17–20 and 19: 15. The day and the year are contrasted. The time of the Lord's wrath is short, for "the Lord will execute His word upon the earth, finishing it and cutting it short", Rom. 9: 28.

The tenderness of the heart of the Lord towards His people, His by covenant and promise, is manifested in the rest of His response to the second question, "And I looked, and there was none to help; and I wondered that there was none to uphold: therefore Mine own arm brought salvation unto Me; and My fury, it upheld Me. And I trod down the peoples in Mine anger, and made them drunk in My fury, and I poured out their life-blood on the earth " (vv. 5, 6).

In the 7th verse Isaiah, speaking as representing his people at the time of their deliverance, as just mentioned in verses 1 to 6, and by way of response to the Lord's goodness, says " I will make mention of the lovingkindnesses of the LORD, and the praises of the LORD, according to all that the LORD hath bestowed on us; and the great goodness toward the house of Israel which He hath bestowed on them according to His mercies, and according to the multitude of His lovingkindnesses."

Such language befits our lips who have been granted Heavenly and spiritual deliverances and blessings, in addition to earthly mercies.

Verse 8 expresses God's approval of His redeemed people, the righteous remnant who have waited for His salvation during the time of the great tribulation, in contrast to the many who will have remained in apostasy, owning allegiance to the Antichrist. This contrast is intimated in the Divine declaration, " Surely, they are My people, children that will not deal falsely." The prophet then records that for this reason " He was their Saviour ", and proceeds to show how He acted as such: " In all their affliction He was afflicted " (verse 9).

Some manuscripts have the word "not" in the latter part of this statement, with the meaning that in all their adversity He was no adversary to them (see the R.V. margin). The weight of evidence, however, supports the rendering in our Versions. In a day long gone by, when Israel returned to the Lord in repentance for their sins as a result of His chastisements, "His soul was grieved for the misery of Israel" (Judges 10: 16; cp. 2: 18). So in the coming time of Jacob's trouble His dealings will have in view both the overthrow of their enemies and the removal of His chastening hand at the appointed time. The statement reveals the tenderness of the Lord's compassions. His chastisements are ever ministered in love (Heb. 12: 5-11). "The Lord doth not afflict willingly, nor grieve the children of men" (Lam. 3: 33). It grieves Him to see their waywardnesses. It likewise grieves Him to be compelled to afflict them.

Next comes the actual mode of His delivering power; " **the Angel of His Presence saved them : in His love and in His pity He redeemed them** " (*verse 9*). Here the thought is carried not only to the future salvation, but back through the past history of His dealings. The presence of God was with His people of old in the pillar of cloud and fire and in the Tabernacle, and the Angel was none other than Christ Himself (see Exod. 23: 20, 23; 32: 34; 33: 2). His presence was more than the mere existence of God in their midst, it indicated the manifestation of Himself in and through the accompanying Angel.

The metaphor of bearing and carrying them all the days of old, recalls verses 10 to 12 of the song of Moses in Deut. 32, where he recounts God's goodness during their journey in the wilderness. Cp. verse 10 with Deut. 32: 19–25. " **They grieved His Holy Spirit** " (*verse 10*), a sin against which we are warned in Eph. 4: 30.

Verses 11 to 14 present the other side of God's dealings, His mercy to them in delivering them from Egypt and giving them rest so that His Name might become glorious. At the end of the 14th verse Isaiah addresses God, reminding Him of His goodness, and this forms an introduction to the prayer that follows.

The prayer for redemption and deliverance (*verse 15*) begins with the request that the Lord will 'look down from Heaven, and behold from the habitation of His holiness and of His glory (or majesty)', indicating that He who had been with His people, manifesting His presence and power, had withdrawn Himself, and was to be approached only in His Heavenly dwelling place. His holiness and His glory are specifically mentioned in contrast to the godlessness and shame of His people. This attitude of distance is borne out by the appeal, " **where is Thy zeal and Thy mighty acts ? the yearning of Thy bowels and Thy compassions are restrained toward me.**"

When God's people are in distress because of their waywardness, the necessity of His disciplinary acts and judgments does not remove His compassion; "whom the Lord loveth He chasteneth." He longs to relieve His people from their afflictions but sometimes necessarily puts a restraint upon His tender mercies.

It is noticeable that Isaiah speaks of himself as the subject of these dealings, thus identifying himself with the condition of his people. So it was with Moses (Exod. 32: 31, 32), and again with Paul (Rom. 9: 2, 3). So it is with every true intercessor in times when the Lord's people are in a spirit of declension from Him.

The prophet appeals in *verse 16* to the relationship of God with His people on the same ground. God has begotten His earthly people by His creative power and loving counsel. He was their Father, though Abraham knew them not, and Israel (i.e., Jacob) acknowledged them not. Abraham and Jacob were no longer present to have regard to their descendants. The words rendered "knoweth" (R.V.) and "acknowledge" convey the thought of intimate recognition and active regard (see, e.g., Deut. 33: 9; Ruth 2: 10, 19). The departed saints do not intercede for anyone. With the Lord, however, the case is different. The relationship is inalienable. So Isaiah repeats the statement " **Thou, O Lord, art our Father** " ; His knowledge and recognition abide. He is their " **Redeemer** ", and His name " **is from everlasting** ", that is to say, in the counsels of the past eternity and in His gracious actings in history.

The prayer in *verse 17* now contains the startling appeal, " **O Lord, why dost Thou make us to err from Thy ways, and hardenest our heart from Thy fear** (or, so as not to fear Thee)? " Isaiah is not imputing to God the responsibility for the sin of His people. Persistent and obstinate rejection of God's will causes Him, consistently with His righteousness, to forego a continuation of His grace and mercy, giving those who have hardened their hearts against Him up to the effects of their own evil ways, rendering them incapable of faith and of walking in His fear. A striking example of this is the case of Pharaoh. The R.V. should be read in Exod. 7: 13, as in both Versions in 8: 19, 32. Again in 9: 7 the statement is "the heart of Pharaoh was stubborn." Then comes the change in verse 12, where it says that God hardened his heart.

This was the case with the greater part of Israel. There were some, however, who remained faithful, and the prophet makes two appeals, first on behalf of these and then on the ground that the nation was God's inheritance: " **Return,** " he says, " **for Thy servants' sake, the tribes of Thine inheritance.** " There was a remnant "according to the election of grace".

The Lord's people had possessed the land "but a little while" (*verse 18*). Adversaries had trodden down His sanctuary, and the people had become " **as they over whom Thou never barest rule ; as they that were not called by Thy Name** " (*verse 19*). Their condition resembled that of Gentile nations.

Believers need to give heed against departing from the will of God and becoming conformed to the world. Persistent Laodicean lukewarmness makes us resemble the unregenerate, and the Lord has to withdraw Himself and stand outside the door (Rev. 3: 15, 20).

CHAPTER LXIV

THIS chapter continues the prophet's prayer. He cries to God to manifest His power against His adversaries so that the Gentile powers might tremble at His presence. The language recalls the way in which the Lord manifested His presence and power at Sinai. There the mountain quaked (R.V. marg.) at His presence. He descended upon the mount in fire; smoke ascended as out of a furnace (Exod. 19: 16–19). Thus revealing His Name to His people, He made them tremble. Would He not now manifest His power and judgment against the foe? (*vv. 1–3*).

This prayer is based upon the fact of the absoluteness and uniqueness of God and His attributes, and of His ways of grace towards those who walk in His fear, having Him in remembrance and seeking to please Him: " **For from of old men have not heard, nor perceived by the ear, neither hath the eye seen a God beside Thee, which worketh for him that waiteth for Him. Thou meetest** (that is, coming forth to shew favour; cp. Gen. 32: 1) **him that rejoiceth and worketh righteousness, those that remember Thee in Thy ways** " (*vv. 4, 5*).

The threefold combination of joy and righteousness and the remembrance of God has a special significance. It is possible to walk in righteousness in strict adherence to religion, without delighting ourselves in the Lord. It is possible to do what is morally right and virtuous without actually having God Himself in remembrance. The enjoyment of the secret of His presence is the key to the manifestation of His power in effective service for Him. The Lord delights in those who know in practical experience what fellowship with Him is. His eye is upon them that fear Him. The Apostle Paul precedes his desire for the realization of the power of His resurrection by the desire "that I may know Him". Enoch walked with God, and so had this testimony that he pleased God. He 'delighted himself in the Lord' and his life of witness in a godless world issued in his translation to the very presence of God.

In the latter part of the verse Isaiah acknowledges the guilt of his people both past and present, and, calling to mind the long continued state of their apostasy, he asks the question " **shall we be saved ?** " (R.V.). This, his rhetorical question, makes acknowledgment that they have no claim to be delivered. They had " **all become as one that is unclean** ", and all their righteousnesses were " **as a polluted garment** ". Consequently they all faded as a leaf and their iniquities like the wind had taken them away.

All this provides a warning as to the effects of persistent departure from the ways of God. Wilful apostasy leads to forgetfulness of God. So it was in Israel. There was none that called upon His Name, that stirred up himself to take hold of God. Insensibility to sin produces insensibility to God's claims and to His mercies.

The consequence was that God withdrew His mercies from them, hid His face from them, and consumed them by means of their iniquities (*verse 7, R.V.*).

In the reality and power of this confession the prophet calls to remembrance the alienable relationship which the Lord had established between Himself and His people, and the way in which He had formed them according to His own counsel. " **But now,** " he says, " **O Lord, Thou art our Father ; we are the clay, and Thou our potter ; and we all are the work of Thy hand** " (*verse 8*). This implies the possibility of the remaking of the marred national vessel. Certainly that will be the case when the Redeemer comes to Zion.

The national foe had been permitted under the retributive hand of God to make the cities of the land a wilderness and Jerusalem a desolation. The very dwelling place of God in Zion, which in days gone by had rung with the praises of the Lord, had been burned down. By God's appointment it had been indeed "a beautiful house" but it was so no longer (*vv. 10, 11*).

And now the prophet makes his closing appeal for deliverance and restoration: " **Wilt Thou refrain** (i.e., restrain) **Thyself for these things, O Lord ? Wilt Thou hold Thy peace and afflict us very sore ? "** (*verse 12*).

CHAPTER LXV

THE answer of the Lord was not immediately by way of the promise of restoration, though that was to be given (*vv. 8 to 10*). The condition of the people however was so grievous that further reproach and warnings of judgment were necessary, so obstinate and incessant had been their resistance to God's grace.

There are two ways of understanding the opening words of this chapter. Primarily the meaning of the Hebrew is by way of Divine denunciation of Israel, and that is continued in the succeeding context, in *verses 2–7*. The original has the past tenses, as in the R.V. margin: " **I was inquired of** (or rather I was discernible) **by them that asked not for Me** (i.e., who refused to turn to God and seek Him); **I was found** (to be found) **by them that sought Me not."** God was ever ready to reveal Himself, had there been a heart to approach Him in humble desire to walk in His ways. Further, " **I said, Behold Me, behold Me, unto a nation that hath not called upon My Name "** (R.V. margin). In keeping with this the Lord goes on to say " **I have spread out My hands all the day** (that is, throughout the long period of His dealings with Israel) **unto a rebellious people, which walketh in a way that is not good, after their own thoughts ; a people that provoketh Me to My face continually "** (*verse 2, R.V.*).

With regard to the other interpretation, the Septuagint version is different, and we have to remember that the Apostle Paul in Rom. 10: 20, 21, uses the Septuagint, as he frequently does elsewhere. Thus verse 1 is regarded as referring to the Gentiles; for it is of these that the statements are made, "I was found of them that sought Me not; I became manifest unto them that asked not of Me." It was by the direct guidance of the Holy

Spirit that the great missionary to the Gentiles thus made use of this passage and in the next verse referred to the apostate conditions of Israel.

In the ensuing passage in *verses 3, 4* there is a terrible revelation of the idolatrous practices of God's people. Sitting among the graves probably had to do with a form of spiritism, in an effort to hold intercourse with the dead. Lodging in the secret places (R.V.) probably represents the practice, in crypts or caves, of a form of idolatry accompanied by abominable sacrificial meals.

Those who practised these abominations were accustomed to boast in their own special sanctity and so to say to the un-initiated " **Stand by thyself** (or stop): **come not near to me, for I am holier than thou** " (*verse 5*). Such made themselves fuel for God's wrath and called forth the most grievous and righteous retribution.

In contrast to all this, the Lord now makes mention of those who were His faithful servants, for whose sake He would not bring about the universal destruction of the nation (*vv. 8–10*). These, who foreshadow the godly remnant in the future time of Jacob's trouble, were like clusters of ripe grapes, in the midst of a degenerate vineyard producing sour grapes or fruitless tendrils. From amidst all God will bring forth " **a seed out of Jacob, and out of Judah an inheritor of My mountains** (representing the land of Israel; cp. Ezek. 6: 2, 3): **and My chosen shall inherit it, and My servants shall dwell there** " (*vv. 8, 9*). Election always has an object in view. For example, the "elect of God the Father" according to His foreknowledge, are chosen "unto obedience and sprinkling of the blood of Jesus Christ" (1 Pet. 1: 2).

In this connection mention is made in *verse 10* of two places, Sharon, the plain of rich pastures and famous for its flowers, stretching along the coastal region from Joppa to Carmel (see Joshua 17: 9; 1 Chron. 5: 16; Song of Sol. 2: 1; Isa. 33: 9; 35: 2), and secondly the valley of Achor (a place lying in the plain of Jericho and associated with the sin of Achan, Joshua 7: 1), called Achar in 1 Chron. 2: 7. There the people humbled themselves before God, dissociating themselves from the evil. There, in the language of Hosea 2: 15, the nation, in the days of her youth, made answer to God (R.V.). Consequently the valley is to become "A door of hope." The whole region is to become "a garden of the Lord", a scene of fertility and productiveness.

There is always hope for those who humble themselves in the sight of God and seek to walk in His fear (Ps. 33: 18; 39: 7).

In *verse 11* the prophecy returns to the guilty ones who were threatened in verses 1 to 7. They forsook the Lord, were unmindful of His worship, substituting for it idolatrous feasts. Two objects of their veneration are mentioned, Fortune and Destiny (R.V.). They prepared a table for the one and filled up mixed wine for the other. The reference is rather to the spreading of cushions upon which the images of the gods were placed during the feasts in their honour. Accordingly the Lord declares that He will " **destine** " them (the word rendered "number" in the A.V. is associated in idea with that rendered "Destiny") to the sword, and as they bowed down to their images so they would bow down to the slaughter.

The Lord was longsuffering with them; He called, but they did not answer. He spoke and they refused to hear but deliberately chose that in which He found no pleasure (*verse 12*).

In *verses 13 to 16* the Lord presents a vivid contrast between them and His faithful ones who walked so as to please Him. They would eat and drink and rejoice and sing for joy, whereas those who turned away from God would suffer want and shame and anguish and vexation. Their name would become a curse, referring to the oath with which the priest had to administer the water of jealousy (see Num. 5: 21–24), for Israel had acted as an adulteress. On the contrary, the Lord would call His servants by another name, so that He who blessed Himself in the land and He who uttered a solemn oath, would do so by " **the God of Amen** " (margin). That is, the God who fulfils His word and will carry out His covenant promises to His people. So now in Christ "how many soever be the promises of God, in Him is the Amen, unto the glory of God through us" (2 Cor. 1: 20, R.V.; see also Rev. 3: 14). In the coming day the redeemed nation will stand in firm and uninterrupted relationship with the Lord.

All this brings home the folly, futility and sinfulness of pursuing our own way, carrying out our own designs and turning after that in which God cannot take pleasure, instead of waiting upon Him, listening to His voice and delighting in the fulfilment of His will. Through our walking with God He fulfils, and will fulfil, all the promises of His Word. He responds to delighted confidence in Him, by adding an Amen to His assurance. The peace of an obedient heart and a trusting spirit is that which enjoys the sunshine of His countenance and the calmness of holy communion with Him.

With the assurance that the former troubles are to be forgotten and hidden from His eyes (*verse 16*), the Lord now foretells the unspeakable blessedness and joy to be ministered to redeemed Israel in the coming Millennial day. But this, which begins at *verse 18*, is preceded by the declaration of what is to be brought about after the Millennial period is over. For it is only when God creates the new heavens and the new earth that unalloyed and perfect blessedness will be granted, and " **the former things shall not be remembered, nor come into mind** ".

When the Lord sets up His Kingdom of righteousness and peace He will fulfil what is now about to be stated in a passage which, perhaps more than any other passage in Scripture, describes the prosperity and bliss of this coming time. He calls upon us to be glad and rejoice perpetually in what He is about to create, and says " **for, behold, I create Jerusalem a rejoicing, and her people a joy. And I will rejoice in Jerusalem, and joy in My people ; and the voice of weeping shall be no more heard in her, nor the voice of crying** " (*verse 19*).

True, there will be death and there will be sin, but these evils will be under severe restraint. And the explanation of this lies in the double fact that Christ and His Heavenly people as well as His earthly will be reigning, and, secondly, the evil one will have been cast into the abyss for the thousand years (Rev. 20: 1–3). Under these conditions there will not be " **an infant of days** (that is a suckling only a few days old), **nor an old man that hath not filled his days : for the child shall die an hundred years old, and the sinner being an hundred years old shall be accursed** " (*verse 20*). That is to say, that one who is a hundred years old will be a youth, and one who, being a sinner, will suffer death as punishment, will not come under this judgment before the hundredth year of his life. The longevity of the earliest times of human history will return.

The next promises, (*vv. 21–23*), give the assurance that His people will enjoy what they have worked for and reap the fruits of their labour without plunder by foes. The duration of their life will be like that of trees which lived for centuries. They will be a generation blessed of Jehovah and their children will share with them what they enjoy, without being removed by premature death (cp. Job 21: 8).

The Lord declares that before they call He will answer and while they are speaking He will hear (*verse 24*). That is to say, the desire in the hearts of His redeemed will be in perfect harmony with His own will. Often now there is an interval between the prayer offered and the answer given, but not so in the day to come (cp. Dan. 9: 20-3 and Isa. 30: 19). This provides a striking testimony to that which will be the outcome of the very presence of the Lord in their midst. Prayer that is the Lord's delight can only arise from the enjoyment of close fellowship with Him.

There is also to be a change in the nature of rapacious animals (*verse 25*). Natural conditions have been full of discord, but then the wolf and the lamb will feed together. The fodder eaten by the ox will be that of the lion. This passage recalls in an abridged form what the prophet had said in 11: 6-9. This and similar correspondences between the later portions of the book from chapter 40 onward, and the earlier, again give plain testimony to the unity of Isaiah in contrast to the higher critical suppositions.

What is new in the present passage is the prophecy that dust shall be the serpent's meat. Its form will be the same but it will have the food appointed for it in Gen. 3: 14.

These conditions will not be the outcome of evolutionary processes but will result immediately from the decree and power of Israel's Messiah. To imagine that what is here said of the changed condition of creatures is mere allegory is utterly without foundation. Isaiah has not used allegory in any of his descriptions of the coming period.

CHAPTER LXVI

THE opening part of this chapter is a continuation of the glorious vision of the future just given, but the great point of connection with the preceding chapter is the contrast between the true and faithful servant of God and the apostate and worldly character of most of the nation. It is to the latter and their ideas of establishing a temple in Jerusalem that the Lord protests that, as the Creator of heaven and earth, He does not stand in need of a house erected by man. What He looks for primarily is the spirit of contrition and godly fear: " to this man will I look, even to Him that is poor and of a contrite spirit, and that trembleth at My word " (vv. 1, 2). From those who are not so characterized He looks for no efforts at temple-building and for no animal sacrifices. With scathing denunciation the Lord makes a comparison between the offering of hypocritical worshippers and gross iniquities; " He that killeth an ox (i.e., in sacrifice) is as he that slayeth a man ; he that sacrificeth a lamb, as he that breaketh a dog's neck ; he that offereth an oblation (or a meal offering), as he that offereth swine's blood ; he that burneth frankincense as he that blesseth an idol " (verse 3).

They had chosen to follow the ways of the heathen in their abominations. To this the Lord replies that He has a choice to make, and will choose their mocking devices (A.V., and R.V., "delusions", but see the margins) and will bring their terrors upon them, because they made no answer when God called and refused to hear His Word (verse 4).

At verse 5 the Lord turns to the minority, consisting of those who with reverence and awe tremble at His Word. He promises them that He will deal with their brethren who have hated them and persecuted them, thus enhancing the grievous character of their sin, and who with scornful unbelief dared to take the Lord's Name in vain, saying " Let Jehovah be glorified (or rather 'Let Jehovah glorify Himself'), that we may see your joy " (the R.V. rightly so connects the clauses). These apostates regarded any hope in God as mere deception, but the Lord determined that they should "be ashamed". Whereas the city and the Temple were lying in ruins, the time will come when there will be a voice of tumult from the city, a voice from the Temple, and that a voice of the Lord rendering " recompence to His enemies " (verse 6), not only those of the Jewish people but the Gentile nations, who will hereafter be gathered together "against the Lord, and against His anointed" (Ps. 22, and for the voice see verse 5; cp. Joel 2: 11; 3: 16; Amos 1: 2; Isa. 63: 1 and 2 Thess. 2: 8).

In view of this mention is made in verse 7 of the future time of Jacob's trouble and the fact of the Incarnation of Christ: " Before she travailed (before the great tribulation which the nation is yet to experience at the hands of the Antichrist) she

brought forth; before her pain came, she was delivered of a
man child." This experience of the nation is contrary to conditions of natural birth. The order is reversed, and this draws
forth the surprised questions, " Who hath heard such a thing?
who hath seen such things?" There is evidently a connection
with Rev. 12: 1–6. The nation is there spoken of as having
brought forth a "man child". Some regard this as the godly
remnant among the Jews in the coming day. Surely the reference
is to the Lord Jesus. The Roman power, energized by Satan,
fulfilled what is said in Rev. 12: 4, and "stood before the woman
which was about to be delivered, that when she was delivered,
he might devour her child." Herod would have accomplished
this had he been able to, but the Man Child was to be "caught
up to God and His Throne." This could scarcely be said of the
remnant, who are to enjoy the Millennial reign. The birth, death,
resurrection and ascension of Christ have already taken place.
The great tribulation is yet future. This explains the inversion
of the natural order of the circumstances of birth as mentioned
in this Isaiah passage.

The next questions, in *verse 8*, point to the effect and issue of
the travail of the nation. These two questions demand a positive
answer, whereas the two preceding ones were asked so as to
produce negative answers. Now it is asked " shall a land be
born in one day?" The R.V. margin gives what is probably
the correct rendering, " shall a land be travailed with for but
one day?" Then follows the question, " shall a nation be
brought forth at once?" The positive assurance is immediately
given, " for as soon as Zion travailed, she brought forth her
children." First the birth pangs and then the birth, and thus
different from the preceding circumstances!

Accordingly the immediate outcome of the great tribulation
will be the issue of God's earthly people as a nation in peace and
joy and righteousness under the mighty hand of its Messiah
Deliverer. The nation thus delivered is not the same as the
Man Child in verse 7.

In view of the certainty that His people will be delivered from
their time of unprecedented trouble, and that speedily (*verse 9*),
the Lord calls upon all who delight in Him and His purposes,
all those who love His earthly people, to rejoice with Jerusalem,
and be glad for her. Those who mourn over her woeful condition
are invited to rejoice for joy with her (*verse 10*). Those who on

earth will thus feel for her in the coming time will themselves derive benefit when she is established in the earth.

In *verse 11* Jerusalem is looked upon as a mother, ministering of her personal nourishment to her children with an overflow for others. The Lord declares that He " **will extend peace to her like a river, and the glory of the nations like an overflowing stream.**" Israel will receive the riches of the Gentiles, who will care for the nation with the utmost devotedness and attention (cp. 49: 23 and 60: 4). That is what is indicated in the promise, " **ye shall be borne upon the side, and shall be dandled upon the knees** " (*verse 12*).

In *verse 13* the Lord declares how He Himself will care for His people: "**As one whom his mother comforteth, so will I comfort you ; and ye shall be comforted in Jerusalem.**" Their heart will rejoice and their bones will flourish like the tender grass, a vivid description of the flourishing condition of Israel when the Lord reigns over the earth (*verse 14*).

How all this blessing will be brought about is described in *verses 15 and 16* by a renewal of the prophecies of the overthrow of their foes. In His indignation against His enemies " **the Lord will come with fire, and His chariots shall be like the whirlwind ; to render His anger with fury, and His rebuke with flames of fire. For by fire will the Lord plead, and by His sword, with all flesh : and the slain of the Lord shall be many.**"

In *verse 17* the Lord deals with those among His people who will have corrupted themselves and become like the heathen. They are to be brought to an end. They will share the doom of the adherents of the Antichrist.

Now by way of contrast the prophecy turns again to the future of Israel and to the favourable dealings of the Gentile nations with them in the Millennium. The statement that the Lord knows their works and their thoughts, forms a transition from the apostates in verse 17 to the redeemed nation and the way the Gentile peoples will assist them.

All nations and tongues are to be gathered to Palestine, and there they are to see the glory of the Lord (*verse 18*). To this end the Lord will set a sign among the Gentiles (*verse 19*), and this for the recovery of His people in far distant places. What the actual sign will be is not disclosed. From Exod. 10: 2 and Ps. 78: 43 and 105: 27, where the R.V. renders by this very phrase, and where the reference is to the miracles wrought by God in

delivering His people from Egypt, we may gather that there will
be some form of supernatural intervention in the world's affairs.
Moreover, God makes clear here that He will send out the Jews
as His messengers to nations in all parts of the world, to Tarshish
in the west, to Pul and Lud in the south, to Tubal and Javan
in the north, and to far off coastlands such as those in Asia and
other continents, to peoples who have not heard His fame or
seen His glory, that they may make known His glory in all the
earth (*verse 19*).

The Gentile peoples will bring the Jews " **out of all the nations
for an offering unto the Lord** ". They will be brought to His
holy mountain Jerusalem, just as the children of Israel were
accustomed to bring their offerings in clean vessels into the Lord's
house. A considerable variety of means of conveyance will be
used, and it is quite possible that motor cars, etc., are referred
to in the mention of chariots and litters. Further, what was
said in chapter 60: 8, in a passage similar to this, about those
who will "fly as a cloud and as doves to their windows", is
indicative of air-travel. The mention of the clean vessel shows
that all the Israelites who are brought into Millennial glory will
have been purged from their old sins and brought to walk in
the ways of the Lord, and accordingly He will take of them
for " **priests and for Levites** " (*verse 21*).

Isaiah's prophecies end with a striking contrast. First there
comes the pledge that " **as the new heavens and the new earth
which God will create will remain before Him, so the seed of
Israel and their name will remain** " (see 65: 17). For Christ,
who is of Israel as concerning the flesh, and who is "over all,
God blessed for ever", Rom. 9: 5, will be identified with His
earthly people. Owing to His presence in their midst all flesh
will come to worship before Him at every new moon and at
every sabbath. There will in that day be every facility for
speedy and frequent journeys from all parts of the world.

The nations will thus have a vivid reminder of the grievous
nature and consequences of rebellion against God. For as they
assemble in the land on the stated occasions, they will ' **go
forth, and look upon the carcases of the men who have transgressed against Him**,' and the Lord declares that " **their worm
shall not die, neither shall their fire be quenched ; and they shall
be an abhorring unto all flesh.**" The region would seem to be
the valley of Hinnom outside Jerusalem.

Yet in spite of this, such will be the spirit of dissatisfaction with the righteous and firm reign of the Lord, that the nations will break out in rebellion at the end of the thousand years, when, under the permissive will of God, Satan will be loosed from his prison to deceive them (Rev. 20: 7, 8).

No merely natural conditions, however peaceful and blessed, can ever regenerate the human heart. This, with its consequent loyalty to Christ, must ever have as its foundation the efficacy of His atoning blood.

APPENDIX

Some of the details that bind together the two parts of the book:

(1) God's abhorrence of mere formal worship, 1: 11, 13, and 66: 3.

(2) The Lord's Throne in the high and holy place, 6: 1, and 57: 15; 66: 1.

(3) His regard for the lowly soul, 6: 5–7, and 57: 15; 66: 2.

(4) His House and Mountain as a resort, 2: 2, 3, and 56: 7; 60: 12-14.

(5) His making every high thing low, 2: 11, 17; 5: 15, 16, and 40: 4.

(6) His overruling of human pride and violence, 10: 5, 7; 37: 26, and 47: 6; 54: 16, 17.

(7) The chastisement of rebellious Israel, 1: 2, 5; 31: 1, 2, and 63: 8, 10.

(8) The sickness and healing of the nation, 1: 5, 6; 6: 10, and 57: 18, 19.

(9) People and land forsaken, 6: 12; 17: 9; 27: 10; 32: 14, and 49: 14; 54: 6, 7; 62: 4, 12.

(10) Judicial deafness and blindness, 6: 10; 29: 18; 32: 3; 35: 5, and 42: 7, 18.

(11) A remnant saved, 1: 27 (marg.); 4: 2, 3; 10: 20, 22; 37: 31, 32, and 59: 20; 65: 8, 9.

(12) A sign or covenant concerning the sure mercies of David, 7: 14; 9: 6, 7, and 55: 3, 4.

(13) The Spirit of the Lord resting upon Messiah, 11: 2, and 61: 1.

(14) Israel fruitful by the Spirit of God, 32: 15, and 44: 3, 4.

(15) Waiting for God, who has hidden His face, 8: 17, and 64: 4, 7.

(16) The setting up of a standard, 5: 26; 11: 10, 12; 18: 3, and 49: 22; 62: 10.